THE FIRST YEAR AT A GLANCE

5 MONTHS

6 MONTHS

DEVELOPMENT

From the *fifth* month on, the baby's little hands go *after* things that are farther away as well (see page 181).

Amuse your baby with a game of peekaboo!

Lying on his belly, the baby practices "dry-land swimming." He discovers what fun playing with his feet can be.

D1518013

HEALTH

The next scheduled checkup is at age six months.

At 6 months, your baby should have a checkup and immunizations.

Toward the end of the first 6 months, your child should have approximately doubled his birth weight.

FEEDING

You may begin to add new solids (purees) now—one at a time.

Now you can begin to give a variety of pureed fruits and vegetables. Remember— one new food at a time.

YOU AND YOUR FAMILY

Now that your baby is becoming more mobile, this is the time to think about getting a playpen—this will allow you more freedom for daily household activities.

Dagmar von Cramm

Eberhard Schmidt, M.D.,
Professor of Medicine

Consulting Editor: Mark A, Goldstein, M.D.
Chief of Pediatrics
Massachusetts Institute of Technology
Cambridge, Massachusetts

Consulting Authors:

Ellen Bass. M.D., M.P.H.
Pediatrics Service
Massachusetts Institute of Technology
Cambridge, Massachusetts

Dante Pappano, M.D.
ABC Pediatrics
North Andover, Massachusetts

OUR BABY:
THE FIRST YEAR

■ *Feeding, bathing, and diapering*
■ *Watching your baby develop and grow*
■ *What to do when your baby gets sick*

BARRON'S

Parenthood: Getting a Good Start 10

The baby's finally here—and still sooo tired at first ...

Making Your Baby Feel Good All Over 36

Most babies love being diapered and bathed—an ideal opportunity for the father to get close to his child.

HELPING YOUR BABY GROW BIG AND STRONG 88

*The "nursing hour" belongs to
you and your baby alone.*

HELP FOR THE ENTIRE FAMILY 144

*Spending time together is important.
But don't forget about your own needs.*

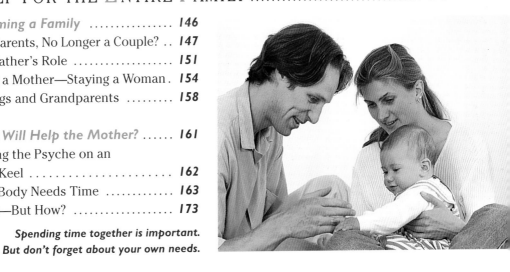

HOW YOUR BABY DEVELOPS 176

Completely helpless at first—and very active
before you know it ...

HEALTHY FROM THE OUTSET 202

Every healthy child is ill
from time to time.

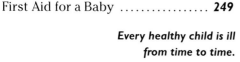

GETTING THE HANG OF IT ALL 252

*A little organization will create
free space and give you more energy
for life with baby.*

Important Note

This Barron's parenting guide provides advice and information about the first year of your baby's life. We suggest that you yourself decide whether, and to what extent, you want to follow the recommendations given in this book. For health problems and illnesses involving either the baby or the mother, you should always seek the advice of a physician!

ABOUT THIS BOOK

Nothing is more thrilling and important—or more arduous—than the birth of a child and the task of seeing him through the first year of life. This statement reflects the positive experiences of the team responsible for this book: Dr. Eberhard Schmidt, who not only has seen four children of his own grow up, but also, as a pediatrician, has been responsible for the medical care of a countless number of children; Dagmar von Cramm, who has three school-age sons; and editor Corinna Gieseler, who—as the mother of a daughter just turned one—was especially close to the subject of the book.

We always kept in mind how particularly difficult the early days of parenthood can be and how complicated the simplest things in the world can suddenly become. The first year is a period of apprenticeship. Doing a good job with a baby is not something that happens automatically; it has to be learned. These days, however, young families are completely on their own for large parts of this journey. The goal of our book is to fill in some of these gaps and to make our experiences, practical tips, and other essential, up-to-date information available to other young parents—while giving a thorough grounding in the basics.

Consequently, the first section begins with some tips you should consider before the birth. We then turn our focus to the delivery, because a great deal occurs between you and your baby in your first hours together.

In the second section, you will learn the essentials of baby care. From a basic "diapering course" through bathing an infant to nail-cutting, everything you need to know about taking care of a baby on a daily basis is presented here. Also included is information about the benefits of fresh air, exercise, rest, and sleep.

An additional area of emphasis in this book is the subject of nutrition—the authors' specialty. As a member of the [German] National Commission on Breastfeeding, Dr. Schmidt is involved in efforts to improve nursing conditions in hospitals; Ms. von Cramm is especially concerned with nutrition for breast-feeding mothers and supplementary foods for babies between the ages of six months and one year. We discuss in detail all you need to know about breastfeeding, as well as bottle feeding.

Our fourth section is devoted to the family as a whole. Happiness is not automatically complete with the birth of a child. The first year with the baby requires many changes for the parents—their relationship as a couple and their individual lifestyles. We don't want you to become discouraged along the way—neither the father, to whom we have dedicated special "info-boxes," nor the mother, who has physical stresses of her own to cope with during this time. Consequently, we have also given some thought to exercises to help her get her strength and figure back, as well as to tips on relaxation and personal grooming.

During the first year your child develops at breakneck speed. You will find a detailed discussion of this process in the fifth section of the book.

And what kind of baby book would this be without a section on health? You'll find all the advice you need here, from well-baby checkups through vaccination to typical diseases of infancy, even if things should get critical.

Life with a baby is often unpredictable—and expensive. You need to be informed about ways to organize your daily routine more efficiently, as well as about your legal rights and other matters.

Our tips on buying equipment and clothing may keep you from making many unnecessary purchases. Important

addresses and books for further reading are listed at the end of the book.

We all have enjoyed working on this book. As we wrote, we learned quite a few new things and recollected other bits of knowledge. Each of us has put his or her heart into the writing; in fact, this book was almost like another baby. . . . We hope our book will make things easier for you as you begin your own personal adventure of raising a child. It is wonderful that you have chosen to be a parent. It is a decision that we have never regretted (with the possible exception of one second of exhaustion in the tenth sleepless night, but we'd rather not think about that . . .). We hope you will savor to the fullest a marvelous first year with your child. For that is what it will be—in spite of all the stress and strain.

Note that throughout the book we have referred to the baby as "he." This was done simply for ease of reading and to avoid confusion when using "she" to refer to the mother.

Dagmar von Cramm
Prof. Dr. med.
Eberhard Schmidt

PARENTHOOD: GETTING A GOOD START

Nothing else will change your life so completely as the birth of your first child. It is wise to be prepared for it. In this chapter you will learn what is important during the first few days of your child's life, what to expect as your body undergoes physical and hormonal changes after childbirth, and what needs to be done when you arrive home from the hospital.

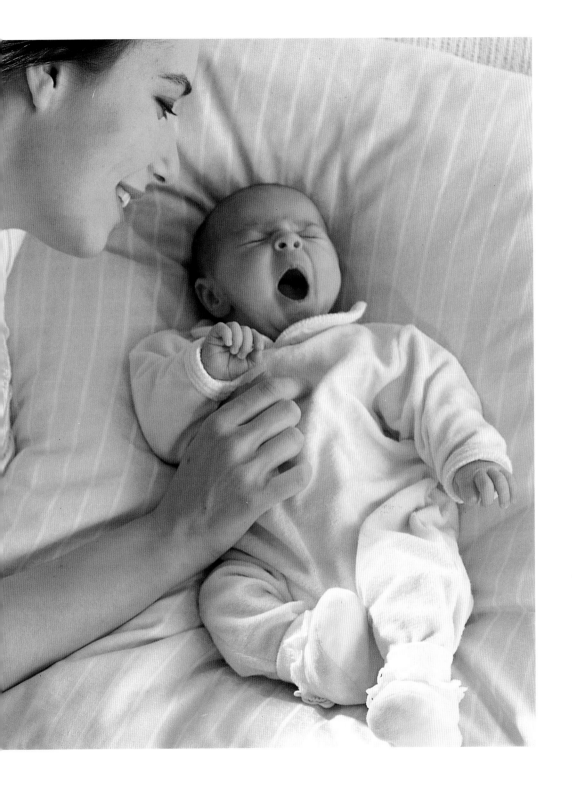

BEFORE THE BABY IS BORN

Routine prenatal care under the care of an obstetrician

should begin as soon as you know you are pregnant.

It will not be addressed further in this book.

Naming your child can be a difficult task. It is probably best begun before your child is born, but the final decision may wait until it is time to sign the birth certificate before leaving the hospital. The name should reflect the desires of both parents, and may incorporate family, religious, or cultural preferences.

Also, before your baby is born, consider touring the labor and delivery floor and nursery in the hospital where your baby will be delivered. You can arrange this through the hospital's obstetrical admitting office or the parenting and childbirth education office.

It is best to choose your baby's pediatrician before your baby is born.

Your friends, neighbors, and relatives may recommend pediatricians to you. You should plan on setting up "prenatal visits" with several different pediatricians before deciding. Important considerations in choosing a pediatrician include insurance plans and HMOs that you may belong to, the office hours, as well as the training and personality of the physician and staff.

If you know that your baby is a male, or do not know the gender, you should make a decision about the option to have a circumcision. Medical science has not determined if it is medically indicated, so cultural, religious, and personal beliefs play a strong role in this decision. Consider raising this topic during your prenatal visits for further opinions. The circumcision is usually done in the hospital before you and your baby are discharged.

THE FIRST DAYS WITH THE BABY

During the hours immediately after the delivery, time stands still. You may be euphoric,

or you may be disappointed or simply tired. Everything has changed for you,

though the rest of the world continues in its customary course.

Your husband can be your best ally, helping you deal with all these

feelings once you come home.

Every woman reacts differently to the first few hours with her child. Don't be disconcerted if you don't feel enormous happiness immediately: This is completely normal. You and your baby have just gone through an overwhelming experience, and you first need time to recover. On the other hand, mother and child are usually wide awake during the hours after birth, ready for each other. If you feel fit enough, keep your child with you during this period, because all of the first few minutes are precious.

During the days following the birth, your body will undergo great hormonal changes, which may be very stressful for you. During these first few days, your milk will come in and you will learn to breastfeed.

At the outset, your baby probably will sleep a great deal. Try to keep your child close to you during this time, so that you can get acquainted in peace and quiet. This will relieve your postpartum blues, the feeling of depression that affects many young mothers after the baby is born.

When you come home from the hospital, knowing how to take care of your baby will make you feel a lot better. Now you can reap the benefits of the hours you spent preparing everything at home before the baby was born.

The postpartum period is an exhausting time for you. Indulge yourself, as much as possible, and read our tips to find ways of making the initial phase easier. Give other people a chance to help, so that you can devote yourself to your child and get back on your feet quickly.

After the Delivery

There it is, the first cry, tentative or lusty. Your baby draws breath and thus announces his or her arrival—a profoundly moving movement!

If everything goes according to plan, your baby will be laid on your abdomen, so that you can feel his skin on yours. A blanket placed over the two of you will keep his body, still damp, from losing heat. Along with the father, enjoy these first few minutes as a new family, keeping the focus on your baby. You will not be left undisturbed for long, because the umbilical cord has to be cut. In some instances, obstetricians allow the fathers to perform this procedure. The length of time your child is allowed to rest on your belly depends on how vigorous he is, whether he has good Apgar scores (see page 206), and whether he is in danger of losing too much heat. Sometimes, if everything has gone well, and after the umbilical cord has been cut, he may stay there until you have been cared for. Then the baby is diapered and wrapped in a warm cotton blanket and handed to you again for a few minutes of peace and quiet. Now is the time to begin nursing your child, if you have opted to breastfeed him (see page 15).

Enjoy this first hour, and let us hope that there will be time and peace enough, despite the bustling activity of a delivery room, for your new family to experience these irretrievable minutes.

If you have a home delivery, you assuredly will have a chance—if everything has gone without a hitch—to spend these first hours in extraordinary intimacy.

Bonding: Accepting the Child

Usually, both mother and child are wide awake during the first hour after the birth. They are ready to become acquainted and to establish an attachment to each other. For this reason, it is important not to separate mother and child during this precious space of time by performing hospital routines or to disturb their moments of intimacy with unnecessary activity and confusion. The baby is now fully ready to nurse. If you put him to your breast now, things usually go easily and well. During this time your baby also hears your voice, sees—though dimly, at first—your face, and commits your specific body smell to memory. The converse is true as well. The more intense the contact in these first hours, the closer the bond between mother and child thereafter—so close that it is even possible for them to recognize each other blindfolded!

Your breast is not just a source of milk: Your baby smells, feels, and tastes safety and security there—and enjoys it.

Include the Father in the Reception Committee

The father has experienced the pregnancy and childbirth as a helping spectator. The first time he touches his child, this passive role is at an end. He, like the mother, will feel inclined to establish an early relationship with his child. This inclination can be best satisfied if he is present during the delivery. The "Hollywood" depiction of the father-to-be pacing the floor in a specialized waiting area while his child is born does not—and should not—happen. Instead, he can stand right beside the mother, and hold her hand during the difficult moments. Later, after checking that it is all right, he can go ahead and touch his child, appreciate the softness of the infant's skin, take him in his arms, and look into his eyes. This early contact with

the father becomes especially important for the baby if the mother, for reasons of health, is unable to take care of her child immediately after birth.

The process of mutual exploration takes up not only the first hours, but the first days with the baby. It is the basis upon which parents and child understand each other and are understood. Both parties have intuitive knowledge of the correct behavior patterns—they have no need to learn them. All they need is time and peace and quiet.

Important!
Don't despair if the first hours and days don't go according to plan if you or your child needs medical treatment. Your relationship to your child does not operate according to the "all-or-none" principle. Later on, you will make up for what you missed at first. Nevertheless, you and your husband should try to spend as much time as possible with your baby.

The First Attempt—Getting Ready for Breastfeeding

The first time you put your child to your breast is an exciting and moving moment. Let the delivery room or nursery nurse show you how to do it, so that your child doesn't become too chilled during the process.

By the way, even if you think your milk hasn't come in yet, your child still will get small quantities of colostrum. Colostrum is produced during the first few days after birth and is yellowish and translucent. It is more viscous than mature milk and is richer in protein and many minerals. It also contains a great many antibodies to safeguard against infections.

Giving the baby the breast as soon as possible after birth is important in

PREVENTING EYE INFECTIONS

It is standard practice in the United States to place some antibiotic medications into the eyes of each newborn at the time of delivery. The medication helps to prevent several different infections that can be passed to the infant's eyes during the birth process. These infections could potentially cause an inflammation of the eyes called conjunctivitis. Before antibiotics were used in the eyes of newborns, some children with untreated eye infections became blind.

Most hospitals typically use erythromycin ointment, which has virtually no side effects. A few hospitals may still use silver nitrate drops, which can cause a mild inflammation of the eyes. Some parents worry that the antibiotic will interfere with the infant's visual bonding with them, but this has never been demonstrated. If possible, request that the hospital use erythromycin ointment in your newborn's eyes.

the process of milk production. It is helpful if you familiarize yourself early with nursing techniques. This will make the initial efforts easier during the next few days. Most hospital labor floors will offer breastfeeding classes you can attend during your hospital stay. Here are some ground rules to help with nursing success:

■ Nurse lying down or sitting up, whichever is most comfortable for you.

■ Giving a baby the breast is not difficult at all, since your child will help the process along by "rooting," moving his head back and forth to search for the nipple. If you place your middle finger and index finger around the nipple, you can gently guide it in the direction of the baby's mouth. Hold your breast slightly away from the baby's nose to give him space to breathe. The baby's mouth should surround the areola, not just the nipple itself, otherwise it can be quite painful for you and can quickly result in sore nipples.

■ Once your baby is sucking continuously, you can let go of the breast and let him drink in peace. To stop the feeding, you should not simply pull him off the breast. Instead, slip your little finger into the corner of his mouth to break the suction.

In the section beginning on page 96, you will find more on breastfeeding techniques, nursing time, and nursing schedules, along with quick solutions for problems.

If You Had a Cesarean Section

Sometimes the delivery doesn't happen the way you imagined: A cesarean section becomes necessary, to prevent problems.

In most cases, a cesarean section is performed under anesthesia delivered by way of an epidural catheter placed in the lower back just outside the spinal cord. With this type of anesthesia, the mother is fully awake during the cesarean section. And in many cases, the father will be able to be present in the operating room sitting next to the mother's head, behind a sterile curtain. After the baby is delivered, he will be warmed and dried on a warming table and examined by a pediatrician right there in the operating room. After the baby is examined, he will be diapered and wrapped in a warm cotton blanket with a cotton hat placed on his head to prevent heat loss. Then the baby will be brought to the mother and father and first introductions can be made. As long as the baby is doing well, he will be able to stay in the operating room with you—probably on the warmer though, because operating rooms are kept on the cool side. After the cesarean section is complete,

HOME BIRTH

The possibility of bringing the baby into the world in familiar surroundings, far removed from hospital routine, is tempting, for some expectant mothers. The prerequisites are supervision by a trained midwife, a prenatal visit with a pediatrician, and an obstetrician and pediatrician available immediately if there are problems with the delivery or the newborn baby. In only a few minutes the baby and mother can develop serious life-threatening problems. You should determine the distance to the nearest children's hospital with an intensive care facility. Before delivery, have the fastest route to the hospital worked out, and have transportation readily available should the mother or newborn need to be taken swiftly to the hospital.

mother will go to the recovery room. Again, your baby will be able to accompany you.

No matter whether you knew the cesarean would be necessary in advance or had to decide shortly beforehand—you may be disappointed not to experience fully and in its entirety the great moment you have been awaiting for months. If you are feeling this way, you should not hide your feelings, but express them to those around you for support during this time.

Recovery will be slower after a cesarean section than after a vaginal delivery, and you should expect to stay in the hospital about 3 to 4 days. If you were planning on breastfeeding, you will still be able to start breastfeeding on the first day.

Breastfeeding After a Cesarean

Even after a cesarean, you still can nurse your baby! Lactation will be slightly delayed, and during the first few days, the nursing position will be somewhat uncomfortable for you. Usually there will be no opportunity to put the baby to your breast right after the delivery, but quite soon you will be able to roll over onto one side to try, with the nurse's help, to breastfeed.

■ Please don't be impatient if things aren't working yet. Generally, lactation begins 2 to 3 days after a C-section, but then it usually proceeds quite normally.

Precautions in the Delivery Room

Doctors have had to learn slowly that the birth of a child is not primarily a medical event, but a family affair.

Since babies usually are delivered in hospitals for safety's sake, however, a number of medical procedures performed during the first hour are part of the process.

■ While still in the delivery room, your baby will undergo a brief physical examination. If the delivery was a normal one, the examination will usually be done by the nurse in the delivery room, and the Apgar score will be assigned at this time (for detailed information, see page 206). The results are recorded on the baby's hospital chart. In some cases, extra precautions need to be taken during delivery, and in these circumstances, a pediatrician will be at the delivery and be performing the initial assessment of your baby.

■ Some newborns will swallow mucus during birth; if so, it will be suctioned out by the delivery room nurse. If he is somewhat slow to breathe initially, a breathing mask can be helpful at this time. Usually this takes only a few minutes.

■ Standard practice, if your baby is delivered in a hospital, is the administration of an injection of vitamin K, which will be given in your baby's thigh muscle to prevent blood clotting problems (see page 207).

If the Baby Has Problems

Complications can occasionally arise in making the transition from intra-uterine life to life outside the womb. You will be aware of it quickly—the bustling activity around your baby will make you uneasy and give you a hint that something is not quite right. Experienced obstetricians can often predict when difficulties are likely to arise and will call a pediatrician or neonatologist experienced in easing the transition. Every hospital delivery room is equipped with all the tools necessary to provide effective help in such situations. Usually the problems are nothing more than brief adaptive difficulties than can be resolved with a little oxygen and stimulation.

More serious neonatal problems may announce themselves earlier, before delivery (see page 206). The delivery room personnel will have responded long before delivery in this circumstance and will have contacted a neonatologist. They will be standing by to help your baby after delivery. In addition, if need be, your child will be transferred to the nearest neonatal intensive care unit, where they are equipped to handle serious neonatal problems.

If Your Baby Has to Be Transferred

■ Keep in regular contact with the nursery where your baby is staying.

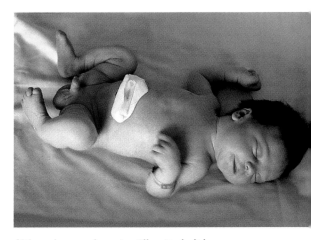

Although a newborn is still quite helpless physically, he already has amazing mental abilities!

The nursery staff will welcome phone calls.

■ If the mother is confined to bed, the father can visit the baby, caress him, or—if possible—pick him up, talk to him, and tell you all about it. Research indicates that fathers can substitute for mothers in this role.

■ As soon as it is at all possible and your obstetrician agrees, have someone take you to your baby. You need to see him and hold him—that will eliminate a good part of your anxiety about his illness and reduce the initial scariness of being separated from your baby.

■ If you are not supposed to breast-feed your baby at first, possibly because he shouldn't be making the effort yet, don't just give up. Use a pump to express your milk (see page 109)—in some cases, it can be fed to your child from a feeding tube or miniature nipple. Once your baby has recovered, you can still try to breast-feed him. Go about it carefully, and let the baby suck for only a short time at first. Be patient if things don't work well right away. Even after weeks have passed, children will learn to nurse at the breast—and both parents will rejoice at their success.

The Newborn

A child that has just been born is in no way reminiscent of the picture of a rosy, plump baby that dominates our imagination. The term "human young" would be much more apt. There the baby lies, covered by the sticky white vernix, probably somewhat bloody, bluish to reddish, and still linked to the placenta through the long umbilical cord. But, when the cord has been cut, the baby dried and placed in your arms, and when he has been put to the breast, you will look into your baby's eyes—and be fascinated. In the first hours and days after birth, babies have a special, almost wise, look and facial expression, and I always have the instinctive feeling that they have a special knowledge, as if they have the experience of having already traveled a long road.

Biologists see this quite matter-of-factly. They also refer to a baby as a fetus born too early, with an immature brain, and needing approximately one year to become fit for life. On the other hand, newborns are equipped with a multitude of instinctual responses, which serve them very well while they are beginning to adapt to the world. Through neonatal research, we now know a great deal about their astonishing abilities. Little is known, however, about their emotional life and their psyche—we can only guess.

Frederic Leboyer, a French gynecologist and obstetrician, taught us to look at birth from the perspective of being born and to receive the newborn accordingly. This attitude of respect, love, and reverence for the little being and this knowledge of the significance of the first hours and days have led us to treat newborns differently.

The Great Change

The birth events are usually seen from the mother's and father's point of view. But what does the strenuous journey from the protective confines of the womb into the light of day mean for the child?

■ After the uniform warmth of his mother's body, he is subject to a *cold shock*. The temperature of his ambient environment has dropped from 98.6 to roughly 70 degrees Fahrenheit. Furthermore, since he is wet, he loses heat more quickly. Consequently, it is important to dry off the newborn immediately and, ideally, cover him with a cloth and lay him on his mother's belly or, if need be, under warming lights. From now on, his body has to maintain its own temperature independently, by using energy that has been stored to generate warmth. At first, a cushion of brown fatty (adipose) tissue around his neck, shoulders, kidneys, and major blood vessels will help him accomplish that. This tissue, which the baby loses

INNATE REFLEXES

Reflexes are actions or responses that are not consciously controlled and can be involuntarily triggered. They are controlled by the most primitive part of our brain, the "brain stem." The newborn has many reflexes that he loses over the course of the early months of life. We now assume that these early reflexes refer to the history of our origin—relics of our primitive ancestors. Only the disappearance of these reflexes makes it possible for conscious thought and movement to develop. You can easily trigger some reflexes in your baby yourself.

■ *When you press your index finger into the palm of your baby's hand or onto the sole of his foot, his fingers will close around your hand—his feet also will try to grasp—albeit unsuccessfully.*

■ *If the baby has the sensation of a change of equilibrium, he will extend his arms and legs to all sides, literally stretching out all fours, and then draw his arms back again (Moro reflex).*

■ *If you hold a newborn so that his feet are touching a surface, he will make stepping motions, as if he were about to march off.*

■ *The first smile, the so-called "angelic smile" (see page 197), is another of these involuntary reflexes. It is interpreted as a reaction of surprise. You frequently can trigger it by merely blowing lightly on your baby's cheek—no earlier than the end of the first week, however.*

■ *One vitally important reflex is the rooting reflex, which will help you get started at breastfeeding. If you touch your baby's cheek with your breast or with a finger, he will turn his head back and forth until he has found the nipple, and then purse his little mouth. Only then will he be ready to suck.*

after a while, has the capacity to generate warmth automatically whenever the baby cools down too much.

■ Before birth, the amniotic fluid allowed the baby to almost float inside his mother's body. But now, the force of gravity acts on his body. Suddenly, every movement—especially the movement of his relatively large head, requires unprecedented effort. When he is lying on his back, all he can do is let his head roll to one side and move his arms and legs. He is not yet able to change position.

■ The skin, which previously came in contact only with the soft amniotic fluid, now is confronted with the sensation of dryness, and with touches that the baby finds rough and scratchy. For these reasons, a warm bath before being dressed the first time is often helpful for the newborn.

■ While inside the mother's body, your baby's lungs were filled with amniotic fluid. Not until the moment of delivery does the infant breathe air! During the passage through the birth canal, the amniotic fluid is squeezed out of his airways. To be safe, the delivering physician will suction the remaining fluid out of his upper respiratory passages. When the baby draws his first breath, air will enter the lungs and displace the fluid that has remained in the air sacs. This sets pulmonary circulation in motion.

■ The filling of the lungs with air is accompanied by a reduction in the blood pressure that is needed to pump blood through the lungs. These changes, along with increases in the amount of oxygen in the blood and alterations of hormonal levels, are sensed by three valves within your baby's circulation. During the minutes, hours, and days after birth, these valves clamp down, effectively changing your baby's circulation from being fully dependent on its mother's breathing to being fully independent.

■ Inside his mother's body, the baby knows no hunger. Through the umbilical cord, he received a continuous supply of nutrients. Only after his blood supply becomes separate does he have to have his own energy source. For this reason, the first few sips of the colostrum he gets from you after birth are especially important. The sooner you start breastfeeding, the sooner your milk will "come in." Formula-fed babies will also receive their first feeding within a few hours of birth.

■ The baby literally beholds the light of the world after birth. In his mother's body, he kept his eyes closed, and only dim light pierced his lids. Once born, he opens his eyes for the first time.

■ Before birth, he perceived sounds, including his parents' voices, indistinctly from inside his mother's body.

Now, every noise reaches his ears unhindered. Mothers are aware of this subconsciously, and they speak to their newborn in muted tones. It's a good idea for everyone else in the room to do likewise.

In general then, the newborn is subjected to an enormous change. We can make his entry into the world easier. If your baby is healthy, however, there is no need to be overly worried. Although fragile and helpless looking, he is able to cope with the demands of life with your help.

What the New Arrival Can Already Do

■ We'll start with the most important thing: The full term newborn can already suck. From ultrasound pictures, we know that fetuses sometimes suck on a thumb or finger while still in the womb—a good way to practice. During the first hours after birth, the inclination to suck is especially pronounced. For this reason, the mother should give her newborn baby the breast as soon as possible (see page 15). The so-called rooting reflex will help him locate the nipple and take it in his mouth. Later on, it will no longer be so easy for the baby to learn to suck.

■ Babies are not blind. In the womb, however, they can only distinguish between light and dark. At birth they can see objects best at about 8 to 10 inches (20–25 cm) away—approximately the distance of the mother's face during breastfeeding. At that distance, the baby can see objects clearly, but at further distances objects are blurred.

■ Babies are able to hear as early as three months before birth. During the first few days after birth, their middle ear is still full of amniotic fluid. This mutes the storm of noises that breaks upon the baby at birth. He reacts most positively to human voices, especially soft, high-pitched tones.

■ His sense of smell helps the newborn find his mother's breasts. Even

---

——*ESPECIALLY FOR FATHERS*——

Show your wife that you are delighted, that you want to protect her, and that you are proud of your baby. Be sure she knows this: It will help her get through the adjustment period of the early days and may also keep postpartum blues within tolerable limits.

Whether your wife succeeds or fails at breastfeeding depends more on you than you may think. If you deny her your support, you will trigger a serious conflict that will impair her chances of breastfeeding successfully.

If the milk should fail to flow properly, encourage your wife, bolster her self-confidence, and ease her burden. Give her a sign that you, too, are willing to do your utmost to attain this common goal. You will be amazed at the positive effect you can have.

in the dark, he can locate his milk source. This seems to be the most mature of all the senses.

■ A newborn's sense of taste already has a preference for sweet-tasting fluid.

■ Finally, a newborn is already able to cry. This will be the first sound he makes. Thus, he possesses an ability vital to his survival: He can summon his parents to his aid.

The First Week

If you have not had a home delivery, then you will be confined to the hospital for the next few days. Take advantage of this situation to get acquainted with your baby, start learning how to diaper, bathe, and breastfeed or bottle feed him. Ask for support if things are not going well at first. This is altogether normal; the period after childbirth is tough. Try to get your strength back as much as possible during this time, since a host of duties are sure to be waiting for you back home.

You and Your Baby

During the first days, you will probably find, to your amazement, that your baby sleeps most of the time, makes himself heard in a soft little voice, and leaves you plenty of time for yourself. Keep in mind, the baby has to recover from a great ordeal, and adjust to his new existence. Things will not stay as they are, however, and you need to use your child's resting phases to

advantage, for your own recuperation. Then, being awakened at night later on may not be so exhausting for you.

Rooming-In:
Ideal for Feeding and Sleeping

The rooming-in plan—with the baby in the mother's room, instead of in a nursery—is a perfect way for you to get to know your baby quickly. Your baby will know you from the outset, and you will be there whenever he needs you. Rooming-in is also an ideal way to ensure frequent opportunity for breastfeeding, which is important for success.

■ Generally, your baby will be next to your bed in a bassinet, a sort of plastic tub on wheels. You should feel free to hold him in bed with you, feed him, caress him, and just relax with him. But if you begin to feel drowsy, you should place him back in the bassinet. An infant falling from an exhausted mother's arms can have tragic consequences. But while you are awake cuddling him, your familiar closeness and body warmth will do him good in his surroundings!

■ Rooming-in allows for "feeding on demand" (see page 93)—a term used to describe feeding the baby when he appears hungry, rather than on a schedule set by an external source, such as a parent or the nursery nursing staff. If you are breastfeeding, then rooming-in is optimal because of the frequency of his feedings (every 2 to 3 hours as compared to every 3 to 4 hours for bottle-fed babies).

■ If you are sharing a double room with another mother, things may be more difficult. One baby's crying may stimulate the other baby, and already sleep-deprived mothers may get even less sleep. So, in some cases, nursery rules may dictate limiting "rooming-in" to the daytime hours.

■ The critical point in this initial phase is the frequent disturbance of your nightly rest when your baby wants to be fed (see page 106). However, there is every reason to continue feeding your child yourself at night as well. Please keep in mind that the better use you make of the first few days, the better acquainted you will be with your baby. Once you are back at home, you, the father, and the baby will appreciate the sacrifice you have made. If you didn't wake up to feed your baby in the hospital, it will be harder for you to deal with night

Especially in the first days, put the baby in bed with you as often as you like: It will do both of you good.

feedings at home—and that will create problems. The days you spend in the hospital are your "honeymoon" with the baby: You are waited on, so that you really can devote your full attention to the new arrival during this period. In addition, you know that your baby is close by, but your baby "knows" that only when he actually feels your closeness.

Important!
Many maternity wards will offer to put your child in the nursery at night, to let you sleep better. The nurses will bring your baby to you to be fed if he is hungry at night. However, realistically this will more closely approximate an external schedule of feeding than demand feeding. And occasionally there may be intervals between feedings that are longer than is optimal.

The Postpartum Period

When the placenta separates from the uterus at birth and is expelled as the afterbirth, it leaves behind a broad wound. This sounds worse than it really is. The blood vessels in that area clamp down quickly, and postpartum contractions (see page 28) ensure that the bleeding area decreases in size. For the next 3 to 4 weeks, however, this wound will continue to produce a discharge, as in menstruation. At first the discharge, called lochia, is bloodstained, but after a few days it becomes paler, and after the tenth day it becomes white or yellowish-white. The uterus regains its usual nonpregnant size within 5 to 6 weeks after delivery.

What's Happening in Your Body

The reality is different: Convalescent treatment is important, if only because secondary bleeding can occur. Besides, your body is undergoing dramatic changes at this time:

■ Your uterus is becoming smaller, going from 2.2 pounds (1 kg) to 2.5 ounces (70 g).

■ After the delivery of the placenta, there is a sharp decrease in the level of the hormones estrogen and progesterone, and a release of the hormone prolactin, which stimulates milk production.

■ Another hormone, oxytocin, is released by stimulation of the nipples during nursing. This hormone is responsible for the "letdown reflex" and the subsequent release of breast milk.

■ Enlargement of the breasts during breastfeeding is due to hormones that stimulate the growth and development of the breast's milk-secreting apparatus.

■ In nonlactating women, the first menstrual flow usually returns within 6 to 8 weeks after delivery, with ovulation occurring 2 to 4 weeks after delivery.

■ In nursing women, ovulation will occur later, but as early as 10 weeks after delivery, and menstruation can occur around three or more months after delivery.

■ The body gets rid of the fluid stored during pregnancy.

In other words, your energies are taxed to the utmost—and, this occurs after the exhausting process of childbirth. In this changeable situation, the sleepless nights with the baby are an additional burden. If your home environment presents additional demands in a nonsupportive atmosphere, you are programmed for crisis.

Lochia

Lochia is discharge from a wound, nothing more. In earlier times, it was thought to be unclean, and connected with puerperal fever and mastitis. Thirteen years ago, I scarcely dared to put my first child into bed with me in the hospital. Today, mothers are even allowed to take a full bath during the postpartum period.

■ Lochia lasts for 6 to 8 weeks. As long as it is heavy, use large sanitary napkins that are available in the hospital. Later, you can switch to normal sanitary napkins. It is too soon to use tampons.

■ As long as you do not overdo it, a little caution certainly is appropriate. Taking a shower during the postpartum period is safe, if you soap yourself down from top to bottom. Generally you lack the time for a full bath anyway, and after perspiring at night, getting under the shower every day will feel wonderful.

When the Milk Comes In

During the first few days, only very small amounts of colostrum will be produced, though your baby will drink it with enthusiasm. Then, between 2 and 3 days after the delivery, your milk will come in. If you do not have the opportunity to nurse frequently enough, your breasts probably will swell considerably at first. If the breast becomes too hard and distended, the baby will have trouble getting the nipple into his mouth. Thus too much enlargement may prevent adequate

nursing by your baby. Stimulation of the nipples during normal breastfeeding causes the release of the hormone oxytocin. If your baby is unable to latch on and suck adequately, there will be lower levels of oxytocin. Without this stimulus, the breast will not release the milk it has produced. So your breasts will continue to get larger and larger as milk is produced but not released. If this situation continues, total engorgement and infection may result (known as *mastitis*). I remember feeling as though there were two blocks of wood in my bra.

■ The best means of preventing this potential problem is frequent nursing. It is a happy coincidence that your baby is becoming more alert again, just at the time the milk is coming in, and is as eager to suck as he was during the first hours after birth.

■ If for some reason your baby cannot feed frequently, or your breasts are already too engorged, breast pumps may help, but they do not provide the same stimulation of the nipples.

■ Call the nurse if you feel unsure. A warm compress can help relieve the distension.

■ For ways to prevent mastitis, see page 107.

■ After a day at most, your breasts will be soft and smaller again—but not yet ready to produce the enormous quantities of milk you expected when you first felt the milk come in.

The Afterpains

The birth is successfully behind you, and now, totally relaxed, you are nursing your baby. For the first time he is sucking vigorously—and all at once you give a start or wince. You may be experiencing what is called afterpains, referring to the contraction of the uterus after childbirth. It can be frustrating: What you thought was all behind you has suddenly reappeared. The reason: The baby's sucking produces a surge of the hormone oxytocin, which causes the uterus to contract. And that can be so intense that it resembles a labor pain. But your motivation for tolerating these unpleasant feelings has simply vanished.

■ Try to look at things positively. With every afterpain, your uterus continues to become smaller, and that contributes substantially to your physical regeneration. As you did during the delivery, continue to breathe into the pain.

If You Don't Want to Breastfeed

If you are quite certain from the start that you don't wish to breastfeed or are unable to do so, you need to discuss this as soon after the delivery as possible. Hospital nurseries are equipped with bottles of formula that they will give you after the delivery—most will send you home with several days' supply.

Try to bottle feed your child yourself. If you leave that to the nurses from the outset, your relationship will have a hard time developing. For more on bottle feeding with infant formulas, see pages 118–128.

Perspiring Is Normal

After childbirth, the body gradually gets rid of the water stored in its tissues. At the same time, while nursing you need to drink plenty of liquids to promote lactation. For these two reasons, you probably will need to go to the bathroom more frequently at night. Some of the excess water in the tissues will be sweated out—you may not be accustomed to this form of water loss, but it is normal.

■ The perspiration may make you unpleasantly cool while you are nursing at night. For that reason, even in the hospital, you should have a bed jacket or a shawl with you. At first I smiled at the relic of bygone days that my mother provided me with, but later on, I was grateful. Being out of bed for 15 minutes on a cool night when you are soaked with sweat is unpleasant.

If the Perineal Area Is Sore

The first few days with the baby would be much more enjoyable if it were not for the episiotomy: Two-thirds of the women who had this surgical incision during delivery or experienced tearing have problems with the site. They don't know how to sit comfortably, they fear every trip to the toilet, they are in pain. However, there are therapies for relief of these various complaints:

■ The best therapy is sitz baths (special therapeutic sitting baths. Your hospital may supply you with the special equipment needed.)

■ Use only clear, lukewarm water when you wash; soapy substances will burn.

■ If going to the toilet is painful, rinse with lukewarm water after urinating.

■ If there is inflammation, cooling the area will help. Take a cool washcloth or place a few small pieces of ice in a washcloth or disposable bag, and cool the incision site for about 2 minutes.

■ An inflatable rubber ring (often called a "donut," and available in a medical supply store, pharmacy, or toy store) will make sitting less painful during the first few days.

After 1 or 2 weeks, the episiotomy site should be completely healed. If you continue to have problems, consult your obstetrician.

Getting Digestion Back on Track

The lower part of your body still hurts—and you spend hours sitting on the toilet. Nothing works anymore! And you are a little afraid of pain as well. The sudden change inside the abdominal cavity and the hormonal readjustment are responsible for the constipation. The problem will not go away on its own; it will just get worse. Your body is drawing more and more fluid away from the rectum.

■ Two to three times a day, take 1 tablespoonful of psyllium with some yogurt, then drink 1 cup of liquid.

■ Drinking plenty of liquids not only stimulates digestion but also is conducive to breastfeeding.

■ Fiber-based laxatives are not absorbed and will not get into the breast milk.

■ Postpartum exercises get the intestinal tract in motion (see page 168).

■ Avoid black tea, chocolate, cocoa, and sweets.

■ If necessary, have the nurse give you a suppository.

Newborn Screening Test

During his stay in the hospital, your baby automatically will undergo a screening test for the detection of silent metabolic diseases. This screening is necessary because a number of serious chronic diseases can lead to brain damage if left untreated. These include inherited metabolic diseases such as PKU (phenylketonuria) and congenital hypothyroidism (insufficient production of thyroid hormones). This screening test is sometimes referred to as "the PKU test" because this was one of the first silent metabolic diseases tested for in newborns. The test is important because these diseases are silent in newborns, meaning that on a physical exam these infants appear normal, and only by testing the blood can these diseases be detected. Metabolic diseases are often the result of missing proteins that help to break down other proteins that are produced during the body's metabolic processes. If a particular protein accumulates in

the blood, it can be toxic to the developing brain.

The PKU test is performed on the second day of life, in the hospital. Blood is taken from your baby's heel and then tested in a special laboratory. Results of this blood test are sent directly to your doctor, and if abnormal, treatment is initiated at once.

Important!
The PKU test is an absolute must for every infant. Should you wish to leave the hospital with your baby before 24 hours, or if your baby is delivered at home, then you should contact your doctor's office to have the test performed there.

Other Examinations

Before you leave the hospital, your pediatrician or a pediatrician on staff at the hospital where you deliver will perform a physical exam on your baby and be available to answer any questions you may have. Also, the first hepatitis B vaccine will probably be given to your baby before leaving the hospital, or it may be given in the pediatrician's office at the 2-week visit.

Getting Started at Home

The longed-for moment has arrived: At last you can go home with your baby. Instead of experiencing the happiness you anticipated, however, all too often you feel like crying. The contrast between the well-ordered world of the hospital and your home—where you bear many responsibilities—is too great. The changes that occurred in your mind and body over the last few days are too overwhelming. Your household and your family have remained the same—only you yourself have changed. In this unstable situation, it is helpful to try to eliminate some potential sources of upset and let the "store" mind itself, as much as possible, without your help.

Coming Home with the Baby

The first time you reenter your home after the delivery, you think you're coming from another world. Hypercritically, you look around the house, paying special attention to the nursery. You may be very emotionally unstable at this time. When I came home with my first child, within a matter of minutes I was sitting on the edge of the bed sobbing because everything wasn't quite perfect. With the third child, my family was prepared for my hypersensitivity: Everything was letter-perfect, and our firstborn, along with his entire school class, had painted a "Welcome Home" banner. I was critical—but happy.

In other words, a sympathetic family makes the return to the everyday world much easier, and a few "frills," such as a bouquet of flowers, a little sip of something, a well-stocked refrigerator, and a few hours of leisure with close family members—without guests!—can cheer you up tremendously.

Plan Ahead!

Your husband or your parents can help take responsibility for running the household now: You don't need any additional work awaiting you.

—— ESPECIALLY FOR FATHERS ——

You may not recognize your wife during the weeks after the delivery. At times you may think you have two babies in the house. This situation is normal. The stress and strain of giving birth and taking care of the baby place an enormous burden on your wife. In addition, hormonal changes make her emotionally fragile. At this time she is especially dependent on your support, in every respect. Even though you may not believe it, at this moment you are the most stable part of the family.

■ It is crucial to have time for each other and for the baby on the first day home.

■ If you don't have an answering machine, have someone else answer the phone.

■ Your husband also needs to make his calendar as free as possible at this time. Even grandparents may need to wait a while longer.

■ Most important of all, while still in the hospital, you need to make your wishes and ideas clear. Don't expect your husband to read your wishes in your eyes; he, too, has his hands full with the new situation.

Ideal and Reality

Rarely is there such an enormous gap between the ideal and the real as in one's new life with a newborn, one's maternal feelings, and what one imagined the joys of motherhood to be. That makes it very difficult for new mothers to look their problems straight in the eye and acknowledge them. They expect themselves to be supremely happy, contented, and radiant. The depressed feeling after delivery is something most new mothers have heard about, but while still in the hospital one is being cared for with understanding and sympathy. On returning home, however, the fact that the following weeks will not be all sunshine and roses comes as a total surprise to most new parents. Husbands in particular often are completely flabbergasted by their wife's mood swings.

Sources of Physical Stress

■ The hormonal swing places the mother under enormous stress. In some women it triggers depression, while others experience at least a temporary decline in efficiency. Possible attendant symptoms are low blood pressure, listlessness, lack of appetite, and even shortness of memory.

■ Episiotomy or C-section healing incisions are additional handicaps that cause you to be physically under par.

■ Continual loss of sleep, in addition, frays the mother's nerves. After a few weeks, my husband and I understood why sleep deprivation is used as a form of torture.

■ If there are problems with breast-feeding, the adjustment period is further made more difficult.

■ And last, but not least, your spirits may be affected by the fact that even after the delivery, your figure will not be ready for a bikini for quite some time to come (for tips on taking good care of your body, see the section beginning on page 163).

THREE GROUND RULES TO PREVENT EXCESSIVE STRESS

■ *Don't ask too much of yourself; don't give in to the high demands of people around you.*
■ *Ask for help, and accept it.*
■ *Don't stay in isolation at home; talk to others around you: your husband, friends, other mothers, family members, or your doctor.*

Problems with the New Situation

■ In earlier times, children were accepted as part of one's lot in life. Today they are usually our heart's desire, and are associated with great expectations of happiness that simply cannot match the reality of the first few months. Maternal feelings just do not arise spontaneously at the moment of birth; they have to develop slowly—as does the routine of dealing with the baby during the first weeks and months.

■ Usually, the new mother is completely isolated with her baby. She may be tied down to her house or apartment, able to go out only if she takes the baby along. She no longer has a life of her own, she may be separated from her circle of friends, and her partner may have already returned to work. This realization can place additional stress on the new mother. New ways of coping need to be found (see page 154).

■ In this fragile state of mind, many women are simply overwhelmed by their responsibility. Often they realize only after the delivery that they can never run away from this job, that their life is permanently changed, and that this helpless baby is dependent on his mother.

■ Thanks to the advertising industry and parenting manuals, we all know how a new mother is supposed to live: She is extremely pretty and well-groomed, she is a perfect housewife and lover, she has infinite patience with her sweet baby, and she always has time for a friendly visit. And, of course, she also continues to have her sights set on her profession. After all, it is only a question of organization and a strong will. We all strive to equal this superwoman and are surprised when we simply can't match her impossible performance. On pages 257–259, you will find ways to create some free space for yourself and get better organized.

Important!

If you notice that you no longer have the strength to cope with everything and that you can't get out of this dark hole on your own, you should see your physician at once. Postpartum depression—the feeling of discouragement after the baby is born—is a real illness and requires psychiatric treatment.

Arrange for Help

In the early period, it is nicest if you and your husband can be alone with the baby. Then you can concentrate completely on each other and come to grips with the new situation without outside disturbance. You may want to arrange for someone to help with the house cleaning and laundry during the first several weeks after delivery. Your physician or your baby's doctor can arrange for a visiting nurse or a nurse's aide to assist you in the days after discharge from the hospital.

Help from Family or Friends

If you are a single mother or if work keeps your husband from spending the first few days at home, ask your family—or his—for help. Grandmothers who live in the same area are a blessing when they are willing to act as a dependable "visiting nurse" for a while. When it comes to intimate understanding, grandmothers are hard to beat—provided they are prepared to accept your views on baby care and don't try to boss you or criticize everything you do.

■ If these ground rules are accepted, subsequent participation by the grandparents in the baby's care is both possible and desirable. Almost no one else is as interested in your children's development and welfare as "Grandma and Grandpa."

■ If no grandmother is available to help out, a relative or friend may be able to lend a helping hand.

SELF-HELP AND BREASTFEEDING GROUPS

Self-help and breastfeeding groups can give you great moral support. You will get to know like-minded women who are in a situation similar to your own. Knowing that there are others in similar circumstances is a big stress reliever. Also, these groups offer mutual support. This does not make you dependent, but rather strengthens your self-confidence and individual initiative. There are sure to be such groups in your area (for addresses, contact La Leche League or family planning organizations, or your doctor or obstetrician may know of local groups).

■ It is important that your helper not take over the baby's care, but concentrate on the housework. In addition, your helper should never come between you and your husband; that could lead to alienation.

Visitors: Only as Desired

After a short night with your child, you probably want to catch up on some sleep. But then the telephone rings, your baby cries, and a neighbor with a bouquet of flowers is standing at your door—determined to visit the baby. What you would normally enjoy at any other time turns into an ordeal! Make sure that you are not defenselessly at the mercy of outside disturbances, however well meant. Before your child is born, don't assure all your friends and fond acquaintances that they will be welcome at any time. Don't schedule large get-togethers with the baby in advance. Allow for the fact that adequate rest is what you need most of all in the beginning. Don't trust that other people will be tactful and sensitive; treat yourself with consideration. And keep in mind that your child probably also needs peace and quiet at first. Not all infants love hustle and bustle; after all, they are still just trying to get used to life "outside."

Protecting Yourself
The following tips may sound harsh, but they are necessary if you are to get some privacy. People who want to visit the baby are often extremely stubborn!

■ Buy an answering machine ahead of time. Then *you* can decide when it's time to chat!

■ Arrange in advance a good day and time, according to your schedule, when visiting might be agreeable.

■ Sleep whenever your baby is sleeping. The housework can wait!

35

MAKING YOUR BABY FEEL GOOD ALL OVER

*Your baby is still relatively helpless.
He needs a special kind of daily care and special
handling, along with understanding,
tenderness, and a great deal of loving attention.
In this section, you will learn to
take care of your baby,
how to deal with him,
and how to understand him better.*

GENTLE CARE FROM HEAD TO FOOT

Clean and sweet-smelling—that's the way we want our babies to be. For the newborn, just home from the hospital, washing with a washcloth is most appropriate until the umbilical cord stump falls off. Shampoos and lotions are not necessary at this time, and bubble baths are not recommended. What's most important is your baby's sensory experience of feeling your tender touch on his skin. This close contact will benefit his overall development—and you as well!

Your baby's skin is highly sensitive. Because of this, your baby needs a very special kind of care. The assortment of items available in catalogs and stores to help you care for him is enormous and confusing. An entire industry has grown up around caring for babies. The flood of complicated tips and offers can be overwhelming for new parents.

To help you keep a clear head, this chapter presents factual information about your child's needs, so that you can decide which purchases and directions are truly useful. After all, you need to decide on a specific diapering system, and you want to know how to go about keeping your child clean and well cared for—from head to toe. And new questions will arise repeatedly during your daily routine. On the following pages, you will find all you need to know about equipment and daily care. Of course, you aren't required to follow all the advice; instead, just take whatever suits your needs. Every baby—as well as every mother—is a little different.

■ One tip right off the bat: Every time you touch your baby—whether it be for bathing, cleaning his nose, or changing his diaper—you need to first wash your hands thoroughly.

Diapers: What Your Options Are

Today there are many options for diapering. In addition to traditional cloth diapers and disposable diapers, new approaches—such as washable diaper pants—have gained a foothold.

All the methods have their advantages and disadvantages. Information is available in your prenatal class, from breastfeeding and baby play groups, from friends with new babies, or from diaper services, though these are not available everywhere.

Consider carefully what is best for you and your child.

You should try to think about the options before the baby is born. If you can't decide what to do about diapers, to be on the safe side, you should buy a package of disposable diapers (see below) with which to start off. For a list of what your layette should include, see page 268.

Cloth diapers are available in a wide variety of styles. Choose a brand that is made of 100 percent cotton, has a soft surface that won't produce lint, and is absorbent without being overly thick.

Disposable Diapers

Disposable diapers have made the lives of new mothers easier. They have turned diapering into child's play, and made outings with the baby much less complicated. By now, almost all manufacturers have discontinued the use of perfumes and optical whiteners (test dated 1992), and even unbleached diapers have appeared on the market. Different sizes and styles are available, making it easier to find the right fit for your baby.

The disadvantage of disposable diapers is the mountain of diapers that have to be purchased and brought home weekly. The mountain doesn't disappear after use—disposable diapers are a major contributor to our overflowing landfills. Furthermore, disposable diapers are more expensive that cloth diapers and diaper services, and they tend to promote

DIAPERS: PRICE AND TIME EXPENDED

Prices and diaper styles can change. But on the whole, relative costs will remain the same. Note that the most expensive diaper is not always the best. This is one place you can save money with no risk to your child. (*$ = least expensive; $$$$ = most expensive.)

Type of Diaper	Expenditure of Time	Costs per Year*	Comments
Disposable	Purchase	$$$$	Convenient, easy; fills landfills
Cloth with diaper service	Minimal	$$$	Difficult to find a service
Cloth with at-home laundering	Washing, drying, folding	$$	Very time-consuming; costs also include soaps
Cloth with plastic pants	Washing, drying, folding	$$	Very time-consuming; decreased ventilation to skin
Cloth diaper pants with liner	Washing, drying, folding	$$$$	Easy to use, but lots of work
Cloth diaper pants without liner	Washing, drying, folding	$$	Less absorbent; easy to use, but lots of work
Cloth diapers with tie-on wraps	Washing, drying, folding	$	Not good for crawlers; tend to leak; lots of work

diaper rashes more readily. To learn how to put disposable diapers on your baby, see page 51.

Helpful tips for shopping for diapers:

■ The diapers should not be too big—otherwise, they will leak around the legs—and, also, they should not be so tight that they fit too snugly around the legs.

■ The weight recommendation alone is not an adequate guide: A baby with a wider frame may wear a diaper designed for a higher weight category.

■ Newer styles include differently padded areas for boys versus girls, to absorb urine where it is most likely to accumulate depending on gender.

■ Environmentally, the disposal diaper does pose more of a waste management problem—adding solid waste to our already overflowing landfills; but don't forget that detergents used to wash cloth diapers contribute to water pollution, and the energy used to run your washer and dryer may come from burning fossil fuels. You really need to choose the best diaper for your particular situation and lifestyle.

Cloth Diapers: The Traditional Method

Our mothers knew nothing but the square, soft cotton diapers. Today, these diapers are again increasing in popularity, and for good reason. Cotton diapers are washable and less

harmful to the environment; they are less expensive than disposable diapers; they are easier on the skin; and they are less likely to cause diaper rashes (see page 221). The main disadvantages are time-consuming laundering and the inconvenience of storing soiled diapers while traveling. You may want to consider using a combination of the two.

If you decide on cloth diapers, you can choose between a velcro fastening or diaper pins. But remember, when pinning the diaper use diaper pins, not safety pins, and always place your hand between the baby and the pin. Diaper pins are available in most baby aisles and are equipped with prick guards and safety locks.

You will also need to use a diaper cover when using cloth diapers. Covers, sometimes referred to as rubber pants, used to be made of thick plastic, which was not a breathable material. Today, covers are made of polyester and polyurethane or nylon. As with the diapers themselves, the covers also are available with velcro and snaps or pins.

The Right Quantity and Quality

At the beginning, you can get by with 24 gauze diapers.

■ Make sure that half the diapers are somewhat thinner, otherwise, the finished diaper will simply be too bulky for the first few weeks. If you continue using cloth diapers, you can stock up again later on, buying 12 thicker gauze diapers and using the thicker one to form the triangle (see page 50). Then you can simply use the thinner ones for the lengthwise piece (see page 50).

■ If your child sleeps through the night, or if you are away from home for a fairly long time, you also can lay a cottonized (flock) diaper (see page 44) inside the lengthwise piece for added absorbency.

■ You also can lay a diaper liner (available in drugstores, some department stores, and by mail order) on the folder diaper; it will make it easier to remove all traces of bowel movements. With a child who is breastfed exclusively, however, there is no need for it, because the stool is so liquid that it all "seeps" into the diaper anyway.

■ Give preference to unbleached diapers without optical whiteners (brightening agents). White diapers are environmentally harmful, because of the bleaching process.

Over the Diaper: Waterproofing

In any event, something has to be put on over the diapers to help protect against "accidents"; otherwise, your baby, along with his crib, will be "floating."

■ *Rubber or plastic pants* are not a good choice; they don't allow air to reach the baby's bottom.

■ *Wraps*, which are tied together over the diaper, breathe somewhat better but still keep the baby dry.

■ Unbleached sheep's wool soaker pants (available in stores that carry all-natural products or baby products) or pants that have absorbent cotton inside and microfibers outside (available in baby stores) offer optimum "ventilation" and high absorbency at the same time.

These *wool pants* still let some moisture through; but they are decidedly friendly to the environment. They are ideal for use in the daytime, when you are changing the baby more frequently anyway.

One other advantage: Untreated sheep's wool, which still contains lanolin, has self-cleaning action. That means that the wool pants, even if they get wet, never smell of urine. There is no need for you to wash them every day. When you buy them, check the label to make sure that they are machine washable.

Microfiber pants keep the baby drier and help him sleep through the night. Here, too, give preference to styles that can be washed by machine.

■ At the start, two pairs of pants to wear over the diapers will be enough. Choose the material that suits you best.

For more on diapering techniques (folding and putting on cloth diapers), see page 50.

Washable Diaper Pants

Washable diaper pants combine the advantages of cloth diapers with the comfort of disposable diapers. Velcro closures or other patented fastener designs make them just as easy to put on as disposable diapers (see page 39), but they are completely washable. They are expensive to purchase, however.

You can choose either of two versions: all-in-one types or diaper pants with separate diaper covers.

The following applies to both versions:

■ The quality of the fabric on the inside of the diaper pants is important.

This diapering method keeps the baby's legs spread slightly, which is good for healthy hips.

Terry cloth should have a very fine pile with short loops, and flannel should have a compact, tightly woven surface. Only if the weave is extremely tight will the surface stay smooth and soft and not irritate the baby's bottom.

■ You can increase absorbency by using cloth diaper inserts or cottonized diapers (unbleached products!).

■ Put them on exactly the same way as disposable diapers (see page 51).

■ The pants should be machine washable.

■ In the store, ask to see the various designs and try them on your baby, because diaper pants have to fit snugly and comfortably. Obviously, it makes sense to wait until after the baby is born to buy these diapers.

The All-in-one Type

With all-in-one designs, the water-repellent outer shield is already "built-in," by means of an external layer containing synthetic fibrous materials or a sheet of PVC or rubber. The disadvantage is that, because of this layer, the pants are slower to dry after being washed.

■ If you opt for this type, you will need 15 to 20 all-in-one diaper pants.

The Two-part System

With the two-part system, you have cloth diaper pants and a separate diaper cover, which also keeps water from soaking through. As far as

43

absorbency, protection against "accidents," the baby's comfort, and affordability are concerned, this design is advantageous.

It is also more practical; the inner diaper pants dry more quickly after being washed, because there is no layer to block the air. In addition, you are free to choose any over pants you like.

■ You will need about 15 to 20 diaper pants.

■ For the *diaper cover*, you have a choice of various qualities.

Over pants made of pure sheep's wool are highly recommended for daytime use, because they allow air to reach the baby's bottom and because you will be changing the baby more frequently during the day—wool, after all, does not waterproof completely.

Covers made of coated cotton or coated synthetics are preferable for nighttime, when there is a long break between changes, because they keep wetness from soaking through and drenching the bedding.

■ You will need approximately 5 covers for daytime and 3 for nighttime.

Important!

During the first months, you should make it a rule to put the diaper on so that the baby's legs are kept separated. That means that the crotch piece between the baby's little legs has to be wide enough to keep them in a slight straddle position. That will help the hips develop properly.

If your disposable or cottonized diaper has a crotch piece that is too narrow, you can fold a cloth diaper into a strip (see page 50) and place it between the disposable diaper and the cotton pants. In critical cases—with a congenital hip problem (see page 226), for example, the orthopedic doctor will prescribe a special splint or harness to keep the hips in the proper place.

Cottonized (Flock) Diapers

These diapers are the precursors of the cloth diaper pants, cut and styled to resemble disposable diapers: wide strips of cellulose that either are kept in place by tie-on wraps or worn inside diaper covers (often made of rubber or plastic). They are easy to use and relatively inexpensive—but decidedly disadvantageous for the baby. Your child's skin is constantly in contact with the wrap or with rubber, and the diapers collapse when wet and then absorb poorly. They also do not promote healthy hip development. The upshot: Not recommended; at best, suitable for use in addition to cloth diapers (see page 41). If you want to use them as inserts for reasons of economy, you should change your baby after every bowel movement—and often in general.

Diapers on Wheels: Diaper Services

Diaper services devote themselves to the laundering of cloth diapers or cloth diaper pants. About twice a week, the company brings you clean diapers and takes away the dirty ones. As a rule, these firms supply the diaper pails with liners as well as the diapers, so you don't have any costs up front. The total cost is going to be a little less than that of disposable diapers. These services are not as common as they once were; therefore, you will need to check the yellow pages in your area to find out if this service will be available to you.

Washing Diapers—No Problem

The following tips apply to all washable types of diapers:

■ In earlier times, diapers were softened and then actually boiled. If your child is healthy, washing them in hot water is adequate (make sure your hot water heater is set no higher than 120 degrees Fahrenheit [49° C]).

■ Coated pants are not heat resistant; never put them in the dryer or lay them on the radiator.

■ Keep the soiled diapers or diaper pants in a diaper pail with a lid, and launder them every three days.

■ Drying the diapers in the clothes dryer or hanging them outdoors in the sun makes them soft and absorbent. If

WHERE TO BUY DIAPERS

Diapering is a science that requires study and method—you need some advice.

In baby superstores or baby specialty stores, you can examine the entire range of baby products. These larger stores are usually located in larger cities. You need to check your yellow pages for stores near you.

Specialty shops downtown usually offer an adequate overview of the various diapering systems, along with good advice.

Mail-order companies that sell baby products publish comprehensive catalogs that are good sources of preliminary information. If you know what you want, you can buy it quickly and easily through these companies.

Stores that carry natural products have environment-friendly systems in stock: unbleached disposable diapers and reusable systems. But not every small shop will carry baby articles.

Drugstores carry primarily disposable diapers, though they sometimes have diaper systems as well. Don't expect to get advice here.

Department stores have a limited selection available in their baby department.

Grocery stores have entire aisles of disposable diapers for customers who know what they want.

you have to hang them indoors to dry, you should "knead" them a little after drying to soften them.

■ If there is a diaper service available in your area, it will be less labor-intensive for you.

■ When washing cloth diapers, use soap instead of detergent; it will leave the diaper softer. Do not use fabric softeners or static guards; they may irritate your baby's skin. Wash in hot water, and double rinse.

There's More to Diapering than Cleanliness

Very few parents understand this clearly: During the first year, they will spend a great deal of time with their baby at the changing table. These are often the moments when you can cuddle with your baby, and have fun with him—with no barriers of cloth in between. At the same time, regular changing of diapers is crucial not only for the baby's emotional well-being, but for his physical welfare as well. It is well worth it to give some hard thought to your diapering setup ahead of time.

Ready for the next change. All the diapering supplies are within easy reach—for you, not for the baby.

The Ideal Changing Area: Warm, Clean, and Safe

In most cases, you will be setting up the diapering area in the nursery, though many parents today have the baby's crib in their bedroom. Thus, it may well be that the changing table will be in your room.

■ The first order of business is organizing your changing table so that everything you need—diapers, wipes, ointments, and diaper pail—are all in easy reach. This way, you will not have to step away from the table.

■ Choose a changing table that is sturdy and stable, and not likely to tip over.

■ You will need a surface at least 28 inches (70 cm) deep and 32 inches (80 cm) wide—more room is nice. Make sure the surface of the table is approximately at the height of your hips (Caution: Take fathers into account!); otherwise, your back will ache.

■ *A changing table with shelves or drawers* is still unbeatable, because it provides a large enough surface for diapering as well as room to store the baby's things. There are also styles that can be used later on as desks. If space is short, you also can get lightweight *wheeled, folding tables* that can be unfolded easily and require only a minimum of floor space. Alternatively, you can change the baby on a flat top that fits over the bathtub. Specialty stores carry a large selection of such space-saving designs.

■ On the changing surface, place a changing pad (available in baby stores) that is padded with foam and can be wiped clean. Cover the chilly surface with a thick, washable piece of terry cloth.

■ Within reach of the changing table—but out of the baby's reach—there should be a place for baby lotion, diaper cream, a brush, and a small washbasin as well. One practical solution is a shelf next to or high above the changing surface, where fresh diapers and clothes can be stored within reach.

■ Next to the changing table, place the diaper pail, a second pail for other dirty laundry, and a small trash container.

■ Finally, arrange the lighting so that you can see adequately but your child is not blinded by the glare and cannot reach up and touch the hot bulb.

■ One important factor is warmth, especially if your child is born in winter. Otherwise, your moments of cuddling will come to a chilly conclusion. A warm-air fan heater will provide warmth, but the air current should not flow directly across the baby's body. Infrared light is not a good source of heat, because it will dazzle your child.

■ *Remember, never leave a child unattended on a changing table for even a moment!*

Diapering: When and How Often?

Theoretically, the baby should be changed as soon as he is wet, because the urine can irritate his sensitive skin. But some of the disposable diapers are so wonderfully absorbent that you may not notice that the baby is wet until quite a bit of urine has accumulated. Your nose will still let you know when a bowel movement has occurred.

For these reasons, we offer you a few ground rules to keep the baby from spending too much time in a wet diaper:

■ If at all possible, change your baby after every feeding. Because feeding causes reflex defecation, your child probably will have a bowel movement while he is being fed.

■ You should also change your baby's diaper first thing in the morning, before a long outing, and before naps or bedtime.

The Right Way to Diaper: Step by Step

■ *What you will need at the changing table:*

• Clean clothing for the baby
• Diapers (cloth or disposable)
• A fresh washcloth, a small basin for water, mild soap, cotton balls, or disposable wipes. (Some babies' skin is sensitive to disposable wipes, and using warm water with or without mild soap is a good alternative.)

How to Change the Diaper

1 Lay your baby down in front of you, with her back on the changing surface, and pull off her pants. Raise her top and undershirt up over her navel, and undo the diaper.

2 Hold your child's feet with one hand, and lift her bottom. Next, wipe her bottom gently with the lower portion of the old diaper. Then toss the used diaper into the diaper pail.

3 *Next, wipe her bottom with a damp washcloth or disposable wipe.*
Important: Always wipe from front to back. Otherwise, germs can get into the urinary tract and may result in infection.

4 *Blot the baby's bottom dry and let your child kick her legs in the air. This is a good time for cuddling—skin contact is good for the baby, especially if she has been wrapped in thick winter clothing.*

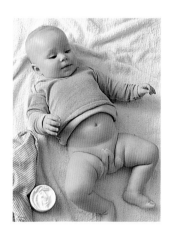

5 *If your baby has a diaper rash, apply a layer of diaper ointment or petroleum jelly over the irritated area as a barrier from further irritation caused by urine and stool. This will also allow the skin to heal more quickly.*

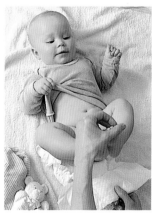

6 *Now put on the new diaper. For more on how to do this, see the following pages.*

Tips on Using
Square Cloth Diapers

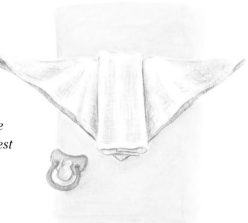

1 Fold one diaper to form a triangle. Fold the second diaper into a rectangular strip about 16 × 6 inches (40 × 15 cm) and place it lengthwise on the first diaper, i.e., from the top of the longest side of the triangle to its lower tip.

2 Now lay your baby on the diaper. Bring the rectangular strip along with the lower tip of the triangle onto her abdomen.

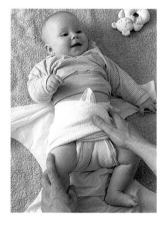

3 Next, join the two outermost tips of the triangle smoothly over her abdomen.

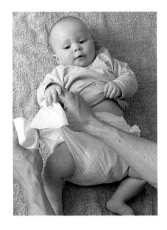

4 Now put something over the diaper for protection against wetness (a diaper wrap or plastic pants), to keep the surface underneath the baby dry.

**Tips on Using
Disposable Diapers**

*1 Your hands need to be free of ointments
and creams; otherwise the fastener won't stick.
Unfold the diaper, and place it under
the baby's bottom.*

*2 Pull the front part of the diaper between the baby's
legs and onto his belly. Fold the upper edges over to
the outside: Plastic has no place on a baby's skin.*

*3 Remove the protective covering from one tape, and
stick the side panel to the front part of the diaper. Then
do the same with the remaining panel on the other side.*

*4 Make sure the elasticized sides around the baby's
legs aren't turned under; that would leave
pressure marks.*

- Diaper pail and wastebasket
- Diaper ointment/cream or petroleum jelly (for use as a barrier cream if your baby has a diaper rash)

Make certain that all the equipment you need for changing the diaper is within easy reach. Once your little "diaper package" has been unwrapped, don't take your eyes off the baby.

■ To clean the baby's bottom, you can use a small paper towel dipped in baby oil (room temperature) instead of the washcloth. That is not quite so hygienic, however, but it is easier, especially when you are away from home, because there is no need for fresh water and a washcloth. Commercial wipes—cellulose cloths impregnated with lotion—are also good for this purpose. Use them with caution, however: Some children have a sensitive reaction to them and may develop a diaper rash.

Especially practical, for bigger children in particular: Attach a holder for toilet paper within reach of your changing table. There are extra soft brands of toilet paper that you can use even on a baby's skin, and they are far less expensive than baby wipes or cosmetic wipes.

For Sore Bottoms

An infant's skin is sensitive and susceptible to irritants from a variety of sources such as stool and urine, from diapers themselves, from laundry detergents, or less frequently from a new food in your baby's diet or antibiotics. A diaper rash will appear as patches of red, inflamed skin or small red bumps around the baby's genitals, buttocks, thigh folds, and lower abdomen.

Tips on Preventing Diaper Rashes

■ Change the baby frequently.

■ Make sure that disposable diapers or plastic pants are loose fitting, so that air is allowed in.

■ If the diaper area starts to become red, use either petroleum jelly or a zinc oxide-based ointment after each diaper change as protection from further irritation.

■ Keep the area dry. Keeping the diaper off when possible exposes the baby's skin to the air, preventing the growth of yeast.

■ If the rash does not clear up after 3 to 4 days, call your pediatrician. Yeast is ubiquitous in the environment, and yeast likes warm, moist, and dark environments—all present in a diaper. With the skin irritation of an irritant diaper rash after 3 to 4 days, yeast is likely to set up house.

Umbilical Care—Not a Problem

After birth, the umbilical cord is clamped and cut off about 1 inch (2.5 cm) from the navel. (There are no nerves in the cord; therefore, your baby will feel no pain during this procedure.) The clamp is then removed when the cord is dry—usually the day of discharge from the hospital. The cord will fall off on its own sometime between 10 days and 3 weeks after birth.

The Most Important Rules

■ Wash your hands thoroughly before touching the umbilical stump and the surrounding area.

■ Keep the stump of the umbilical cord dry and clean. Use cotton balls dipped in isopropyl alcohol or alcohol pads with each diaper change to clean the umbilical stump until it falls off. Your baby may cry when the stump is cleaned with alcohol, which is normal, but it is only because the evaporation of the alcohol makes the skin feel cold.

■ Keep the diaper folded below the cord to protect it from friction. You can fold the front of the diaper over or cut a notch in the diaper just below the cord. Some diapers already have a notch cut out in the front.

■ You may notice a few drops of blood at the cord site when it falls off. This is normal. If there are more than a couple of drops or bleeding does not stop, you should call your doctor.

■ You should call your doctor immediately if you notice any signs of infection at the cord site: redness surrounding the base or pus coming from the base of the cord, or your baby crying when your finger touches the base of the cord or the skin around the base.

Bathing and Washing

Let's dispense with the old prejudices right off the bat: Your baby does not have to be bathed daily; there is no need to restrict baths to the morning hours; getting water in his ears will not cause problems; providing a full range of shampoos, lotions, and creams is not necessary; and bubble baths are not recommended. Washing and bathing your baby is far less complicated than it seems.

For a list of equipment that you will need, see page 271.

How Often and When?

If you bathe your child two or three times a week, you will completely satisfy the requirements of good hygiene. Older babies love bath time, and there is nothing wrong with bathing every day if you both enjoy it. Most newborns, though, have not yet acquired

Don't let anything but water touch your baby's skin—with very few exceptions!

the love of water and nakedness that an older baby loves—so 2 to 3 times a week is fine.

It is not an easy matter to find the ideal time for washing and bathing. After feeding, a baby is tired and usually doesn't want to be bathed; yet, a hungry baby wants to be fed, not to splash in the tub. So, choosing the best time for him can be difficult. And, the bath routine has to fit into *your* own daily schedule as well. Don't take your child outdoors just after his bath—don't bathe him before you go shopping, for example. Some babies are wide awake after a bath, while others are tired. Observe your child closely, and try to choose a time that is truly convenient for you or your husband. Once you have decided on a time, you need to stick to it as closely as possible, to make planning easier. Besides, a regular routine will benefit your child as well.

Cosmetics—What Is Wise?

Today our children have problems not only with infectious diseases but also with allergies, rashes, and diseases of the respiratory system. A wide variety of chemical irritants are responsible for some of these problems. Unfortunately, baby products are not necessarily less irritating than products formulated for adults. Keep in mind: Healthy baby skin produces its own oils, and does not need oils or lotions from an external source in principle, unless it has been dried out by bath additives or too much soap. Resist using the sweet-smelling, attractively packaged "baby cosmetics." You may contact consumer groups for information about these products, or you can save yourself the time and restrict your purchases to the essentials.

Some tips on what to use and what not to use:

■ A newborn baby's skin may appear dry and peeling in the first few days after birth. It is not necessary to apply oils or lotions to the baby's skin; this will go away on its own.

■ Few infants need shampoo on their hair—whether they have a full head of hair or not. You can use a wet washcloth on the scalp with or without a mild soap.

■ For the body, use children's bath products sparingly, if at all, or instead use a mild soap. Start by washing the face with a plain wet washcloth, then you may use a mild soap for washing the rest of the body.

■ Don't use powder on your baby. He could breathe in a cloud of powder, which could be irritating to his respiratory tract, or it could form clumps and irritate his skin.

Sponge Bath on the Changing Table

Your baby does not absolutely have to be given a tub bath to get clean. You also can give him a "head-to-toe" sponge bath on the changing table. It is especially important to clean his face, hands, bottom, and genital area, since those are the areas of a baby that are likeliest to get dirty. Wiping his arms, legs, belly, and back with a damp cloth is sufficient.

Make sure you have everything you need within reach before you start the sponge bath. The room should be warm and free of any drafts.

What You Will Need
• Fresh clothing
• Clean diapers
• Several clean washcloths

- A basin of warm water (Remember, you should always test the water with your wrist or elbow to make sure it is not too hot or too cold.)
- A towel
- Mild soap

■ Now, to get started:

1 Spread out a large bath towel on the changing table, and fold the bottom half of it up at first. (You will unfold the towel after cleaning the baby's bottom.)

2 Undress your child completely. When you pull off the pants and diaper, wipe the baby's bottom with the old diaper, then clean the bottom with a wipe or washcloth as you normally would when changing a diaper. Then you can unfold the towel fully.

3 With another dampened washcloth, wipe the baby's eyes—going from inside to outside. Then go over the forehead, mouth, and nose.

4 Next, wash the external parts of the ears and back of the head. (Do not try to clean inside the ear canal, as this can potentially cause harm to the inside of the ear and is unnecessary.)

5 Finally, dry the head, taking care to be gentle and not to rub too hard.

6 Always wash starting with the head, and remember to rinse and squeeze out the excess water after washing an area of the body.

7 After each "wash cycle," or each area of the body washed, such as the head or the chest and back, dry the damp areas of skin immediately, to keep your child from getting cold.

8 Clean the baby's neck, arms, and hands next. Wash his abdomen before his back, then wash the legs and feet.

9 Last, wash the genital area and bottom. If your baby is a boy and is uncircumcised, you should not attempt to pull back the foreskin to wash—this is not necessary and can cause irritation and potential problems if it is forcibly pulled back.

——ESPECIALLY FOR FATHERS——

The first bath is a moving and exciting experience. The brand-new mother probably is feeling a little unsure of herself. Why don't you make it a joint venture, or even do it yourself? One of you can bathe the baby while the other gives support, then holds out the towel to take him and dry him.

You'll see, it not only works better, it's more fun, too.

In the future, you may want to consider taking over the evening bath altogether. If you are always gone in the daytime, you should reserve the right to bathe the baby yourself in the evening. That will be your special time to enjoy your child, a time you can look forward to. And a great help to your wife!

During the early weeks at home, when the newborn is still very small, it may be easiest to bathe him in the sink: The preparation is brief, you don't have to bend over, and you have a good hold on your child. Fill the sink with only 2 inches of water (cold water on first, off last), and always run your wrist or elbow through the length of the sink to assure there are no hot spots.

In Between: A Small-Scale Sponge Bath

If you bathe your child about every other day and wipe his bottom with a damp cloth or baby-wipe every time you change his diaper, a small-scale sponge bath will be adequate in between.

■ Get everything ready just as you did for a large-scale sponge bath and begin:

1 Lay your child on the bath towel. Remember to always wash starting with the head first and the bottom last, and dry his skin after every "wash cycle" (each successive area of the body washed).

2 Wash the baby's eyes, face, and head as previously described.

3 Soap both hands using a soapy corner of the washcloth, then wipe away the soap with the remainder of the washcloth. Then pat them dry with the towel.

4 Take off the baby's pants and diaper, and wipe his bottom with the old diaper. Wash the baby's genital area and bottom as previously described.

A Bath Your Child Will Enjoy

In the first few months babies feel happiest in an *infant bathtub* (or bathinette). You will find a great many styles available in stores that carry baby products. You can set the tub up in the bathroom or kitchen, placing it either directly into the bathtub or on a stable surface. Placing it within the bathtub or a large sink ensures that it won't be at risk for falling as it might on a sudsy countertop. Also available are lightweight changing tables on wheels (see page 47), with a top that lifts to expose a baby bath.

Features to Look For
■ A drain hole and an attached plug; then the water is easy to drain.
■ A pocket or tray at the side is practical for holding supplies.

What You Need to Get Ready
■ Before the bath, lay out all the things you will need, within easy reach.
■ The room should be warm and free of drafts—ideally the room temperature at about 75 degrees Fahrenheit.
■ The water temperature should be warm—not hot—to the touch of your

The First Bath—
Step by Step

■ What you will need: mild soap, a cup for rinsing with fresh water, two fresh washcloths (use clean ones for each bath), bath towel, clean diapers, fresh clothing.

1 Fill the tub with 2 inches of warm water—cold water on first and off last. Before placing the baby in the tub, test the water temperature with the inside of your wrist or elbow—it should feel pleasantly warm.

2 Undress your baby. Place your left arm under the back of his neck, so that his head rests on your forearm (near your wrist), and take hold of his upper arm near the shoulder. With your other hand, support his bottom.

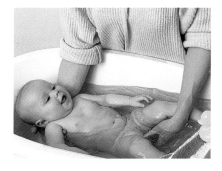

3 Slowly lower your child into the bathwater. With your right hand, which is now free, wash his head, ears, and face, then the rest of his body. Use soap to wash his hands, feet, and finally, his genital area and bottom. If some soap gets in his eyes, take a wet washcloth and wipe his eyes.

4 Once the bath is finished, with both hands, lift your child out of the bathtub again. Wrap him in the bath towel from head to toe, to keep him from becoming cold. There are baby towels available with built-in hoods.

5 Gently blot him dry inside the towel. Dab or blow on the places where skin touches skin: under arms, bend of the arm, behind the ears, neck, bottom crease, and hollow of the knee.

6 Now diaper (see page 48) and dress (see page 60) your baby, making time for plenty of cuddling during the process.

elbow or wrist. Make sure your water heater is set no higher than 120 degrees Fahrenheit.

■ Put only 2 inches of water in the tub or sink and remember never to leave your infant alone in the tub even for a moment—if the doorbell or the phone rings, take your baby out of the tub and wrap him in the towel before answering.

■ If the bathtub and the changing table are not in the same room, make sure you wrap him in a towel on the way to the bath and again on the way back to the changing table. This little trick will enable you to have the bath towel close at hand to keep him warm:

• Stick one corner of the bath towel into the waistband of your pants or skirt. After undressing your baby on the changing table, throw the towel over him. Now, with him nicely wrapped up, you can proceed to the bathroom.

• Next to the tub, let the towel slip off—the corner will stay in your waistband; after the bath, the baby can be wrapped up in the towel again right away and carried back to the changing table, without having to find some place to put him down.

Rompers and pants that fasten at the crotch are practical: There's no need to half undress your baby every time you change him.

In the Tub: Important Information

• If your child ever slips out of your hands and gets his head under water momentarily, no harm is done. A baby's ears and nose have mechanisms that keep water from getting inside.

• Please don't let the bath last more than 5 to 10 minutes. Being in the water longer will wash away the skin's natural oils, and leave the baby with dry skin. Also, the water will begin to get cold.

• Whether your baby has only a thin layer of hair on his head or a full head of hair, it is not necessary to wash with anything but a wet washcloth, unless your doctor orders differently. You can use a nonirritating baby shampoo or mild soap to wash

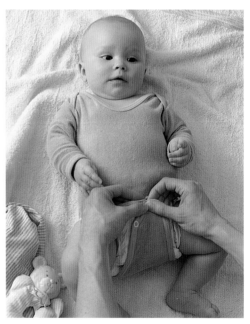

the hair if you wish, but only 1 to 2 times a week. For treating cradle cap (a harmless condition resulting from a dry, scaly scalp), see page 221.

Important!
- <u>Never</u> leave your infant or child alone in the bathtub, even for a moment.
- Never leave the faucet water running while the baby is in the bath.

When Bathing Becomes Stressful

Some babies desperately resist being bathed. They are frightened by their unaccustomed nakedness and by the water—and possibly by their own state of agitation as well.

■ If your baby seems to be upset by his bath, you can make bath time very short at first—several minutes at most. This is usually only in the newborn period. Most older babies love bath time.

■ If your baby protests greatly each time, this can be very stressful for you. If that's the case, then you can give a sponge bath for a week or two, then try the tub again.

■ You will inevitably get wet during bath time, and therefore should be prepared in advance by wearing an apron or an old sweatshirt.

■ I bathed my third child in the big bathtub with his brothers in his third week of life, because I simply couldn't find the time to arrange a special bath for the baby. All three children thought it was wonderful!

CLOTHING RULES AND REGULATIONS

For the essentials of your firstborn's layette, see page 269.

■ *Underwear, stretch suits, and little sweaters are standard wear for daytime when indoors. The combination of sleeveless stretch suits, plus long-sleeved sweaters is practical, because you can change both articles of clothing separately if your baby spits up or gets the pant legs wet.*

■ *As long as your child spends the entire day in his bassinet or crib, you can dress him the same way at night. There is something to be said for having special pajamas: Pajamas and sleepers designed for very small babies can be quickly opened at the crotch with a row of snap fasteners, so that you don't have to completely undress your baby to change him at night. You will get back to bed faster, and your baby will not become so wide awake. Baby pajamas are extremely comfortable and light. They tell your child that another part of the day is beginning. Even if the baby will scarcely register that message at first, it still may help him get into the day to night rhythm.*

■ *Most babies need little cotton or fleece booties at first, to wear over the feet of the stretch suit, because their circulation may not keep their feet warm enough in infancy. With bigger babies, too, it may still be a good idea to put thick terry socks over tights or socks, or to use socks with a skidproof coating on the bottom.*

■ *What you will need for a walk, depending on the season, is discussed on pages 81–83.*

Dressing and Undressing with Care

Babies usually don't like to be dressed or undressed, and often they protest with a howl. Their movements are still uncoordinated, and it will take all of your attention and energy to get the job done.

Don't let that annoy you: Do the dressing and undressing as quickly as possible, to keep the baby from getting chilled unnecessarily. In the first months, the changing table is the best place for these procedures. Once the child can sit without support, it is practical to dress and undress his upper body with him on your lap.

It may help to distract your child. Talk or sing to him. A colorful mobile over the changing area can also accomplish miracles.

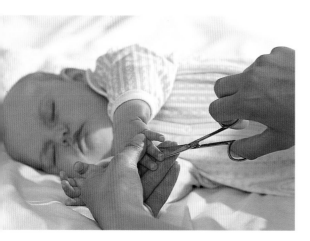

It's easiest to cut the baby's fingernails while she's asleep, because her hands are totally relaxed then.

The Most Important Rules

■ Dress your baby in one more layer than you are wearing.

■ Many newborns do not like being naked, nor do they like being dressed and undressed. You should undress or dress him step by step. Leave his upper body dressed at first, and start by changing his diaper.

■ Although undershirts and shirts in previous times were open at one side, today pullover styles are more common, because they don't shift around so readily. Stretch the neck opening wider with both thumbs and index fingers in a scissors position, bunch up the little shirt like an accordion, and pull it carefully but swiftly over your child's head.

■ If the shirt has long sleeves, bunch up each one in accordion fashion over one hand, while with the other, you push the baby's arm through, helping things along from the other side. Make sure the baby's hand is closed, because a tiny finger can quickly catch in the sleeve.

■ With one-piece underwear (bodysuits) or rompers, always dress the baby's top half first, then stick his legs through and fasten the garment.

Important!

Newborns often react in a panicky fashion when something is pulled over their head. When you get the baby's layette, it might be wise to look for shirts that close in front or in back, with ties, if possible.

Manicure for Tiny Nails

Some babies—particularly if they were born after their due date—come into the world with long fingernails. These fingernails can cause scratches on the baby's skin, and you may notice some facial scratches in the first few days of life. This won't hurt your baby, but at this point you should trim the nails. You can do this with either a soft emery board or with blunt-tipped nail scissors. Note that toenails grow slower than fingernails and will not need to be trimmed as often.

How and When to Trim the Nails

■ You can trim your baby's nails either after the bath, while the baby is sleeping, or while he is lying on your lap.

■ If your baby is awake, then it is best to have 2 people in order to do this safely. Take his hand, or foot, and cut or file the nails into ovals. It will be easier if your baby is distracted by his father, siblings, or exciting views, or if he is being fed.

And in Conclusion: Ears, Eyes, Nose, and Teeth

■ Clean only the external parts of the *ears*, using a damp washcloth. It is not advisable to use cotton-tipped swabs: They can cause injury if inserted too

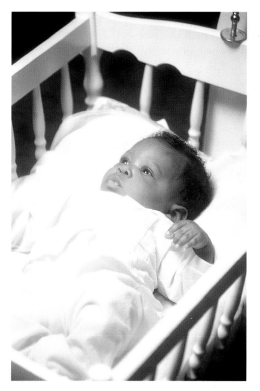

Clean and content.

far into the ear. The ear canal will clean itself. All you need to do is carefully remove the visible earwax in the entrance to the canal with a paper tissue, twisted to a point.

■ The same applies for stuffy *noses* as well: Do not stick anything inside the baby's nose! If your baby has congestion or dried mucus inside the nose, you can use a bulb syringe placed at the entrance to the nose to help remove the mucus.

■ Always clean the *eyes* by wiping from the inner corners toward the outer corners. Use a soft, clean, damp washcloth. If the baby has a severe cold, or conjunctivitis (pink eye), the lashes may stick together. It is advisable under these circumstances to call your doctor.

■ When the first *teeth* appear, you may use a clean cloth or soft toothbrush with warm water to clean the teeth. Perhaps the single most important step in the prevention of tooth decay in the first year of life is resisting the urge to put your baby to bed with the bottle in his mouth. If he falls asleep with the bottle in his mouth, this can lead to what is called "bottle caries," or tooth decay due to the pooling of formula or juice around his teeth. Fluoride is also important in the prevention of tooth decay, and you should find out if your town water supply has been fluoridated. You can do this by calling your state department of public health, or asking your doctor or dentist. Take note that often the "baby water" sold in the "baby aisle" of your supermarket or drug store contains adequate fluoride. If you are not using fluoridated water, check with your doctor about the possible need for fluoride supplementation. If needed, the supplements are usually started after 6 months of age. Later on, the second molars will come in (between 20 and 24 months of age), at which point it is important to have a regular brushing routine with a fluoride toothpaste.

HANDLING THE BABY SAFELY

Babies need a very special kind of treatment. If you know how to hold and carry your child, where he should lie and sit, what temperatures are comfortable for him, why he cries, and how to rock him to sleep—then you will be able to enjoy him with far fewer worries about "mishandling."

When your child is born, he is a strange, puzzling being. You cannot deal with him as you do with adults, and he often reacts in ways that you did not expect. Some things will remain a puzzle to us—but there are many things we can learn. If you use the appropriate handling techniques, it is not at all difficult to pick up, hold, and carry even the most fragile-seeming newborn. You can easily learn how to lay and set him down properly. Later, we will discuss other handling issues such as carrier versus baby carriage. Part of learning how to "handle" him has to do with dressing him—when you leave the house with the baby, is his clothing appropriate for the weather?

Although proper holding and handling techniques are simple to learn, not all the difficulties that you encounter while caring for your child can be resolved according to such simple rules. For example, when your baby cries, you may be at a complete loss as to the reason and how to console him. When he simply won't go to sleep, you sometimes will become desperate. The information in this book concerning the reasons behind babies' crying and difficulty sleeping may help you; one of the tips may possibly succeed with your child. There is no patent solution. Console yourself with this: Whether a baby is "difficult" or "good" does not depend on the parents' performance in their child-raising roles. Babies simply have different temperaments. Don't let other people put pressure on you; take your child as he is.

63

Holding and Carrying

In the first days you may scarcely dare to touch your baby. To overcome this irrational fear, you need only think of how much pressure his little body has already withstood during his passage though the birth canal. With your help, he has been prepared for life "outside." Touch your child gently, but firmly and with assurance; this will give your baby a feeling of safety and security. A newborn likes to be closely embraced because it approximates the way he felt inside his mother's body.

Where your movements are concerned, however, make sure not to do anything suddenly: Your child will react sensitively to that.

On the following pages, we will present the "correct" ways to handle a newborn. You'll see quite soon that picking up, carrying, and rocking your baby will become second nature for you.

Handling Newborns Properly

In the first weeks, the baby's head and spinal column need extra support, because his muscles are not yet strong enough to control his head. He becomes frightened when his head flops backward, and he reacts by thrusting his arms and legs into the air: a protective reflex to counter the sensation of falling. On these pages, you will find several positions in which you will have a good hold on your baby and he feels comfortable as well.

Lifting the Baby
Slide one hand behind the baby's head and back, and support his bottom with your other hand.

Eye Contact Position

His head lies in the bend of your arm, his body rests on your forearm, and your hand supports his bottom. If you carry him this way for a fairly long time, it is better to place your other hand beneath him as well to support his body. This position affords you excellent visual contact with your child, at the correct visual distance— the same as with the breastfeeding position.

"Presentation" Position

Hold your child in a sitting posture with his back against your abdomen, so that he can look all around. This "presentation" position is ideal when you want to show your child something or distract him—or when you would like to show him off. (That's legitimate as well, from time to time.)

Work Position

One variation of the position described above: You have a good grip on your child, and at the same time you have one hand free— this is the best position for all the situations when you need to take care of something else without putting the baby down.

Burp Position

Hold him upright, with one cheek resting on your shoulder. This position is very effective when your baby has to be burped or when he is coughing or crying: The slight pressure on his stomach and the upright posture help to relieve stomach distention by releasing air bubbles. You can pat his back gently with one hand; often that has a soothing effect.

For Stomachache: The Flying Position

Hold your baby so that he is "flying" in the air, belly down. Being suspended in this position can help the abdomen relax. In addition, you can massage the baby's abdomen gently. Let his upper body rest on your forearm while you put your hand under his armpit. With the other hand, support his abdomen.

An ideal variation for long-armed parents: Let the baby's entire length rest on your forearm, with his head in the bend of your arm and your hand around one of his legs. With your free hand, you can stroke and pat the baby.

How to Hold an Older Baby

During the third and fourth months, your child will gain better control of his head (see page 181), and the muscles in his back will become stronger. When you notice that he is starting to balance his head with less help, you can use your supporting hand less frequently. Practice is the best way for the muscles of the head, neck, and back to strengthen themselves.

Picking Him Up under the Arms
Place one hand under each of your baby's arms, and lift him up toward you. You can pick him up this way and carry him on your shoulder, in the bend of your arm, in front of you, or on one hip.

Hip Position
When the baby gets heavier, it will be easiest for you to carry him on one hip. First he has to be able to hold his back straight—that ability will develop sometime during the fifth to the sixth month. If you set him on one hip with his legs straddling you, he will have a wide field of vision, while remaining able to communicate with you, and you will have one hand free.

The Right Place to Sleep

A newborn can neither raise his head nor turn over on his own during the first several months. He will stay wherever you put him down. In the first months, he will spend most of his time in a crib, cradle, bassinet, or papoose. It is now recommended by the American Academy of Pediatrics that infants sleep on their back. They should therefore not be put into the crib on their stomach for sleep. There have been several studies linking stomach sleep position with SIDS (sudden infant death syndrome). In addition, for newborns and young infants, the crib should be free of pillows, stuffed animals, thick comforters, loose bumper guards, and toys.

Crib, Cradle, or Bassinet?

In the first weeks, your baby needs the security and warmth of his baby bed. There is no need to leave your child in a quiet room all the time, however. When he is awake, push his bed into whatever room you are in, and let him participate in family life.

Of course, the baby's "nest" needs to be prepared before he is born. There are a great many options when it comes to buying the necessary equipment.

Bassinet

A bassinet is a small, wheeled baby bed, usually with a fabric hood or canopy. It is very lightweight and can be rolled anywhere in your home, so you can keep your child with you at all times, if you wish. This is practical at night, especially if you are breast-feeding.

The newborn will like being in the small confines of the bassinet, since that will help him adjust to his new

Ideal for the first few months: a bassinet on wheels, with a canopy.

life. The hood will shield him from the sun and screen out a great deal of noise at the same time. In addition, by moving the bassinet rhythmically, you can rock the baby to sleep or soothe him with the greatest of ease. The only drawback is that your baby will outgrow the bassinet by the time he is five or six months old, if not sooner.

Consequently, since you will only be using the bassinet for a short period of time, you should try to borrow one or buy one secondhand—you can dress it up with new bedding and trimmings.

■ One alternative to the bassinet is the carrycot. Both woven basket types and collapsible fabric types are available, and some come with a wheeled stand (available in baby stores). They allow you to tote your child from one room to another without much trouble.

■ A good solution for small babies: If you have purchased a combination stroller/carriage with a built-in fabric bassinet and there is enough space in your living room, your baby easily can nap in it during the day. At night, just remove the fabric bassinet from the carriage/stroller and put it in the cradle or the crib.

The Good Old Cradle

Cradles are available either in wheeled styles with hoods, similar to bassinets, or in truly old-fashioned styles, made from a single piece of wood, with floor rockers.

Bassinet cradles also employ some type of rocking mechanism. They are similar to bassinets in most other respects, including the fact that they are used only during the first several months. The heavy wooden cradles, however, are often so large that a child can sleep in them until he is one year old. The disadvantage is that they cannot be rolled, and you always have to bend over to pick up your child. These are more comparable to cribs. If you have a large cradle, then you can easily make the transition to a large crib next, one that can convert into a junior bed later on.

Practical: Beds with Rails

Today, many parents put their baby in a crib with wooden slats right from the start, because he will be able to use the crib right up until the time he is ready for a twin bed. It is important to shop carefully and wisely when buying or borrowing a crib. Strict safety standards for cribs went into effect in 1974, and new cribs will have a label that states whether the Consumer Product Safety Commission (CPSC) standards have been met. If you are borrowing a crib or have a crib that has been in the family for generations, then you should make sure that it conforms to the following safety standards:

69

You can lower one side of the crib later—to let your child climb in and out of bed, once he's old enough. Be sure to put something soft on the floor next to the crib!

■ Bars should be no more than $2^3/_8$ inches apart. Larger openings may permit your child's head to become caught in between the bars.

■ There should be no decorative cutouts in the headboard or footboard. This is also an area where your child's head can become caught.

■ Minimum rail height of 22 inches when the mattress is at its highest setting, and the rail is at its lowest setting. When lowered completely, the top of the side rail should be at least 4 inches above the mattress. Remember to always leave the side rail up when your child is in the crib.

■ Any corner posts or knobs that are higher than $5/_8$ of an inch should be removed, if possible.

■ Inspect the wood for splinters, sharp edges, stability, and lead paint (if borrowing or if a family heirloom).

■ The mattress should be firm. The baby's back should not sink into the surface.

■ The mattress should fit into the crib snugly, and you should not be able to fit more than 2 fingers between the mattress and the sides or ends of the crib.

■ The bumper guard should fit tightly to the crib rails and be secured with at least six ties, and the ties should be no longer than 6 inches.

■ Once your child is able to pull to a standing position (between 8 and 10 months), you should then remove the bumper guards.

■ Never place the crib near a window.

What Every Bed Needs

The Right Foundation

The mattress should be neither too hard nor too soft: The baby's back should not sink into the surface upon which he lies.

■ For the first months, a polyurethane foam mattress is sufficient for your baby's flyweight. For a basket that you set up yourself or a bassinet that is incomplete, you can have a mat cut to order. Then you will need two mats of different sizes because the basket is larger toward the top. At first, lay only one mat inside—then the sleeping area is smaller. When your child grows larger, adding the second mat will expand the sleeping surface as well.

■ For a crib, however, you need a crib mattress. Latex or foam mattresses should be purchased in high-density varieties; they are especially recommended if there is a risk of allergies.

■ On top of the mattress, place a thick cotton pad; then put a waterproof mattress cover over that. The mattress cover should be washable and permeable to air. Caution: Do not use plastic or rubber covers because they interfere with the baby's respiration. Finally, put on a fitted sheet.

■ There is no need for a pillow, and it would get in the way. Instead, protect the head end with a diaper folded into a triangle, with its edges tucked under the mattress. You can change a covering of this kind whenever your baby spits up, without having to put on a fresh sheet every time.

Warmly Covered

Recent studies have shown that certain types of soft bedding, including pillows, comforters, and soft mattresses may be linked to sudden infant death syndrome (SIDS). The theory is that soft bedding can create pockets that trap the carbon dioxide your baby has exhaled, and he then rebreathes this carbon dioxide, which can result in suffocation. The following are recommendations for bed coverings:

■ Make sure your mattress sheet is tightly fitted.

■ Use a light blanket for covering the baby.

■ Avoid heavy comforters: Nightgowns or *cotton sacques* with drawstring bottoms or *newborn sleepers* will keep your child warm. You will need different thicknesses and material depending on the season.

■ Newborn sleepers are practical for little babies who still have to be changed at night. There is no need to undress your child completely; you simply unfasten the crotch panel of the garment to gain easy access to the diaper.

Well Positioned for Sleep

At first, your baby will be unable to change his position by himself. The recommendation by the American Academy of Pediatrics is that all infants sleep on their back. This is because of the association between sudden infant death syndrome (SIDS) and the prone (stomach) sleep position. It is advisable to place the baby on his stomach only when he is awake and under your supervision, to let him play, look around, and strengthen his

Only during the first few weeks does the baby need to be propped while lying on her side.

muscles to help prepare him for crawling.

■ Because your child will mostly be lying on his back when in his crib, you can hang a toy or mobile overhead for him to look at. Make sure that you hang it high enough so that he cannot pull it down onto himself.

■ In the first several months, many babies will spit up a little after feeding; therefore, right after feeding you should lay him on his side. A newborn cannot remain in the side position without a little help. Roll up a towel into a sausage shape and lay it against his back. Change him from one side to the other regularly.

Important: A Change of Perspective

Your child's eyes will always be drawn by brightness or movement. If his crib stands next to a wall and if he spends most of his time there, he will begin to hold his head to one side. You need to rotate the bed a little every day. Alternatively, switch the head end and the foot end once or twice a week. You can also put a crib mirror on the side facing the wall.

Sitting and Crawling in Safety

When your three- or four-month-old child starts raising his head and showing increasing interest in his surroundings, and when his legs become stronger and more active and he makes his first attempts to roll himself over, you need to begin carefully enlarging his "area of action." The crib will eventually get boring for most children.

This moment arrives at different times for different children. Don't force these changes on your child, just experiment from time to time, and watch his reaction. You can place him on a clean blanket or colorful mat on the floor for "play time." It is important, though, that you do not leave your baby alone in a room without supervision.

For the Transitional Phase: An Infant Seat

As long as your baby is still unable to crawl and cannot sit up to look around on his own, he will have the best view of things from a semiupright position. An infant seat can be propped up in such a position, and the seat belt will keep him from falling out—he is safer there than in a mountain of pillows. In addition, the infant seat can easily be carried from one room to another, and it does not take up too much space. These types of seats are ideal for young babies during the brief transitional period between lying and sitting.

Keep in mind that infant seats are not covered by federal regulations.

■ Here are some tips on buying and using your infant seat:

- Look for a wide, stable base with a nonskid bottom, and crotch and waist restraint straps.
- Check the weight guidelines that are provided by the manufacturer on the box.
- A carry handle makes transporting from room to room convenient.
- A rocking mechanism is a nice additional feature.
- Never use an infant seat as a substitute for a car seat. Infant seats should be used for propping up the baby so that he can see more easily and be fed more easily.
- Always use the strap when your baby is in the seat, even if the seat is stationary.

Your baby still can't sit for long on his own. A pillow behind him will protect him if he falls over.

Important!
Never set the infant seat down on a table or counter. The danger of falling off is just too great!

Attempts to Exercise: Playmat and Playpens

At the age of five to six months, your child's radius of action becomes considerably larger. He tries his first pushups, rolls over, and is beginning to sit by himself. He no longer has to spend all his waking hours in his crib, bassinet, or infant seat. Now the floor is his element.

■ A large, quilted cotton mat or pad for playing on the floor is ideal for his first attempts to exercise. The larger the playmat, the better. When your baby starts to sit without falling over,

WALKERS

With good reason, walkers have almost completely disappeared from the scene: the contraptions meant to encourage babies to walk. These devices are dangerous—the injury toll in walker-related accidents is high—and they force the baby to make unnatural movements. The claim that they make babies walk sooner is entirely false. The truth is that every child develops at his own pace and learns things when he is ready for them.

place a pillow behind him on the mat so that if he loses his balance and tips over backward, he won't hit his head.

■ The good old playpen still has a legitimate purpose, provided that the baby is not confined there constantly. In the playpen, the baby has a relatively large amount of space available, and the top rail helps him learn to stand. When you have to race down to the basement, to the front door, or to the telephone, your child can continue to play in safety, without your having to carry him around with you everywhere you go. In the kitchen, while ironing, or while working at your desk, the child can be near you and

you won't have to be constantly on the go. A prerequisite: The play yard has to be big enough (at least 48 by 48 inches (1.2 × 1.2 m)); otherwise you might as well pack your baby off to bed. If the playpen is a wooden model, the slats have to be at least $2^3/_8$ inches apart. A simple model that will fold away is completely adequate, because you will be laying the playmat on the floor of the playpen anyway. Small playpens with fine mesh sides are not something that you need. They are, at most, the size of the bed, and the closely interlaced threads of the mesh side interfere with the baby's view of the surroundings. If your baby can't maintain a sitting position without toppling over, don't leave him in the playpen unsupervised. If he falls backward, he could injure himself on the slats of a wooden playpen. Lay him on his back if you are going to leave the room for a moment.

By the way, don't just set your child down in the playpen when you are busy with chores. Always play with him for awhile, and help him get used to the enclosure and the possibilities it offers for having fun. Otherwise he will always feel that he is merely being deposited there, and he will protest it vigorously.

When the Baby Cries . . .

Our ideal image is of a baby who sits or lies on his playmat, rosy, rounded, and smiling, and plays contentedly by himself while we watch in delight. The reality: Your child doesn't even think about allowing you to take a breather, he just keeps crying—and how!

Nothing brings us so close to our wits' end as a crying child, and in the first months of life that is a frequent occurrence. I was seldom able to tell what my child really wanted when he cried, and often I could not comfort him. Especially with my first child, his crying often haunted my dreams.

But, a bad conscience, feelings of failure, and self-reproaches are only additional burdens during this trying period. Although other mothers may make claims to the contrary, there is no ingenious solution, no button you can push to turn off the excruciating sound of the "siren." With the birth of your child, you do not automatically acquire intuitive knowledge of his needs. You have to get to know each other first. Be patient with your child—and with yourself. It will take a little time to figure out what each particular cry is intended to mean. Always keep in mind that your child is not crying in order to annoy you. The following pages may enable you to understand your child better, and that will help a great deal.

Why Do Babies Have to Cry?

Let's put the old prejudices behind us for good: Crying is not healthy, nor does it strengthen the lungs.

A baby cries
- because he is hungry,
- because his diaper needs to be changed,
- because he is too hot or too cold,
- because he has a stomachache,
- because he wants someone nearby,
- because he is overtired, and
- because he is bored.

You, as his mother, will try to rule out these causes by nursing your child, diapering him, feeling the back of his neck to check his body temperature, rubbing his tummy, picking him up, or giving him some attention. Often you will succeed in calming your child—a wonderful feeling.

75

Your baby isn't always sleeping or smiling. She has bad days and moments, just like the rest of us. Stay calm—and don't blame yourself.

Sometimes, however, the baby is simply inconsolable. He has apparent discomfort without any obvious source.

Usually we suspect adaptive problems of the baby's immature digestive system, the infamous "colic" (see page 226). Because the baby is unable to move around much at first, he has a hard time getting rid of the gas that distends his abdomen.

Researchers have found evidence of additional difficulties of adaptation to life outside the mother's body:

■ The baby has not yet developed a day to night rhythm. Since he is always a little on edge just as his sleep phase begins (a situation that changes later), his parents pick him up. That disturbs him, and he has trouble falling asleep, despite his fatigue. The baby may have difficulty establishing a rhythm and become tired, irritable, and cranky.

■ Even in the first weeks, a baby wants to understand and to influence the world around him. He wants to be integrated. In his efforts to become part of his new world, he frequently encounters limits and experiences helplessness, lack of understanding, and despair.

How Much Babies Cry

Babies are very different, and their crying is different as well. Behavioral research, however, has determined certain average values:

- In the first two weeks, two 45-minute periods a day of crying—a total of about $1^3/_4$ hours—are considered normal.
- From weeks 3 to 6, the baby will increase his crying, especially in the evening.
- From weeks 6 to 12, the duration of the crying increases by one hour; then from the twelfth week on, it slowly decreases to one hour per day.
- Excessive criers are babies who cry longer than three hours per day on more than three days of the week, for longer than three weeks. Of these babies, 15 percent are affected in the first three months, whereas the figure drops to only 3 percent by the end of the sixth month. The typical crying hours are usually between 6 P.M. and 11 P.M.

How You Can Calm Your Child

You can't spoil a newborn baby! In the first several months of life, it is important to respond to your baby's crying by holding and consoling him. The faster you comfort your newborn, the sooner he will stop crying. Check to see if he needs a diaper change. Is it time to eat? Is he too hot or too cold? Is he overtired and in need of a nap?

Some Tips on Consoling Your Crying Baby

- Gently massage his back or his abdomen in a circular motion.
- If your child has not discovered his thumb yet, a pacifier may help soothe him. You can get information on recommended pacifiers.
- Rocking is calming and soothing for babies. Rock him in his cradle or in a rocking chair in your arms.
- Lie down on your bed with your child. Place him on your stomach, cuddle him, and sing to him. That will be relaxing for both of you.
- If your baby has "fixed" crying times, make it a habit to go out for a walk or take him for a ride in the car at these times. Then you won't lose your cool, and the ride, the background noises, and the fresh air will help calm the baby.

——ESPECIALLY FOR FATHERS——

If your baby ever has a really bad day and brings his mother to her wit's end, it often helps to have someone else take care of the baby. Find time to get your wife out of the house for a few hours, or take the baby out somewhere on your own. This small effort can help your wife get a little space for herself and replenish her energy, and you will be amazed to see that your little squaller actually stops crying in your company.

EXTRA-TIP

Wrapping your child snugly in a cotton blanket helps many restless babies calm down. This may be because they are reminded of the familiar confines of their mother's body.

Fold a blanket into a triangle, with the tip at the bottom. Lay your child on his back in the center of the long side, so that his head barely sticks out over the top of the blanket. First fold one side around your baby, tucking the tip behind his back. Then wrap the other side firmly around him. Now fold the bottom of the original triangle under the baby's feet, toward the back.

■ If he wants to be close, you can carry him in a papoose or soft fabric front carrier.

■ Sometimes, just holding him in your arms and walking around the house is very helpful.

■ If you think gas may be the cause, turn to page 225 for ways to help your baby.

■ Perhaps he likes music? Try sitting with the baby on your shoulder, and enjoy some relaxing music together. If you wish, you may also dance around the room with him in your arms.

■ Hang a mobile above his crib.

If the Crying Gets on Your Nerves...

Nothing causes more stress for mothers than ceaseless crying "for no reason at all." Don't make things worse by trying to stick too precisely to your daily routine, your plans, or your work demands. If you put too much pressure on yourself, you will become impatient and your child will despair. Instead, turn a blind eye, and go along with your child's rhythm. Then you will have the best chance of eventually getting some time for yourself.

Acknowledge to yourself and your spouse your negative feelings, rage, and anger toward your baby. These are human reactions to constant sleep deprivation, feelings of inadequacy, and excessive stress. But it can be dangerous if you or your husband get carried away by these feelings. In moments of anger I found abdominal breathing and relaxation exercises helpful—the same ones I had learned while preparing for childbirth. Singing and talking can also help keep aggressions from escalating.

Important!

Stress leads to cramping. Keep your chin and mouth areas relaxed; then you will be less tense overall. For a stress-relieving exercise, see page 174. If necessary, it is better to put your baby in another room from time to time, until you recover.

Healthy Sleep Habits

"Sleep like a baby?" Not at all! Babies usually don't sleep the way we parents want them to. They often have trouble settling down; they wake up again easily; and above all, they don't sleep when we are tired—at night. That can make the first months with your newborn highly stressful, since nothing is so exhausting as constant sleep deprivation. Once you understand your baby's sleep behavior, you can adjust to it. Once you have a sense of the schedule, you can count on certain hours to get work done or to catch up on sleep.

Sleeping Through the Night: Wishful Thinking?

Babies sleep differently. Because of the rapid succession of the various sleep phases (see box at right), a baby keeps waking up from time to time. Research indicates that newborns sleep more in the daytime and are alert at night. This is most pronounced at about the age of 1 month. But don't despair, this will not last forever. Your baby will readjust his schedule and sleep more at night than during the day in no time. Many babies will be sleeping through the night (about 6 to 8 hours at a stretch) between three and four months.

Tips for a Good Night

Whether babies can be taught the day to night rhythm is a controversial question. If the rhythm fails to develop, however, and the restless nights are taking too much out of you, you can try to help the adaptation process along.

SLEEP PHASES AND SLEEP TIME

Like adults, babies have two sleep phases: deep sleep and active (REM) sleep. But unlike adults, a baby begins with the restless REM sleep. The sleep phases are cycled through more frequently, and REM sleep accounts for a majority of a baby's sleep time. REM sleep is active: Babies will dream and move around a lot, sometimes more than when awake. During the third to fourth months, the sleep phases become more like those of adults. At this time, deep (non-REM) sleep predominates.

The amount of time babies sleep each day varies from one baby to another. The following data will give you useful reference points, however. These numbers represent the sum of all of the sleep periods in a day—your baby does not sleep these lengths of time at any one sitting.

1–2 months	*16–19 hours*
3–4 months	*15–18 hours*
5–6 months	*14–16 hours*
7–8 months	*13–15 hours*
9–12 months	*12–14 hours*

■ If you use the baby's waking phases in the daytime for play, but offer no attractions at night apart from diapering and feeding, the night is more likely to become a resting phase.

■ Don't have the house all lit up at night. Use soft light and only where you need it for feeding or diapering.

■ In the daytime, wake your child at regular intervals to feed him. If that causes him to drink more milk, he will hold out longer at night.

■ Never let your baby cry for long—he may not settle down again the rest of the night.

Getting Your Child to Sleep More Easily

Often your baby has a hard time falling asleep, as well as difficulty sleeping through the night. If he is too wound up, he may not be able to settle down at all. Then desperate parents come up with elaborate ideas: they pack him in the car and drive around the block; they turn on the washing machine; or they dance the tango.

In the Right Mood for Sweet Dreams ...

Naturally, it is good to find out what will send the baby off to the land of dreams, but don't get involved in anything too extreme. Some techniques

> **EXTRA-TIP**
>
> *Pediatric providers have developed a strategy for babies who cry persistently at night. Start by making a note of the time the baby wakes up each night. After getting a good sense of when he tends to wake up at night, wake your child 15 to 30 minutes before the time he usually cries, nurse or bottle feed him, cuddle him, and put him back to bed. The following night, wake him 15 minutes earlier. Over time, he will begin to sleep longer. If relapses occur, start the process again. This system works by rewarding your baby for sleeping, not crying.*

are useful and others become unhelpful superstitions. These reliable tips may help you.

■ During the time before the baby goes to sleep, make sure peace and quiet prevail. The television, the radio, noisy siblings, and shopping trips will not put the baby in the right mood for going to sleep.

■ Rocking and patting on the back are still wonderful ways to help the baby fall asleep. Be patient, and try to maintain a steady, even rhythm.

■ Some songs have a peculiar soothing effect on newborn babies. Try *Rock-a-Bye Baby, Brahms' Lullaby*, or *Twinkle, Twinkle Little Star*.

■ Being carried or held while you make dancing movements will soothe many infants. Use the fabric front carrier (papoose) if the baby is too heavy to carry around. If you maintain a continuous rhythm for 5 to 10 minutes, your child will become tired.

■ Bedtime rituals that are repeated every evening are also helpful. A goodnight song, a little prayer, or the same light every night may have a recognition effect even in the first months.

■ Your husband can put the baby to bed. He may have more patience at that moment than you.

■ Some children become more alert when they are bathed, but others may become sleepy after their bath. Afterward, don't rub your child dry, but instead wrap him up in a warm towel. After you dress him, put him immediately in his bed.

■ If you have a rocking chair at home, sitting and rocking just before bedtime can be helpful.

■ And the parents' sleep? For tips on ways to get the sleep you need despite restless nights, see pages 174–175.

Going Out with the Baby

Working mothers are usually at home after the birth of their baby for at least 6 weeks. Fathers, on the other hand, usually have returned to work much earlier. In most cases, therefore, the mother is home alone with the baby and will need to take him along on every errand. That is why the selection of car seats, strollers, and baby carriers is so enormously important. But another factor to consider is how much heat or cold can the little one tolerate?

When to Go Outside

Your newborn is created for life on this earth and can tolerate fresh air from the start. Feel free to take him on a walk around the block in his stroller or on a trip to the supermarket. A baby who is ready to leave the hospital is ready for these outings. Take some caution, however, if the weather

What a relief, to see your baby sleeping so peacefully and "sweetly" at last!

is very cold or very hot. If you're uncomfortable, then your baby will be as well. Also, protect your baby's skin from direct sunlight exposure. In the summertime, keep a hat on him and use the weather shield or canopy on his stroller. If you live in an area that has bitter cold winters, then you should limit the time spent outdoors.

In my own experience, nothing keeps a baby busier and calmer than swaying branches in his field of vision and the background noises outdoors (even traffic noise!). He will sleep better after an outing in the fresh air. It is nice if you have a yard, a terrace, or a balcony, because then you don't have to go out for a walk with the carriage.

Caution: Extreme Situations

Your baby is still very sensitive to extremes of weather. Babies have a harder time compensating for temperature differences than adults do. Therefore, guard against overdressing or underdressing in extremes of temperature.

Protecting Your Baby Against Heat

Your baby can become overheated—in the summer months, in winter, or in overheated rooms—if he is too warmly dressed.

Some tips to guard against overheating:

■ It is best to dress your baby in natural fibers, like cotton, that breathe.

■ If your baby is too hot, the back of his neck will perspire. You can place your hand on the back of his neck to check if he is too warmly dressed.

■ On hot summer days, babies need to drink more than usual. Give an additional bottle of formula or an additional meal of breast milk if you are breastfeeding.

■ Never leave your baby in direct sunlight. Always keep a cap or bonnet with a wide brim on his head. After the age of 6 months, you should apply sunscreen to help protect against the damaging rays of the sun.

■ Although drafts and wind are dangerous for a newborn, a gentle breath of air will move the heat away from his body, and therefore is important.

Important!
An overheated child is listless and exhausted. Take him into a cool room at once. Undress him, fan the air toward him, and give him a drink. Sponging him down with lukewarm water will also have a cooling effect. And, inform the pediatrician immediately.

Helping Your Baby Enjoy the Winter

Even when the thermometer drops below 32 degrees Fahrenheit (0° C), your baby can go outside in the first weeks and months of life. Don't make this outing too long, however. It is better to go out twice for 30 minutes each time than once for an hour. The prerequisite is warm "packaging."

Some cold weather tips:

■ As in summertime, in the winter your own comfort should be your guide for dressing your baby.

■ In windy, cold weather, apply a thin layer of cream or ointment to your baby's cheeks to help prevent against chapping.

■ Protect exposed areas such as hands and head with mittens and hat.

■ When it is very cold, dress your baby in several layers—ending with a size-appropriate snowsuit with a hood.

■ If, for reasons of space, your carriage or stroller is kept outside the front door or in an unheated entrance hall, place a hot-water bottle in it to warm it up shortly before leaving the house. And remove the hot-water bottle before you depart.

Important!

Car fumes are toxic. For your walks outside, always choose routes that are away from traffic, if possible. Avoid downtown and heavily traveled streets. The concentration of fumes really is greatest at exhaust-pipe level. In town, a high carriage or stroller is better than a low umbrella stroller.

Plenty of fresh air and sunshine strengthen a baby's resistance to disease and are enjoyable as well!

Means of Transportation: Carriage or Carrier

In Africa and Asia, working women carry their baby on their back, abdomen, or hips around the clock. Both methods—carrier and carriage—have their advantages and disadvantages.

The Baby Carriage and Stroller

The baby carriage places the least amount of stress on the mother's body because she is pushing it, not carrying it. Using a carriage allows parents to take their baby on long walks without becoming exhausted, and it can hold

83

purchases as well. For the baby, it provides a quiet zone, a feeling of security, and protection against cold and noise. Many babies sleep better in the carriage than in your arms. The carriage also offers better protection from sunlight and heat.

On shopping trips, a carriage with a storage shelf and a net basket is especially practical, because you can carry your purchases easily. Nevertheless, selecting a carriage model is not easy. Most parents buy a carriage before their baby is born, relying on their best knowledge at that time, but afterward, experience often leads them to change their mind about options and models that work best for them.

A combination carriage and stroller is a real jack-of-all-trades. It can deal with any situation.

You have many options: plain, heavy carriages (prams); nonfolding strollers; combination carriage/ strollers that can be converted into strollers when the baby is bigger; and lightweight folding (umbrella) strollers in a great many different designs. Since the prices for a carriage with accessories can be expensive, you need to choose carefully.

Some tips when buying a carriage or stroller:

■ Look carefully at the wheels: If you live in the country, you are well advised to buy something with large wheels that can handle country roads and paths. Since the suspension of such carriages usually is softer as well, the baby will ride more comfortably in them. In addition, such models usually are extremely sturdy and roomy—but also heavy, unfortunately.

■ If you use public transportation frequently, live higher than the ground-floor level without an elevator, or have to transport the carriage in a small car, you need to choose a lighter, space-saving model. As a rule, it will also have smaller wheels.

■ Before buying, try out the product to see how it performs. I ordered a carriage/stroller from a mail-order company, and for months I had problems with a clumsy unit that never went where I was trying to steer it. In addition, you need to be able to push it without having to bend over. It is advisable, therefore, to get a model that has adjustable height handles.

■ The unit needs to collapse for convenient transport. Models that automatically lock into place when opened and have to be unlocked before they can be folded are safer for your child.

■ Safety brakes are also an important feature to look for on carriages and strollers.

■ Check the stroller for a reliable restraint belt, secondary safety latch, sturdiness, and stability.

Typical Models

■ The basic model is the *plain, sturdy baby carriage* without a removable pouch, stroller attachment, or other extras. Usually it has large wheels and good shock absorption, but it is not easy to collapse and is quite heavy. It is good for newborns, because is provides plenty of room, security, and peace and quiet. Once your child is able to sit alone, however, you should switch to some version of the stroller. This way they will have a better view of their surroundings.

■ A *combination carriage/stroller* will solve the problem of having to purchase a stroller and carriage separately. The stroller in this model is built-in. Some carriage/stroller models have an upper part that can be removed and used as a bassinet as well as a car seat that meets federal safety guidelines.

■ *Lightweight carriage/strollers* and *nonfolding strollers* generally are not suitable for newborns: Especially in winter, they offer the baby too little room. They are better for older infants who can sit on their own.

■ *Folding (umbrella) strollers* offer a very lightweight alternative for the older child who can sit on his own. They fold up into the shape of an umbrella and are good for traveling.

■ How about the *interior features*? In principle, you need no extra blanket or quilt for the carriage; just take the one from his crib. The carriage usually comes with a mattress, rain shield, and canopy. You can place terry cloth

In the blazing sun, your baby needs a sun hat, even in the front carrier.

towels on top of the mattress. In addition, you will need two cloths to protect the mattress, as well as one foot muff. Also useful are a net shopping bag and a storage basket for the baby carriage.

(For a list of basic equipment, see page 274.)

Carriers (Soft Front Carriers and Framed Carriers)

Despite all the advantages of the baby carriage, carriers have become popular, and with good reason. Your child is right next to you where he can feel, hear, and smell you. In addition, you are far more mobile where escalators, streetcars, buses, and stairs are concerned. You have both hands free to do other chores or to help your older children. Parents who live in the city, therefore, will find a carrier indispensable.

Front carriers are best for the newborn because later on he will be too heavy and it will be more comfortable to have him in a back carrier. For doing housework, it is easiest to have the baby on your back. He is held more closely to you and is outside the danger zone. Carrying him on your back is less stressful for your spine as well. In that position, you have no eye contact with your child, however. Once he can hold up his head on his own, you can carry him in a sling on your hip.

Tips for buying carriers:

■ Until the baby can hold his head up alone, he needs support for his head. Head support should be padded and adjustable.

■ You should be able to adjust the carrier without latch settings, so that the fabric always supports the infant firmly. That is the only way to keep him from being jolted when you walk and to avoid placing any stress on his spine at this early age—this is one advantage of the soft front carriers for small babies.

■ The carrier needs to "grow with the baby," supporting his head at first and leaving the top part of his body free later on.

■ If the carrier wearers—the mother and father—are very different in height, a fabric carrier is not as practical. You will need to keep repositioning it, while a framed carrier is easier to adjust for differences in height.

■ Remember that your child will not be ready to ride in a framed carrier on your back until he can sit alone.

■ Carriers need to be washable. Be sure to wash your carrier before you use it for the first time.

■ Be sure there is a mechanism to secure your baby safely into the carrier.

Car Seats—Good Trip for Babies

Most babies love riding in a car. Almost all of them enjoy watching the passing scene outside the car windows, and many are lulled to sleep by the purring noise of the engine. The manufacturing of car seats is regulated by the federal government. The seat you choose should meet the current Federal Motor Vehicle Safety Standard, number 213. Car seats are available for infants up to 22 pounds and for children 20 to 40 pounds. The infant car seat for up to 22 pounds should be rear facing, and the car seat for 20 to 40 pounds should be forward facing. Also available are convertible car seats that will serve a child from birth to 40 pounds. Some models of the smaller/infant car seats for up to 22 pounds also come with a stay-in car base and therefore double as a car seat/carrier. This enables you to take the car seat with you as a carrier and the base remains belted in the car. These models must also meet current federal guidelines for car seats.

Important!

Many cars today have dual front seat air bags. You should never put your child's car seat in the front seat, especially if your car has dual air bags. In these circumstances, the baby's car seat needs to go in the back seat—preferably in the center section.

Safety in the Car

■ Never take your baby in the car unless he is properly restrained in a car seat.

■ For infants up to 22 pounds, you will need a federally approved *infant car seat*—rear-facing in the back seat, unless your car does not have air bags.

■ For babies 22 to 40 pounds you will need a larger car seat, front-facing—again in the back seat, unless your car does not have air bags.

■ All car seats should be equipped with safety harness, and must be approved by the Federal Motor Vehicle Safety Standard.

More Riding Enjoyment for Infants

■ Avoid drafts in the car. Do not drive with the windows all the way open, and monitor the heating and air conditioning flow settings to avoid having hot or cold air blowing directly on the baby.

■ Your child's pacifier and favorite stuffed animals can help you weather minor crises.

■ Also nice to have in your car are sunshades for the side and rear windows. They do more than keep out the sun: Many babies become tired and irritated on long trips because they try to follow the rapid movements of the passing traffic with their eyes.

Important!

Never leave your child in a parked car. The heat that accumulates can cost him his life. To prevent accidentally locking your baby in the car, keep an extra door key hidden under the car frame.

HELPING YOUR BABY GROW BIG AND STRONG

Whether you intend to breastfeed or bottle feed your

baby—new questions arise repeatedly:

Will my child really get enough nourishment?

What type of infant formula is right for my baby?

How do I wean him off breastfeeding?

When do I start feeding him solids, and which kinds?

How will my child learn to feed himself?

In the following chapter, you will find essential

information and tried-and-true answers to all

your questions on feeding and nutrition

in the first year of life.

INFANT FEEDING— BASIC INFORMATION

A baby needs "special" nutrition that is formulated especially for growing babies.

It is special in the sense that it contains nutrients in the proper amounts

for growth of your baby's brain, bones, and organs.

Luckily, Mother Nature developed a milk for babies that meets all their needs to perfection—breast milk. It is designed to meet the needs of the still-immature functions of the digestive and metabolic organs and the great amounts of nourishment required to fuel the rapid growth of the first year of life.

■ A baby needs many fat calories—50 percent of his energy supply, in comparison with 30 percent in later life. These calories provide concentrated energy, and furnish important components for cell structures, including those for the brain.

■ He needs just enough protein to be able to grow well (7 percent of the overall energy supply), but no more; otherwise, the burden on his kidneys and liver would be excessive.

■ He needs plenty of carbohydrates (about 40 percent of his energy) as available energy reserves, which also can be stockpiled and perform certain chemical functions.

■ Despite the abundance of carbohydrates, breast milk is only one-seventh as sweet as if it were sweetened with sugar. Its salt content is low, in order to spare the kidneys and to leave the infant's body ample reserves of water. Nevertheless, it has enough calcium to guarantee healthy bone growth. With the exception of vitamin D, all the essential vitamins are present in sufficient amounts in breast milk.

This "breast milk prototype" is the model for all man-made formulas. Like breast milk, formula meets the infant's nutritional requirements fully until the end of the sixth month. From that point on, however, a diet of milk alone is no longer sufficient. The iron supply is no longer adequate, and other sources of protein now become important for the baby's nutrition. Roughage or solids also become important for healthy bowel function.

Eating is important—but don't let it become the dominant topic, even if there are difficulties.

The schedule of solid-food feedings now begins. Between the fourth and sixth month of age, solid foods can be introduced into your baby's diet. The first solid should be infant cereal, usually rice cereal first, followed by barley and oat for variety. At this time, you can also introduce apple juice—4 ounces per day. You will find apple/fruit juices in the baby aisle in the store. You may wonder if these juices are any different than fruit juice you buy for yourself. Yes, it is different. Infant juices have less sugar (carbohydrate) than those formulated for older children and adults. This is important because a high sugar content can cause or worsen loose stools.

Between the ages of 6 to 8 months you can start to introduce pureed fruits, vegetables, and protein foods. A good rule-of-thumb is to introduce one new food every 4 to 5 days. If your baby does not tolerate or has an allergy to a particular food, you will easily be able to pinpoint which one it is. Also, between the ages of 6 to 8 months, your baby will become a companion at the family table, since around this time he will be on a more regular schedule of solid meals—breakfast, lunch, dinner, and 2 small snacks—and he will sit in a high chair. Around the age of 10 months, your baby will begin to show great interest in the foods you are eating, and you can begin to expand his repertoire of foods, pureed as well as finger foods.

Eating: When and How Much?

If you feed your baby appropriately for his age and on demand, you don't have to count every swallow or watch every bite. His growth and development will be the best proof of his well-being. Nevertheless, you may have questions about nutrition. On the following pages, you will learn what requires close attention. For more on breastfeeding, see page 95; on infant formulas, page 118; on supplementary solid foods, page 129.

From Milk to a Meal

Some tips on making the transition from milk to a meal:

■ In the first 4 to 6 months, your baby should be fed milk exclusively—either breast milk or infant formula.

■ No sooner than the fourth month, you can begin to give your baby a meal of iron-fortified cereal mixed with either breast milk or formula. You can give this meal with a spoon once or twice a day. After the age of 4 months, your baby is ready for taking solids with a spoon.

■ If you have started cereal in the fourth or fifth month, at the beginning of the sixth month you can begin to give pureed fruits, vegetables, and meats—one new food at a time.

■ Do not force your baby to take a particular food. If he seems disinterested or the taste is not appealing, stop that meal and try again tomorrow.

Feeding Plan for the First Year (by month)											
breast milk and / or infant formula											
				infant cereal							
					pureed fruit						
						pureed vegetables					
						egg yolk					
Note: Depending on your baby, your doctor may change this recommended schedule of feeding.							pureed meat and finger foods				
							table foods				
							junior foods				
									egg whites		
1	2	3	4	5	6	7	8	9	10	11	12

An Eating Pattern Is Slow to Develop

The days when babies were fed at fixed times of the day are over. Not every bout of crying signifies hunger (see page 75). But what is the normal feeding pattern for children?

Feeding on Demand

In the first weeks of life, the baby is not yet able to tell day from night. He still has a very small stomach, and for this reason he requires many small feedings. A newborn baby who is breastfed should receive 8 to 10 feedings a day. At first, he may be hungry every 2 to 3 hours, but at about the age of 4 months, his requirements will drop to 5 to 6 meals a day. Don't try to put your child on a schedule of four meals a day; he would get too little nourishment for the first months of life.

How Much Milk Does Your Baby Need?

The daily amount is only a guideline, because requirements can differ from one child to the next, and it is impossible and unnecessary to measure amounts given if you are breastfeeding. Initially, breast-fed babies should be fed 8 to 10 times a day and formula-fed babies should get 16 to 32 ounces a day in 5 to 8 feedings. A general rule to follow is 2 to 2.5 ounces of milk per pound per day. See the table on page 94 for

DIGESTIVE PROBLEMS

Your child's digestive organs are still sensitive in the first months. For helpful tips on problems such as constipation, diarrhea, gas, and a sore bottom or diaper rash, see the section beginning on page 214.

guidelines for daily amounts needed for breast- and bottle-fed babies.

There are several ways to know if your baby is getting enough milk. One is to check how many wet diapers per day your baby is having. Your baby should have had several wet diapers before leaving the hospital. A good rule-of-thumb is that there should be 5 wet diapers by the fifth day of life. After that, he should have 6 to 8 wet diapers per day. Stool patterns vary greatly from baby to baby. A breast-fed baby may have a stool once a day or once with each feeding. A bottle-fed baby will have anywhere from several stools a day to one stool every 2 to 3 days. As long as the stool is soft and

colored, this is a normal pattern for your baby. Another way to check if your baby is getting enough to drink is by his weight. Full-term babies will lose 8 to 10 percent of their birth weight (about 10 to 12 ounces) in the first week of life, and by 2 weeks of age, he should be back to his birth weight. Then, your baby will gain about $^2/_3$ of an ounce a day during the first 3 months, then 1 ounce per day between 3 and 6 months of age. If you or your pediatrician are concerned about the baby's weight gain, you can check the weight once a week to once every 2 weeks in the doctor's office.

Can You Overfeed Babies?

Only about 3 percent of our babies are too fat; that is, their weight is more than 20 percent above the standard. That is less serious than underweight.

An undernourished baby experiences a delay in his physical and mental development. Baby fat is all right; our ideal of slenderness is misplaced here. Fat babies do not automatically turn into fat adults. After all, babies have to develop fat deposits. A newborn's body is only 10 percent fat, but after the fourth month, fat accounts for 25 percent of a baby's weight. Breastfed babies cannot get too fat, and even infants who are fed cow's milk-based formulas (see page 119) exclusively do not overeat.

■ However: Prepare the bottles and strained foods exactly as directed; do not force your child to drink the entire bottle, and preferably do not give him supplementary foods before the end of the fifth month.

■ For growth and weight curves for normally developing children, ask your pediatrician.

	DAILY MILK/FORMULA INTAKE		
Age	Amount of milk/formula per day	Number of breastfeedings per day	Number of formula feedings per day
0–4 mos.	16–32 oz.	8 or more	5–10
4–6 mos.	24–40 oz.	5 or more	4–7
6–8 mos.	24–32 oz.	5 or more	3–4
8–10 mos.	16–32 oz.	on demand	3–4
10–12 mos.	16–24 oz.	on demand	3–4

Source: Massachusetts W.I.C. Program

BREASTFEEDING IS BEST

Nothing is so natural and at the same time so difficult as breastfeeding.

It is worth the struggle because when you nurse the baby, he does more than eat,

he regains a part of the physical connection to you that was lost at birth.

You give your complete attention to your baby at these moments—

and thus create, again and again, an island of togetherness,

just for the two of you, in your busy daily routine.

Since babies can easily be raised on infant formula, it is by no means a foregone conclusion that every mother will breastfeed. On the contrary, after the end of World War II, the number of nursing mothers was on the decline. Because of this, the present generation of grandmothers have little breastfeeding experience. In the 1970s, more women started to breastfeed their babies again, perhaps related to a broader trend that encouraged more natural, simpler living practices. Later, scientific research indicated how beneficial breastfeeding really was. The research continues today, expanding our understanding of the benefits to both the baby and the mother.

Today, the American Academy of Pediatrics recommends exclusive breastfeeding for the first 4 to 6 months of the baby's life, along with part-time breastfeeding accompanied by solid foods for up to one year of age. A major study in 1995 showed that only 20 percent of babies in the United States were still breastfed at 6 months of age. Midwives, physicians, nurse practitioners, and lactation consultants are making major efforts to support and encourage women who want to breastfeed. La Leche League, a large international breastfeeding organization, has local chapters throughout the United States and has a buddy system to pair new breastfeeding mothers with experienced breastfeeding mothers for support. In addition, there are now a great many small breastfeeding support groups.

In other words, we now have to go to a lot of trouble to relearn the most natural thing in the world. And our daily routine often is so thoroughly planned, our lives so emphatically guided by reason, that many mothers find nursing difficult because of its unpredictability. But by learning to listen to our bodies and accepting the child's eating pattern during the breastfeeding phase, we also become closer to our baby. Go along with this different way of looking at life, this intense awareness of your body. It will be easier for you to attune yourself to your child, and you will be able to understand him better.

Best for Mother and Child

Breast milk is perfectly balanced to suit a baby's needs, in a way that cannot be imitated. It possesses a great many subtle advantages that are only now being discovered. It is the ideal food, perfect for the state of maturity of the child's digestive organs, metabolism, and nutritional needs, as well as for physical growth, particularly that of the brain.

Along with your milk, you also give your baby specific immunity to infections while you are nursing.

In addition, nursing has a positive effect on your own health, since your child's sucking triggers hormonal reactions in your body that help the uterus return to its prepregnancy size.

Important!

If you are uncomfortable breastfeeding, there is no need to reproach yourself or feel that you have failed. You will be just as good and loving a mother if you decide to bottle feed, rather than breastfeed, your baby (see page 118).

Breast Milk: The Basics

Despite repeated assertions that formula approximates breast milk as closely as possible, we have to acknowledge that breast milk, in terms of its composition and its effects on mother and infant, cannot be imitated, and there is unlikely to be a perfect substitute for it. Here are a few of the most convincing reasons:

■ The composition of breast milk, down to the most minute biochemical details, is attuned to the infant's requirements, particularly to the functional immaturity of his organs. Neither symptoms of nutritional deficiency nor oversupplies of substances is possible.

■ The composition of breast milk changes from the time the baby is first put to the breast throughout the entire nursing period. It changes during the day, indeed during a single feeding, in that the caloric content rises toward the end of the feeding, and thus a baby first quenches thirst and then satisfies hunger during the subsequent course of sucking.

■ The baby's digestive organs absorb the nutrients and active substances from the milk virtually in their entirety. When the supply of vital substances—iron, for example—in the breast milk is low, the body compensates with "resorption enhancers," which are not present in formulas.

■ The most convincing advantage is the presence of antibodies in breast milk that prevent infections and allergies. These antibodies are not only specific to humans, but specific to the mother; that is, they are generated in reaction to those infections that the mother has successfully fought off thus far in her life. They render the baby immune against threats from his own surroundings. Of course, cow's milk also contains antibodies—but they only benefit the calf.

Make Your Decision

To breastfeed or not may be considered during pregnancy, but the decision is best made before the birth.

Once you've got the hang of it, breastfeeding is the best and easiest method for both of you.

Although almost every mother is able to nurse, most women expecting their first child are plagued by doubts about whether it will actually work. This has to do with the fact that breastfeeding in the preceding generation was no longer a matter of course; therefore, you may not find the necessary support within your family. You need support in the decision-making process and all the determination you can muster.

If your obstetrician or midwife, your childbirth classes, a friend or relative, or even an easy-to-understand book do not give you sufficiently clear information, you can always turn to a lactation consultant and/or breastfeeding group—both of which can help and advise you. Naturally, you will receive the strongest assistance when your baby is born, and he makes his own vigorous contribution by showing you "what's what." Midwives and pediatric providers can help both of you to manage and dispel doubts about your ability to breastfeed. It is helpful if you make your interest in breastfeeding known before delivery, because once the baby is there, it's time to start.

Your Baby Gives the Starting Shot

Even during pregnancy, your breasts are getting ready. Under the influence of the pregnancy hormones produced in the placenta, the tissue of the mammary glands grows: the lactiferous glands, in which milk is produced, and the ducts through which the milk flows to the nipple. Prolactin, the milk-producing hormone, becomes active during the second half of the pregnancy and stimulates milk production in the lactiferous glands. The baby's sucking will continue to trigger the release of this hormone and thus match the amount of milk to the baby's level of thirst. When he starts to suck, his actions will tell your body to make milk available.

The Let-Down Reflex

The child's sucking action is the key stimulus that activates another hormone: oxytocin. It causes the milk to "let down." The lactiferous glands contract and empty their contents through the ducts into the reservoirs directly behind the nipple. There the milk can be easily drunk by the baby—you will notice that it begins to drip from your other breast as well.

If this stimulus is not triggered, your baby, even with the greatest effort, can get only a little milk. On the other hand, even the thought of your baby or the sheer weight of your breasts, without adequate support, can cause milk to trickle. We hover between these two extremes but are not always successful in our balancing act.

■ In some mothers, the let-down reflex does not function at times because this interplay can be disturbed by emotional stress. When you are relaxed, are concentrating on your baby, and feel in harmony with yourself and the world, then it works like clockwork. Stress, distraction by the baby's older siblings, a disapproving husband, the fear of not having enough milk, and a sore or inflamed breast, on the other hand, can interfere with this process.

■ Other mothers have the opposite problem: their milk keeps overflowing!

■ Finally, it may also be that not enough milk is produced.

■ In all these cases, the following applies: Don't give up right away—there are many ways of getting the breastfeeding relationship back in order again. Working with the pediatric provider, a lactation consultant, and/or a breastfeeding support group will help you get through most of the problems and give you the support you need to stay with it. For more information, see "Nursing Problems" on page 106.

The First Feeding

Milk does not begin to flow on its own but only when you let your baby suck. In general, your baby reigns supreme where breastfeeding is concerned, because he not only stimulates milk production but also determines, through the volume he demands, the amount of milk your body will produce in the future.

The fact that a newborn has a need to suckle shortly after birth is a small miracle. If you leave healthy newborns on the mother's abdomen after an unmedicated delivery, they will slowly creep toward the nipple and begin to suckle within the first hour of life. They can tell by the smell where the milk is to be found. Actually, your baby is especially awake and alert in the first hours after his birth; not until two or three hours later does he become tired again. During the first one to two weeks he will sleep a great deal with brief alert periods.

Signal to the Lactation Hormones

The baby's first sucking movements are an important signal for your body, because they continue to mobilize the hormones that are responsible for milk production and flow. Oxytocin

YOUR BABY IS AN EXPERT ON BREASTFEEDING

From the moment of his birth, your baby has a number of reflexes at his disposal:

■ *Your baby "roots" for the nipple when he feels it against his cheek or when he smells it, and he takes it into his mouth.*

■ *He can perform the complicated act of sucking with "technical perfection."*

■ *He can swallow milk, and the special coordination of his swallowing and breathing equipment enables him to drink and breathe at the same time.*

Nevertheless, there may be difficulties. Some babies keep dozing off, whereas others refuse the breast. Both patience and expert help can solve your problems (see page 34).

performs a dual function here: It causes the tiny muscles surrounding the ducts in the breast to contract, thus ejecting milk, and it also produces powerful contractions of the uterus, so that bleeding ceases. When he first begins to suck shortly after birth, the baby is doing something important not only for himself, but for his mother's health as well.

Important: The Colostrum

The colostrum (first milk) is a wonderful "first food." It consists predominantly of antibodies. Your baby's intestines become coated with a film of this precious solution, which fights off undesirable pathogens and gives a huge boost to the growth of beneficial bacteria in the intestines.

Remember, you will probably not feel the colostrum in your breasts, and you many not even see it come out. But it's there, it's important for your baby to get it, and your baby will get what he needs with short, frequent breastfeedings.

When Your Milk Comes In

Usually three days after your delivery, your breasts will become firm, sometimes to a point of painfulness, at which point they are said to be engorged. Your hormones have been stimulated by your baby's sucking to produce and deliver the milk to your breasts. This unforgettable feeling tells you that your milk is "in." The best thing to do at this time is to feed your baby, again at the short and frequent intervals from both breasts if possible, as described below.

A Supplemental Bottle Until the Milk Comes In?

Sometimes, usually with the first child, the breast milk flows in very small amounts during the first week. If this happens, you may be tempted to give your baby supplemental feedings with either water, sugar water, or formula. This is a good time to talk with your pediatric provider, midwife, or a lactation consultant. If you supplement at this time, your baby may find the artificial nipple easier to use and have a more difficult time getting on the breast. This is sometimes called "nipple confusion." Anything that interferes with the short, frequent sucking that your baby does to your breast in the early weeks may interfere with the normal supply and demand that determines milk production. The need to supplement may indeed occur, but is best done in conjunction with a specific plan to help your baby breastfeed better.

The Right Way to Nurse—A Basic Course

Even though nature has made plenty of preparations, breastfeeding is not a purely instinctual process. It is something you, as well as your baby, have to learn. Don't be upset if it doesn't work right away. It is quite understandable that you and your newborn need a little time for both parties to be successful and free of stress. Use the first days to get a feel for breastfeeding techniques, and turn to the pediatric provider or midwife with whom you have the best connection.

your time, and enjoy the peace and quiet of these irretrievable moments.

■ At every feeding, have a drink available for you to sip. During or after nursing, you will have some leisure time, and it's important for you to drink fluids, something that is easy to forget in these busy days.

After every feeding, try to rest for 15 minutes. If at all possible, have a little snack as well: a serving of oatmeal, a piece of fruit, yogurt, or the like.

Be Relaxed

Always make yourself as comfortable as possible when nursing, even in the hospital. Back at home, set up the corner where you plan to nurse as a place where you feel at ease, and experiment to find the ideal nursing position for you and your child. You may want to use all the positions described here, depending on the time and place. And here are some tips to help you relax:

■ Turn down your telephone, so that the ring is not loud. Even better: use an answering machine.

■ If your baby falls asleep at your breast, you don't need to put him in his crib right away. If you like, take

SUPPLEMENTAL FEEDINGS— THE SAFE WAY

Occasionally your pediatric provider may ask you to supplement breastfeedings, especially if the baby is dehydrated, jaundiced, or not gaining weight appropriately.

■ *Your baby should always be put to the breast first to stimulate the flow of milk.*

■ *You should follow the recommendations of your pediatric provider in regard to using supplemental sterile water, sugar water, or a soy-milk based formula.*

■ *As soon as the medical or feeding issues are corrected, you should discontinue supplemental feedings and return to all breastfeedings.*

The Right Way to Breastfeed

■ Continue to ask for expert help even after the first time you nurse. Don't put pressure on yourself to succeed. Try to relax during these initial breastfeeding experiences. The milk is sure to flow better.

■ Your child probably will move his head back and forth, making seeking movements. Take your breast in one hand, holding it between your thumb and index finger in a "C" position just behind the areola, the darker circle of skin around the nipple. Then gently guide the baby towards the breast.

■ Tickle the center of the baby's bottom lip; he will then open his mouth. Rubbing both lips or the top lip only will often cause him to tighten his mouth and even close it.

■ Your baby will latch on with a wide mouth around your nipple and about one inch of your areola. His top and bottom lips are rolled outward and his nose and chin are touching your breast.

■ Your baby's chest will be facing your chest.

■ If the breast is extremely taut, express a little of the milk beforehand. Place one hand under your breast and, with the palm of your other hand, move repeatedly from the engorged area down toward the nipple using a moderate amount of pressure. Gentle massage may help as well.

■ Make sure that you always guide the baby's mouth towards the areola at a right angle. If it is off to one side and not positioned right in the center of the tongue or oral cavity, the sucking pressure will be unevenly distributed, and sore or even cracked areas on the breast can develop.

■ Experiment by sticking a finger straight into your mouth, then at an angle, and suck on it. Then you will understand that the wrong position stimulates both the areola and the

The Sitting Position
Your baby's entire body is facing you, his head resting on your forearm while he suckles. Important: Maintain a relaxed posture. A comfortable armchair with wide armrests or a big pillow under your arm is ideal. Even more comfortable: Elevate your feet on a footstool.

nipple unequally, and that results in pain.

■ It is also essential that your baby take at least one inch of the areola into his mouth. If he only sucks on the nipple, it will be unbelievably painful and will injure the sensitive skin.

Ending the Feeding

Your baby's suck is often quite vigorous. Your nipple will become very sore if you try to take him off the breast without first breaking the suction.

- To do so, use the little finger of your free hand. Carefully slide it between your nipple and the corner of your baby's mouth. That will break the suction, and your baby will release the nipple.
- Now you can hold him upright for awhile and rub his back a little, to encourage him to burp. Breastfed infants often burp less than bottle-fed babies because they swallow less air during the feeding.

The Cross-Legged Position

The tailor position: Your baby's entire body faces your body, and he lies on your crossed legs. Your arms are supported by your legs. It can help to slide a pillow or a folded towel under the "nursing leg." This position is ideal on a picnic, at the beach, or out in the country.

The Reclining Position

Lie down on one side, with the baby's head at the level of your underarm. Rest on your arm, and with your free hand pull the baby close to your body, so that you are lying belly to belly. It helps to have some back support (a pillow or a person) and a pillow between your knees. To change to the other breast, you and the baby should turn over to the other side.

A Guide for the First Week of Life

Frequent, short feedings will help both you and your baby with breastfeeding.

■ It's normal for all newborn babies to lose weight initially. They all regain and surpass their birth weight within the first 10 to 14 days of life, and often sooner.

■ A good rule of thumb is to nurse 8 to 10 times in 24 hours, usually from both breasts each feeding. This works out to about every 2 to 3 hours during the day and every 4 hours at night.

■ The short feedings help your nipples get used to suckling. It is a good idea to begin with 5 to 7 minutes per breast and work up to 12 to 15 minutes over the first several days.

■ The frequent feedings give your baby the calories he needs to regain his birth weight.

■ Because newborn babies sleep a lot, you will probably have to wake your baby after 3 hours to breastfeed him if he's sleeping—just for the first week of life. Undressing him to his diaper, changing his diaper, washing his face with a wet cloth, walking your fingers up his spine, or doing slow, gentle baby sit-ups are some ways to awaken him. He will go right back to sleep after the feeding, so you are not depriving him of needed rest.

When Is Your Baby Full?

Many mothers are concerned about whether their child is gaining enough weight—especially if they are breastfeeding. A mother who bottle feeds her baby can always tell by the scale on the side of the bottle how much her baby has drunk. The breast, obviously, has no such markings.

■ For many mothers, especially with their first child, there is a bout of anxiety until they have learned their baby's peculiarities. Please don't start weighing your baby before and after every feeding. There are several ways to tell if your baby is getting enough:

• Your baby will pass a colorless urine at least 6 to 8 times in 24 hours.

• Your baby will have a loose yellow seedy stool at least 3 to 4 times in 24 hours—though after the first week, this may occur as often as every breastfeeding.

• You will hear your baby swallow during the feedings and you will see milk in his mouth as well.

• Generally, your baby will be satisfied after the feeding and sleep soundly until the next feeding.

EXTRA-TIP

Usually we forget which breast we used last. Attach a safety pin to your bra strap as a reminder: Always put it on the side where your baby nursed last—and will nurse first at the next feeding.

Your Pediatric Provider Can Help

If you have any questions or concerns about your baby's nourishment or weight gain, it's a good idea to contact your baby's pediatric provider. Often a brief phone call can give the provider enough information to decide whether you need to bring your baby into the office to be checked. Sometimes a referral to a lactation consultant is helpful as well. Most pediatric providers will routinely see you and your baby between one and two weeks after delivery and earlier if it's necessary.

Ideal—Feeding on Demand

Once your milk supply is well established, you and your baby constitute a breastfeeding community; everything that goes on between you is regulated by the principle of supply and demand. If you let your baby decide how much milk he wants—that is, how much milk he needs—then you are feeding him "on demand." At the beginning, that may be as many as 12 times a day, at very irregular intervals. Be prepared for that, and have confidence. Slowly, a certain system will emerge. Every baby handles it differently, but in general a roughly 2 to 4 hour rhythm will appear after three weeks. With a little luck, you will discontinue one of the nighttime feedings around the sixth to eighth week.

Growth Spurts— Don't Get Discouraged

There are times when your child's demand for milk increases rapidly, and he has to be nursed more frequently until your milk supply adjusts to his large appetite. These are called growth spurts and occur after birth at about 10 to 12 days, 4 to 6 weeks, and monthly after that until you begin to feed your baby solid food. These last about two days and can be exhausting for you, since you are constantly nursing. It is especially important at these times to drink fluids, eat regularly, and rest so your body can increase your milk supply to a new baseline for your growing baby. After a couple of days, your baby will go back to more regular feeding intervals.

Unavoidable at First: Nighttime Feedings

A young infant who cries at night needs to be fed. Research has shown that the efforts of older generations to teach children moderation by letting them cry at night were misguided. If a baby cries because he is hungry, he has to be nursed, even several times if necessary.

■ But please, don't get upset if your baby fails to wake up some night to nurse. As long as he is gaining weight well, just rejoice at the first sign of undisturbed nights to come.

■ After the first three to four months, your baby may be able to do without his nighttime feeding. If the disturbance at night gets to be too much, you—or, even better, your partner—can cautiously start to postpone the next feeding a bit by rocking the baby or give him a finger or pacifier to suck on.

What to Do About Nursing Problems

In the first weeks, difficulties with breastfeeding are almost the norm—especially with your first baby. These can cause some mothers to give up breastfeeding even when they would have liked to nurse the baby longer. The advice of an experienced midwife or pediatric provider and the support of a lactation consultant or breast-feeding group can help a great deal with these problems. Try not to be discouraged easily. Sometimes it's easy to think that other mothers can do it much better or that it isn't worth the effort. Most breastfeeding problems can be solved. It's worth getting some expert help and advice so that you don't unnecessarily wean your baby earlier than planned.

Sometimes giving the baby water (see page 127) or clear juice (once the baby is 4 months old) will help when you want to delay the breastfeeding a bit. The father can help.

Painful and Sore Nipples

Naturally, it will feel strange the first time you nurse your child. If he is a "barracuda baby" who sucks vigorously, it can even be somewhat unpleasant. But after the first days, you will be accustomed to it, and then it won't be painful anymore. The situation is different if your baby grips only the nipple (instead of the areola) in his mouth or if the nipple is not in the correct position inside his mouth. This can be corrected with guidance, however.

Things become unpleasant if your nipples get really sore. Women who nurse their babies too long in the first days may quickly develop irritated, cracked, and even bleeding nipples. Be extremely careful in the early days and weeks, because germs can enter your body through the injured nipple and give rise to an infection of the breast (mastitis). Sore nipples and inflammation can quickly make a mother lose interest in breastfeeding. After the first few weeks, your breasts will become accustomed to breastfeeding, and there are steps you can take to prevent these problems.

What You Can Do
■ Let the last few drops of breastmilk dry on your nipples after each feeding—this will help the healing process.

■ When you finish nursing, air dry your nipples.

■ Try soaking your nipples with warm water a few times a day to help the damaged skin heal, followed by a purified lanolin product to hold in the moisture.

■ Before using salves or ointments, you may want to ask your obstetrician or midwife for advice. Some of these products are unhealthy for the baby to consume, may give the breast a bad taste, and/or may irritate your skin.

■ Try changing your nursing position from feeding to feeding so your baby's lower lips are not repeatedly putting pressure on the same place on your nipple.

■ Having cracked, painful nipples does not mean that you have to stop nursing. With nipple care, pumping, and occasional nursing, you can heal your nipples and resume full nursing. This is a time when a breastfeeding expert can help you develop a plan and support you through the healing process.

So Your Baby Wants to Nurse Constantly . . .

You look pale and tired, and you admit reluctantly that your baby is wearing your nerves to a frazzle. He wants to nurse all the time—after a short feeding he rests a little while, then resumes nursing.

Without a doubt, there are restless, delicate, or balky children who need more than the usual number of feedings over a period of weeks, or even months. Very frequently, however, something else is going on.

It's helpful to know that the composition of the milk does not remain constant throughout the entire feeding. Whereas the first milk (foremilk) is more watery, the last of the milk (hindmilk) contains more calories. So if the baby nurses too briefly, he does not have a chance to benefit from the high-calorie milk. Even a longer nursing on just the first breast with a brief nursing at the second breast will often satisfy him.

What You Can Do

Of course, you first have to talk to your pediatric provider to see if your baby is developing well and appropriately for his age.

If his weight gain is slow, it's important to review with your provider the baby's positioning at the breast, his sucking and swallowing, and the amount of urine and stool in his diapers each day. These are the signs of effective feeding:

■ Your baby will latch on with a wide mouth around your nipple and about one inch of your areola. His top and bottom lips are rolled outward, and his nose is touching your breast.

■ You can see your baby's jaws, temple, and throat move when he is nursing.

■ You can hear him swallowing occasionally followed by small pauses in his sucking.

■ He has at least 3 to 4 good-sized bowel movements and 6 wet diapers in 24 hours.

If his weight gain is fine, try feeding him longer on the first breast (15 to 20 minutes) to be sure he's getting the high-calorie hindmilk each feeding. After the first breast, offer him the second breast and stop the feeding if he's not interested or is only briefly interested. The increased fat content in the hindmilk usually will satisfy him for longer, even if it's only from one breast. Begin the next nursing with the breast he nursed on only briefly.

Not Enough Milk

If your baby doesn't seem to be getting enough milk during the first two weeks, it is important to work with your pediatric provider and/or a lactation consultant to help determine the reason for the low milk supply. Usually by increasing the number of nursings, your milk supply will increase. It rarely occurs, but there are other problems related to the breast tissue that can occur. Even once your nursing is well established, the day will come when you suspect that you don't have enough milk. Your baby wakes up at night and cries, tends to be restless in the daytime, or seems unsatisfied after his feeding. You've guessed right—your milk supply is no longer adequate. Presumably your child has grown and gained weight well up until this point.

What You Can Do

Don't panic—trust your baby. He may be in a growth spurt. Nurse him more frequently, day and night, as he demands. After two or three days, your hormonal system will understand the message (see page 98), the milk will be flowing abundantly, and your baby will settle back into a comfortable pattern again.

Sometimes because of the demands in your life, your nursing schedule is altered and decreased for a few days. This results in less milk production (due to less sucking at the breast) and, often, a fussy baby. If you think back and realize this has happened (it's often a subtle process), it's a good idea to spend a day in bed with your baby letting him nurse on demand. During this time you can rest, concentrate on your baby, and simply ignore the outside world. You'll see: After 24 hours, your milk supply will probably be replenished.

In general, good nutrition, adequate fluid intake, and rest are important to keep up your milk production. But the most important variable is to put your baby to your breast often enough. "Often enough" changes as he grows, but he will let you know!

If more frequent nursing, adequate rest, and good nutrition do not result in improved milk production, you may want to consider a supplemental bottle of formula. By doing so, however, you will begin the weaning process. This is another time when working with a pediatric provider or a lactation consultant can be helpful if you are not ready to wean.

What You Need to Know About Breast Pumps

Perhaps your baby had to be transferred to a special care nursery because of some problem at birth. Please don't think that you have to wean him. Often it is especially important for a sick or premature baby to receive his mother's breast milk. For the time being, express your milk with breast pumps so that you develop and maintain your supply. The nursery staff can feed your pumped milk to your baby by bottle or by gavage tube if necessary until he is able to nurse at your breast. This is the best solution for difficult circumstances.

Most maternity hospitals are prepared for this: You will be given an electric pump, and will be instructed

There's nothing wrong with spending a day in bed with your baby to get needed rest. This is often a help when your milk isn't flowing the way it should.

on how to use it. If you are already back at home, you can rent an electric pump in a pharmacy or a medical supply store. Ask a medical provider to certify in writing that you need such a device, so that your health insurance carrier will cover the rental costs.

■ If only a small amount of milk needs to be expressed, a simple hand pump may be adequate. They are available in most pharmacies.

■ A hand pump can also be very helpful if your breasts are engorged. Sometimes when the milk comes in, after the baby is a few days old, the breasts become so engorged that the baby is unable to get a good grip on the nipple. Sometimes it helps to express a small amount of milk to allow the baby to nurse.

■ Basically, the same rules apply to using a pump as to breastfeeding. The milk often flows more slowly because the pump is not as efficient as your baby's sucking at stimulating milk production. Luckily though, it's good enough, and many mothers have supplied their babies with pumped breast milk for long periods of time until their babies were healthy enough to breastfeed on their own.

■ It is important to use the pump regularly, every 3 to 4 hours at least, and express milk from both breasts. If you pump too infrequently, the volume of milk in your breasts will drop.

Storage of Breast Milk

■ Thanks to its antibacterial properties, breast milk will keep for a long time. If it is stored in the refrigerator at 39.2 degrees Fahrenheit (4°C) after being expressed, it can safely wait 72 hours before being taken to the hospital.

■ If you want to store extra milk that you have expressed, it will keep six

EXTRA-TIP

If you have an important engagement that does not include the baby, or if for other reasons you ever want to give your baby breast milk from a bottle, you can express the milk with a pump ahead of time.

months in the back of your freezer. To freeze it, put the expressed milk immediately into clean, sterilized glass bottles or plastic bags, close the top, and attach a label with the date on it.

Important!
After every use, clean and sterilize the containers, as well as the milk pump.

■ To use the stored milk, thaw one portion in the refrigerator. If you are in a hurry, you can place the container in warm water. For the basics of bottle feeding, see pages 118 through 128.

Tips for Nursing Mothers

Breastfeeding will help take off the extra pounds you may have gained during pregnancy! The daily amount of milk you supply to your baby causes you to burn about 500 calories. Not only do you need to eat good, healthy foods, you also have to make an effort to compensate for the lost calories daily. After the first days of fluid loss following delivery, you should not lose any more weight. Weight loss during the time you are nursing means that you are burning up your fat tissue, possibly releasing the harmful substances stored there and passing them on to your baby. Take your time about getting your prepregnancy figure back. For more on this subject, see page 172.

Eating Right Is Important to Your Health

Eat a good variety of foods—just as you did during your pregnancy. Only now you can eat a little more if you want. It's important to know that when you do not eat certain foods, it is not your milk or your baby that will suffer—it's your own health that may suffer. For instance, if your diet is low in calcium (see page 112), your milk will contain adequate calcium for your baby, but it will be drawn from your own bones, thus depleting your bone calcium content. It is recommended, therefore, that you continue your prenatal vitamins throughout the time that you are nursing and continue to pay attention to your nutrient intake.

Your Baby East and Drinks What You Do

In general, you can go ahead and eat what you want at first. When breast-feeding, however, it's a good idea to avoid excesses in any food or drink. An excess of anything has the potential to have some effect on your baby.

■ For some mothers, gas-producing foods (such as cabbage, cauliflower, and some legumes) disagree with their nursing infants. These are good sources of nutrition and fiber, so it's worth trying them and watching your baby for symptoms. All babies will have some gas and even discomfort when passing a bowel movement. If these symptoms are brief, they are not harming your baby, and there is no need to alter your diet.

■ Sometimes acidic juices (such as orange juice) in a breastfeeding mother's diet can cause skin irritation or a rash on your baby's skin. If this occurs, it may be worth a trial period without them to see if the symptoms go away.

■ If there is a history of allergies in your family, you may want to consider limiting your consumption of hyperallergenic foods, such as milk, eggs, fish, and nuts, while you continue to breast-feed. Discussing this with your pediatric provider is a good idea. Once again, your own nutritional needs must be considered if you eliminate food groups from your diet during breastfeeding.

What to Eat While Breastfeeding

■ Eat plenty of grains and cereals, giving preference to whole grains whenever possible. Whole-grain products contain an abundance of B vitamins, have no irritants that could harm your baby, and promote milk production. Vitamin B-rich foods that are especially easy to digest are oat flakes, millet flakes, and rice. Chew them well to help prevent flatulence.

■ Drink about 1 quart of milk each day. Alternatively, eat corresponding quantities of dairy products or other calcium-rich foods. Your body requires 1200 to 1500 grams of calcium every day when you are breastfeeding.

Nothing comes from nothing: A diet that includes plenty of milk, whole grains, fruit, and nonacidic vegetables will help milk production.

■ Eat lots of vegetables. No other food category contains so many vitamins and minerals per calorie! As a rule, all the vegetables we recommend for the baby (see page 132) are good for you as well.

■ Fruits and fruit juices supply vitamin C and betacarotene. The acid in the fruit, however, can irritate sensitive baby skin. These fruits are especially low in acid: apples, bananas, pears, blueberries, blackberries, mangoes, nectarines, peaches, and grapes.

■ Eating iron-rich foods such as meats, legumes, eggs, dried fruits, and nuts regularly will prevent you from becoming iron deficient. Your baby has his own iron reserves from you that will last until his fourth or fifth month; a shorter time if he is premature.

■ It is all right to eat slightly more fat than usual. Olive and canola oils are better fat sources than butter or margarine. Fresh nuts are good for you, too.

What to Drink While Breastfeeding

In addition to calories and nutrients, fluids are passed on to your baby through your breast milk. For this reason, you need to drink at least two quarts of fluids a day. Ideally, drink in order to satisfy your thirst, or try to keep your urine a light color—they are both good indicators of proper fluid intake.

■ Liquids such as water, milk, buttermilk, kefir (a yogurt-like drink), and low-acid juices are good choices.

Medications in Breast Milk

A nursing mother may also become ill and need medication. Many medications may even be transferred to the breast milk—but it is not necessarily harmful. If you have a headache, go right ahead and take a pain-reliever, such as acetaminophen or ibuprofen. The small percentage of it that shows up in your breast milk and reaches your baby will not harm him—after all, he may be treated with the same medications if he has fever. How much of a medication shows up in your milk and whether the amount is harmful depend on certain chemical properties of the medication.

■ If an antibiotic, for example, is prescribed for you, let your provider know that you are nursing, so that he or she can choose a suitable medication.

■ In general, for almost every type of medication (antibiotics, vasopressors, analgesics, and so forth), there are one or more preparations that a nursing mother can take without having to stop breastfeeding.

■ To make sure, ask your medical provider. She or he will give you reassuring information or prescribe a related, innocuous preparation.

CAFFEINE AND NURSING

Moderate caffeine intake causes no problems for most breastfeeding infants. Research has shown that with five or fewer cups (6 oz.) of coffee daily, the baby usually has no problem. The caveats are these:

■ Babies accumulate caffeine in their bodies because they metabolize it more slowly. Therefore, some babies may be more sensitive to caffeine. If you are drinking coffee and your baby is wakeful or hyperactive, it's a good idea to cut down or stop and see if this behavior resolves.

■ When figuring out your caffeine intake, it is very important to include all sources of caffeine—coffee, iced and hot teas, colas, other soft drinks with caffeine, over-the-counter medicines with caffeine, and prescription medications with caffeinelike effects.

■ Theobromine, found in chocolate and cocoa, has similar effects to caffeine on the baby.

If you are inclined to cut down on your caffeine consumption, now is a good time to do it. Though with careful monitoring of your baby's behavior, moderate caffeine use is not contraindicated while breastfeeding.

Smoking and Nursing

Though experts disagree, many believe it is better for you to breastfeed your baby even if you continue to smoke cigarettes. But the fewer cigarettes you smoke, the fewer the health risks to both you and your baby. This is a good time to consider quitting. Sometimes it is easier to do something good for your baby than just for yourself—though you will both clearly benefit in the long run!

A Compromise

■ If you can't quit now, try to limit your smoking to less than 20 cigarettes (one pack) per day. Heavier smoking will reduce your milk supply and may cause gastrointestinal symptoms in your baby from the nicotine.

■ Try not to smoke immediately before or during breastfeeding. Nicotine may interfere with the letdown and ejection reflexes and cause problems with nursing.

■ Avoid smoking around your baby— or letting anyone else! Passive smoke inhalation is a health hazard to your baby. It increases the risk of pneumonia, asthma, middle ear infections, and even colds.

Alcohol and Nursing

Regular consumption of alcohol during pregnancy can harm the baby. The same situation exists while you are nursing, too—whatever you drink is passed along to the baby. He can even get tipsy and doze off blissfully. A baby's system has a very hard time breaking down alcohol. For this reason, it is safest not to consume any alcoholic beverages.

■ Nevertheless, while nursing, if you have company, if a special meal is in the offing, or if the day has been especially tough, then a glass of champagne, a light wine, or a glass of beer—on rare, selected occasions—will not hurt. A little sip is more apt to relax you and let you approach your baby's care with renewed vigor.

■ If you drink a glass of wine, it is best to do so either while feeding your baby or immediately thereafter: 30 to 60 minutes after taking a drink, the alcohol content of breast milk rises to the same level as in the mother's blood. By the next feeding, it will be at least partially broken down.

■ There are lots of ways to relax that you can use instead of drinking a glass of alcohol:
• Lie down and listen to music.
• Take a long, hot bath.
• Read a magazine or book you've been waiting to get to.
• Ask your partner or a friend to give you a massage (or treat yourself to a professional massage).
• Get a sitter for a couple of hours and walk, or go to a movie, the library, or a museum.

When the Time Comes: Weaning

How long are you really supposed to breastfeed? Many mothers, disconcerted by reading contradictory information, ask themselves that question. Through the first year? Longer? Or should you stop when the baby's teeth come in?

Generally, we wait until between the fourth and sixth month to begin feeding the baby strained food from a spoon. Your baby will raise his mouth toward you and proudly enjoy the process of taking food, chewing it, and swallowing it. One after another, the breastfeedings are replaced by meals of pureed food or cereal. And finally the day will come when your baby stops nursing on his own accord; often between the tenth and twelfth month. By this time he will probably drink from a cup. You can begin offering a cup with water or diluted juice at about six months of age to give him practice.

The major advantages of breast milk in terms of intestinal and metabolic function and also in terms of strengthening resistance to infection occur in the first six months of life. But these benefits continue as long as your baby receives breast milk. Basically, every day of breastfeeding your baby will benefit his health.

How Do I Wean My Baby?

■ Begin with the feeding when you have the least milk available. First, let your baby drink from the bottle or cup or eat from a spoon, then offer him your breast. Soon he will be nursing only a little, and your milk supply will start to slowly decrease on its own.

■ What and how much do I feed him? These questions are answered in the section beginning on page 130. Eliminate a breastfeeding over the course of five to seven days, not all at once.

■ Then begin to replace the next feeding bit by bit. In this way, you can wean the baby completely within a period of about three weeks—unless you want to continue the morning and evening feedings for awhile in order to have some quiet, intimate time together.

What Will Help

Here are a few ways to keep the process from being unnecessarily uncomfortable for your breasts:

■ Decrease your fluid intake—and don't drink lactation-promoting teas, of course!

■ Wear a tight bra and pull the straps taut to keep your breasts high.

■ If your breasts hurt, use cool compresses.

■ Don't express the milk with a pump at intervals; this will stimulate milk production.

■ Pills to decrease milk production contain hormones that place considerable stress on your circulatory system. It is better not to use them.

Important!

Sometimes you may have to wean the baby from the breast quite suddenly. Illness or an emergency may force you to be away from your child for a few days. Here you need to ask your obstetrician or midwife to prescribe a medication that will decrease milk production quickly and prevent engorgement, which is painful and could even result in mastitis.

If Your Child Objects

Quite a number of babies who are used to being breastfed will fight like a lion to postpone being weaned and steadfastly refuse the bottle. Faced with that fierce determination, some mothers are forced to give up their weaning plan.

■ What will help: Try to feed the baby the breast milk from a spoon.

This takes patience, however. Often it is easier to ask the father or another person close to you to feed your child, because there will be no breast to offer. You will be amazed how quickly your baby adjusts to the realities of the new situation and accepts his fate, along with the nipple of the baby bottle or a cup (if he is over six months old).

You need to be clear on this point: The older your child is, the less willing he will be to give up the breast. If you have not weaned him by the end of the ninth or tenth month, you probably will continue breastfeeding him after his first birthday. If you are prepared for that, there's no problem. If not, you need to seize the initiative in time.

——ESPECIALLY FOR FATHERS——

It is very difficult for your wife to wean your baby without help. And if your baby needs some consoling in order to lengthen the intervals between feedings (especially at night), she is not the right person for it: The baby naturally will demand her breast at once. In this situation, it is an enormous relief if you can assume this task lovingly but firmly. The baby is more likely to accept his bottle or cup from you than from his "milk source."

Your active participation and support during your baby's weaning will help it go smoothly as he moves to other food sources—ones that you will be able to feed him, too.

THE ALTERNATIVE: INFANT FORMULAS

There are good reasons for deciding to bottle feed your baby.

You may be going back to work, you may be ill, the letdown reflex may be

prevented by stresses at home, or you may have decided that you just don't want

to breastfeed. It may also be that you find nursing burdensome,

aren't having a lot of success with it, or simply want more flexibility in your life.

By this time, you are aware that we think breastfeeding is preferable. But there is absolutely no doubt that the needs of bottle-fed babies are nutritionally fulfilled, and these babies thrive equally well—provided they get the appropriate formula and enough cuddling besides.

Formulas are manufactured to be as close as possible to the composition of breast milk. Manufacturers continue to do extensive research on formula composition. Babies that are raised on infant formula develop no less well than breastfed children. There are many formulas on the market, as well as proper equipment, for bottle feeding your baby.

In this chapter you will learn which baby formula is appropriate for your child, how to prepare it properly, and how to feed it to your baby.

Often, using a bottle leads you to speed up the feeding session. Take plenty of time, and create an atmosphere of intimacy during "feeding time." Feeding, after all, means a great deal more than merely filling the baby's tummy.

The Right Type of Formula

Cow's milk is not suitable for babies. It contains too much protein, too few unsaturated fatty acids, and is a poor source of iron. Therefore, infants should not drink whole milk at all before the twelfth month. Most infant formulas are cow's milk protein-based, meaning that they use the same protein as in cow's milk, but the other components have been formulated to be similar to human milk.

The following types of iron-fortified formulas are available:

- Cow's milk based
- Lactose-free cow's milk based (same protein, but different sugar than the first one listed)
- Soy protein based (different protein and different sugar than the first one)
- Elemental or hypoallergenic
- Specially formulated for metabolic diseases like PKU (phenylketonuria)

(Each of these types of formula have several different manufacturers.)

About 80 percent of formula-fed babies in the United States are on cow's milk-based formula. Soy formulas are used primarily for infants who have an intolerance to the protein in cow's milk-based formula or to the sugar, as with the rare disease galactosemia. The other formulas are reserved for infants with milk or soy allergies or metabolic diseases.

> **EXTRA-TIP**
>
> *When preparing your infant formula with water you have several choices. Use bottled spring water, fresh tap water, or boiled tap water. If you are using tap water, it is a good idea to boil it before preparing your formula for the first several months, especially if you have well water. If you are using bottled spring water, you should discuss the need for fluoride supplementation with your pediatric provider. Supplements are usually started at the age of 6 months. Bottled water that has added fluoride is available in the baby aisle of your supermarket or pharmacy, but it is more expensive than traditional spring water.*

These formulas come in three forms:

- Ready-to-feed
- Concentrated
- Powdered

What the Terms Mean

The *ready-to-feed formulas* come either in cans or in single-serving bottles. They do not need to be diluted or mixed with water, and are ready to serve after opening. They are more convenient but also more expensive. Several things to keep in mind: After

119

opening, the remaining formula in the can must be refrigerated; in the refrigerator, it is good for only 24 hours; and never reuse leftover formula from a bottle your baby has already used.

The *concentrated formulas* come in liquid form and need to be diluted with water. It is very important to read the mixing directions on the can carefully, and measurements must be exact. If too little water is added, the formula will be too concentrated and may cause strain on the kidneys as well as diarrhea. If too much water is added, this may disturb the delicate balance of salts in your baby's body; in addition, he will not be getting adequate nutrition.

The *powdered formulas* also need to be mixed with water, and all measuring must be exact. Directions, again, will be on the can. This is the least expensive form to purchase but also the most labor intensive.

COMMONLY AVAILABLE FORMULAS

Note that the ingredients listed are the proteins, sugars, and fats, in that order.

◼ *Enfamil with Iron (cow-milk based): nonfat milk, demineralized whey, lactose sugar, palm olein, soy oil, coconut oil, HO sun oil*

◼ *Similac with Iron (cow-milk based): nonfat milk, lactose sugar, soy oil, coconut oil*

◼ *Isomil (soy based): soy isolate, methionine, corn syrup, sucrose, soy oil, coconut oil*

◼ *ProSobee (soy based): soy isolate, methionine, corn syrup solids, palm olein, soy oil, coconut oil, HO sun oil*

◼ *Alimentum (for infants with food allergies, protein or fat malabsorption): casein hydrolysate, cystine, tyrosine, tryptophan, sucrose, modified tapioca starch, MCT oil, safflower oil, soy oil*

◼ *Nutramigen (for infants with food allergies): casein hydrolysate, cystine, tyrosine, tryptophan, corn syrup solids, corn starch, palm olein, soy oil, coconut oil, HO sun oil*

Equipment and Hygiene

There is a wide range of equipment available for use with infant formulas: bottles in all shapes and colors, with and without handles; nipples for every age group, usable for everything from baby foods to milk; drinking spouts; bottle warmers; sterilizers; thermos containers; and storage chests. Not all of these products are helpful. Some of them are not practical or not hygienic. For a list of the absolutely essential items for a new baby, see page 272. Be sure to boil new bottles and nipples for five minutes.

A Choice of Bottles

The bottles (feeders, nursers) available are made either of heat-resistant glass, plastic, or pre-sterilized disposable liners for use with a plastic holder.

■ The advantage of *plastic bottles* is that they are lightweight and are shatter-resistant. The main disadvantage is that they are harder to clean than glass bottles.

It's better not to let your child take charge of the bottle himself.

■ *Glass bottles* are heavier and are breakable, and they are not recommended for storing breast milk.

■ *Plastic holders (nursers) with pre-sterilized disposable liners* have the advantage of having a reusable plastic holder that is easy to clean and liners that are disposable and collapse down as the baby drinks from the bottle, which helps decrease the amount of air swallowed during feeding.

All You Need to Know About Nipples

Baby bottle nipples—including pacifiers—also come in several types: colored latex (natural rubber) and clear silicone.

■ Latex nipples have to be replaced after awhile, because they age and become sticky. Moreover, allergy-producing substances have been found in some models—ask for up-to-date test reports.

■ Silicone nipples are scarcely affected by aging at all, and they are very easy to clean. They are dishwasher safe and are odor- and taste-free. They are less "bite-proof," however. Once your baby's first teeth are in, you may need to replace one here and there.

The Right Shape

There are three prototypes for nipples' shapes. Scientists continue to disagree about the advantages and disadvantages of the different basic designs.

121

■ The *natural* or standard shape is designed to resemble the nipple of the breast. It is especially good for newborns.

■ The *square shape*, seen with some disposable bottles, is also said to resemble the breast nipple.

■ The *orthodontically correct* shape is designed to prevent overbite.

You may need to try several different styles to see which best suits your baby.

Nipple Type and Size

Not all nipples are created equal: It is important that the hole in the nipple be the right size, since that determines the rate of flow of the drops. You should try several different types before determining which will be best for your baby. Larger holes are more appropriate for younger babies and for the feeding of formula, whereas smaller holes are better for older babies and for juices. Packages will generally give the age range that is appropriate for a particular nipple and its hole.

A Must: Scrupulous Cleanliness

During the first months, when the baby still has little immunity against germs, good hygiene is very important. Set up a corner of your kitchen as a place to prepare the bottles. It is safest to store the bottles and nipples in one of your kitchen cabinets. There are special bottle stands that usually have a place for nipples as well. However, you also can store the bottles top down on a clean kitchen towel and keep the nipples in a clean glass preserving jar. Set up a corner for the cleaning and sanitizing equipment— brushes and a sterilizer, for example— and use these items exclusively for the baby's things.

Cleaning Bottles and Nipples

■ Remember that formula should always be fresh and all baby equipment should be kept clean.

■ Depending on your town water supply, it is not an absolute necessity to sterilize feeding equipment or use boiled water for formula preparation. You can ask your pediatric provider for advice about this.

■ If you decide not to sterilize, then you should scrub all equipment, including bottles, nipples, caps, spoons, and mixing jars, in hot, soapy water with a bottle brush. Dishwashing liquid detergent is quite adequate.

■ You may also use your dishwasher to clean bottles, caps, and silicone nipples.

■ If you decide to sterilize your feeding equipment, then you should boil the nipples and bottles; make certain they are immersed in the boiled water for 10 minutes.

A PACIFIER—YES OR NO?

Pacifiers are a frequent topic of discussion, because they continue to make the headlines from time to time. They have gotten a bad reputation because in the past, some of these cherished rubber nipples contained harmful substances and some people have put forth theories that the use of a pacifier can interfere with the development of the baby's jaw. There is no evidence that the use of a pacifier will affect your baby's teeth unless he continues to use one after the age of 6 years.

When deciding whether to use a pacifier at all, you may find this matter-of-fact list of the advantages and disadvantages helpful.

What's good about pacifiers:
■ They calm many restless infants and often help them fall asleep more easily.
■ So-called nonnutritive sucking (without eating) is said to have certain benefits for a baby's state of mind.
■ Their use can help parents stay calm as well: They feel less helpless when their baby is restless or cries.

■ You can always make a pacifier vanish during the baby's second year, but that doesn't work with a thumb....

What's bad about pacifiers:
■ They are unsanitary, because they keep falling out of the baby's mouth and are sterilized too infrequently.
■ With a pacifier, you prevent babies and small children from talking.
■ Nursing is best from an orthodontic standpoint.
■ Without a pacifier, you save yourself battles when it comes time to get your child out of the pacifier habit—a five-year-old with a pacifier is quite a peculiar sight

Safety precautions when using a pacifier:
■ Do not tie the pacifier to your child's shirt with a long string or ribbon—your child can choke on the string.
■ Make sure the shield is large enough so that your child cannot swallow the pacifier.
■ Do not dip the pacifier in sugar or juice—this can promote tooth decay.

■ Also, in the first few months, remember to wash or sterilize pacifiers regularly.

As Directed: Preparing Formula

The manufacturer's directions for preparation appear on every package or can of formula. Follow these guidelines precisely. It is a good idea to clip the directions and stick them on the door of the kitchen cabinet where you keep the feeding equipment or on the refrigerator door. Even with easy-to-use instant formulas, there are still some precautions to follow.

■ Before preparing the bottle, always wash your hands well with warm water and soap.

■ Tap water, especially that from a well, should be boiled in the first few months of life.

■ Tests show that in many cases the measuring spoons tend to be generous, and too much powder ends up in the bottle. The upshot: The formula becomes too concentrated. This places stress on the baby's kidneys and increases his need for fluids. Make sure the scoop is level, not heaping, each time! Scrape off any extra powder with the back of a knife.

■ Be sure to check the expiration date of the formula.

■ Formula should always be freshly prepared. Never mix it in advance and let it stand. Similarly, you should discard any leftover formula.

■ To warm up a bottle that has been in the refrigerator you should run warm water over it—then you must test the temperature with a few drops on the inside of your wrist. Note, though, that many babies like their formula cold, directly out of the refrigerator.

■ For traveling, it is easiest to bring along premixed formula.

Important!

Never agitate the bottle as if it were a cocktail shaker. This will produce too many tiny air bubbles, which can cause gas. Instead, just turn it upside down two or three times. Alternatively, you can stir the formula with a long-handled spoon.

What Kind of Water for the Bottle?

■ You can use tap water or bottled water to mix the formula. For the first several months, you should boil the tap water for five minutes, for sterilization, before mixing with the formula.

■ Bottled water may have chemical impurities not found in public water supplies. Check the label or contact the bottler if you have concerns.

■ Be careful if old lead pipes or brand-new copper pipes are relocated or laid in your home. Then you should switch to mineral water, choosing a brand that is approved for the preparation of formula.

■ Always use cold water, not hot water from the tap.

■ Let tap water run for a minute before you take some.

■ A standard water filter will not reduce nitrate levels that are dangerous for your baby. All it will do is filter harmful substances such as pestcides, chlorine, copper, and lead out of the water—and there's no way to tell by looking; you have to go by the length of use. In addition, the germ level in the water can become elevated. Consequently, avoid using filtered water for baby formula.

■ The safe alternative to tap water generally is bottled water.

Bottle Feeding Takes Practice

When your child is fed, he not only has his hunger satisfied but also senses your nearness and feels warm and secure. In the first months, this feeling of well-being is the natural basis of your relationship. Newborns' vision actually is sharpest at the typical "nursing distance."

If you bottle feed your child, try to approximate the nursing situation as closely as possible. Take plenty of time, and don't rush your baby. Don't construct any props for the bottle with pillows and stuffed animals to let your baby feed himself (quite apart from the fact that it could be dangerous). Simply grant your child the moments of togetherness that nature intended. Give him as much physical contact as possible.

Of course it is wonderful if the father gives the baby some of his feedings; your child will be able to attune himself to more than one person without any difficulties. But it's probably not a good idea to hand over the bottle and the baby to a stream of constantly changing baby-sitters.

Whether your baby is breastfed or bottle fed—water or juice is necessary only in special cases.

The Feeding Process

Babies have an aversion to scratchy sweaters and stiff fabrics. When feeding the baby, make sure at least your arms are bare. The more skin contact your baby has, the better, as far as his well-being and development are concerned.

1 Sit down and relax, and slide a pillow under the arm on which the child's head rests. Hold him so that his head rests in the angle of your arm, at breast level. He should not lie flat—his head needs to be slightly elevated, which will make sucking easier for him.

2 With the nipple of the bottle, gently stroke the cheek closest to you. This will stimulate the "rooting reflex."

3 Push the nipple into his eagerly seeking mouth. Make sure that your child doesn't swallow any air: The nipple has to be filled with formula at all times.

4 If your baby sucks so vigorously that the nipple contracts, take the bottle away for a few seconds. You may have to slip your little finger into the corner of the baby's mouth until the vacuum inside the nipple has filled up again. Then continue the feeding.

5 As with breastfeeding, your baby has to be burped after the feeding—possibly even once or more during the feeding (see page 66).

Boil fresh tap water and pour it into a clean thermos container. Then you can prepare the bottle more quickly at night or away from home.

The Right Temperature

Breast milk always flows at the right temperature and rate—with a bottle, you have to control both factors.

■ Formula needs to be at about body temperature when fed to the baby. With plastic bottles in particular, the temperature is hard to tell just by touching the bottle. Always let a few drops of formula trickle onto the inside of your wrist. If the formula feels pleasantly warm, the temperature is right.

■ Has the formula gotten too cold? Run warm tap water over the bottle to warm it. Remember to test the temperature of the formula on the inside of your wrist before you feed the baby.

Important!
After heating, stir the formula thoroughly and test the temperature.

The Rate of Flow

The rate of flow, or rather the rate of feeding, depends in large part on the size of the hole in the nipple: If the hole is too small, the baby usually will

Skin-to-skin contact is very important for your baby—not only when he's being fed.

not get enough formula, and if the hole is too big, he will get too much and may choke. You may find that when feeding water, a single small hole is best, and when feeding formula, a large hole or multiple holes works best for your baby. The size of the hole in the nipple is ideal if 1 to 2 drops per second fall when you turn the bottle upside down.

Do Bottle-Fed Children Need Water?

Modern infant formulas are almost as thirst-quenching as breast milk,

thanks to their low protein and salt content. Additional liquids such as water are unnecessary in the first several months of life—until your baby begins solids. Your baby will get all the water he needs from his formula or breast milk. When the weather is hot, it is best to give an extra feeding of formula or breast milk instead of water. In the early months of life too much water can disturb the delicate balance of salts in your baby's body. If you want to give your baby a little water on a very hot day or if he has fever or constipation, you can give 2 to 4 ounces per day.

Tooth Decay from Prolonged Sucking

Milk and fruit juices can ruin your baby's teeth if he constantly has the bottle in his mouth. In addition, your child will be literally inundated with fluids and minerals—a real strongman act for his little kidneys. Even pure water is harmful to babies who suck too long: It rinses away the protective layer of saliva on the teeth to such an extent that the dental substance is attacked, even without sugar. For these reasons, do not use the easy-to-grip bottles that encourage self-feeding—using heavy glass bottles will avoid this potential problem. Remember, though, glass bottles should not be used once your child can hold the bottle himself—they are breakable, and he may drop them.

EXTRA-TIP

What makes beads of sweat appear on many a mother's brow?: rage-filled cries of hunger long before the formula is cool enough to drink. Put the bottle in a tall container of cool water that reaches all the way to the screw-on top—this is the quickest way to bring it to room temperature if you have just boiled the water. And remember to always test the temperature of the water on the inside of your wrist before feeding your baby.

SPOON BY SPOON: SUPPLEMENTARY FOODS

Between the ages of 4 and 6 months you can start to give your baby his first solids. The best solid to start with is rice cereal. It is easily digested and is fortified with iron. You can start with one to two feedings per day of 1 to 3 tablespoons mixed with formula or breast milk. At this time, you can also offer your baby 2 to 4 ounces of fruit juice per day. At around the age of 6 months you can begin adding strained or pureed fruits and vegetables, and eating from a spoon will gradually take the place of sucking. Be sure the solids are single ingredients so you can readily identify an allergic reaction. Pureed meats are introduced a little later—around 7 to 8 months. The texture can be smooth from 6 to 9 months and chunky from 9 to 12 months. By his first birthday, your baby will be able to join you at the table and literally eat from your plate.

In his second six months, your baby will undergo rapid development as far as his feeding and nutrition are concerned. Sometimes the situation can almost make you sad: Just when breastfeeding was working perfectly, you are supposed to cut back on it. And now that your child is nursing so happily and quickly, you are supposed to start the battle over the spoon and cup. Don't rush into anything! But try to understand that your baby will not stay little; his needs are going to change as he grows. Some mothers will welcome that—they understand that too conservative an approach will delay their child's development. As the menu is expanded, motor abilities are growing at the same time, along with self-confidence: Being able to feed oneself is an enormous accomplishment. If your child is allowed to learn to feed himself—even if things are messy at times—he will develop a positive relationship to mealtime. You need to allow him to do that.

The Meal Plan Changes

After the sixth month, breast milk or formula alone can no longer fulfill your child's needs: The iron stores your baby is born with begin to diminish after 4 to 6 months of age, and his caloric requirements are growing. His digestive system, too, is now mature enough to deal with food other than milk. It is time for the first spoon.

Homemade or Store-Bought?

We want everything to be absolutely safe for our child. In the first year of life, a baby's immune system is not completely developed. This includes the part of his immune system that protects his stomach and gastrointestinal tract. For this reason, precautionary measures are needed early on in his life. Therefore, the little jars of strained foods are an excellent idea. Keep in mind though, if you are so inclined and have the time, home prepared pureed food is perfectly acceptable, provided that it is always fresh. If you are going to prepare your baby's food at home, remember to not allow the food to sit out at a temperature between 60 to 120 degrees Fahrenheit (16 to 48°C) for more than one hour, and always use clean utensils and work surfaces.

Texture is important in early feedings. You want to go from pureed or finely mashed to progressively thickened serving after the age of 7 to 8 months as your baby becomes a seasoned eater.

Important!
Your baby is not a gourmet; his chief aim is to get full! And don't worry that the diet could be too monotonous for him. During the first year, too wide a range of foods increases the risk of allergy.

Quick and Easy:
Glass Jars of Baby Food

■ Give preference to products with as few ingredients as possible.

■ Heat baby food in a small bowl over simmering water or in a heating dish—test the temperature on your wrist after mixing. (Remember, you do not have to heat the food—your baby will probably like it just as well cold or at room temperature.)

■ In the first six months, opened jars that have not been warmed may be refrigerated for one day at most; later, they can be kept two to four days in the refrigerator before use.

■ Leftovers that have already been warmed should not be reheated for the baby. You can add them to a sauce or soup for the rest of your family.

■ Buying premixed baby cereals in a

In the second six months, it's time for solid foods—at first, just a few spoonfuls of strained or pureed foods or baby cereal, but later on something to chew can be added to the menu. You can cook foods for your baby yourself, if you stick closely to our recipes.

jar is really not worth it. Instant flakes make preparation easy, and pureed fruit also can be fixed at home in a flash.

Home-Prepared Foods

■ Give preference to fruits and vegetables that have been organically grown, without pesticides, and prepare them as freshly as possible.

■ Use only cereal flakes that are expressly designed for babies—they are iron-fortified.

■ When your baby is around the age of eight months, before cooking your family's meal you can occasionally set

aside some of the food to prepare for the baby: Boiled peeled potatoes, a little piece of meat, and some broth can be mashed or pureed for his dinner.

Nutritious Fare for the Baby?

The basic idea behind food of high nutritional value is that it should be as close to its natural state as possible. Breast milk fulfills that requirement to perfection: It is a natural food, tailor-made to meet the baby's needs.

For the first year of life, however, this standard cannot be applied to any other foods. Whole cow's milk and

131

raw vegetables, for instance, are taboo in the first year of life. They place too great a burden on your child's digestive tract.

WHAT CAN MY BABY EAT, AND WHEN?

From birth on:
Breast milk and/or infant formula

From the fourth to the sixth month:
Rice, oat, barley cereal
2 to 4 ounces of fruit juice (avoid orange and tomato)

From the sixth to the eighth month:
Strained vegetables: dark yellow, orange, dark green
Plain yogurt mixed with strained fruits
Cooked fruits, applesauce, strained fruits
Cooked egg yolk

From the eighth to the tenth month:
Hot cereals (remember—no added honey or corn syrup)
Finger foods: bread, cheese, pasta (avoid popcorn, whole grapes, raisins, nuts, and hot dogs—choking hazards)
Strained meats: turkey, chicken; or soft meatballs cut into small pieces
Cooked egg whites—9 months on

From the tenth to the twelfth month:
Orange and tomato juice
Soft, cooked vegetable pieces
Small pieces of cooked chicken, turkey, fish, or meat

Is a Vegetarian Diet Harmful?

Strictly speaking, there are different forms of vegetarianism. Strict "vegans," include people who follow a macrobiotic diet, refusing meat, fish, eggs, and cow-based dairy products. Many people in the United States follow a strict vegan diet and remain perfectly healthy. Problems can arise if certain vitamins and minerals—vitamin D, calcium, folic acid, and vitamin B_{12}—become deficient in the diet. Therefore, the strict vegetarian's diet needs to be supplemented—either in the form of vitamins or vitamin-enriched foods. Most people who are vegetarians are very knowledgeable about the important vitamins and minerals that are missing in a strict vegetarian diet and do very well with planning their meals and taking supplements.

Lacto-ovo vegetarians will consume eggs and dairy products but not fish or meat. This is a little easier because dairy products are a good source of calcium, B_{12}, and protein, as well as the major source of dietary vitamin D. Eggs are an excellent source of protein and iron.

Some tips if you are going to raise your child as a vegetarian:
■ It is best to breastfeed your child for at least the first 6 months of life.
■ Look for soy-based milk products that are fortified with iron and calcium.

If you are preparing a meat-free diet for your child, use primarily iron-enriched cereal during the second six months of life. Baby's iron stores from birth begin to diminish between 4 and 6 months of age. Therefore, it is important to replenish these stores with dietary iron, which is plentiful in meat, or other food if "iron-enriched." It is a good idea to mix the cereal occasionally with vitamin C fortified juices—vitamin C aids in absorption of iron from the gastrointestinal tract.

■ Give your baby a vitamin supplement that contains vitamin D, iron, folic acid, and vitamin B_{12}.

■ Once your baby begins solids, give high-protein breads, pastas, and legumes.

Baby Foods: From Sweet to Hearty

For the time being, solid foods are something completely strange and new for your baby. He will first want to check out the consistency and taste—not infrequently he will be disgusted by the first spoonful and, shaking his head, will spit it out again. Once he has become used to the cereal, the strained vegetables and meats will launch the next assault on his gustatory nerves. Consequently, you cannot replace an entire feeding all at once. Here, too—as in all other developmental processes—it is best to begin patiently, taking small steps.

Just a Few Spoonfuls at First ...

Start at midday, with 1 or 2 teaspoonfuls of strained carrots or pureed fruit after half a breastfeeding or bottle feeding. At first you can easily use carrots from a jar, since you need only small amounts.

■ It is best to use a small jar: Once opened, it will keep for only 1 to 2 days in the refrigerator.

■ With fruit you can prepare one portion at a time, pureeing one to two small spoonfuls of banana.

■ See page 140 for directions on teaching your baby to eat from a spoon.

...Then the First "Real" Strained Foods

No earlier than the middle of the sixth month, you can feed the baby a meal of strained potatoes and carrots with meat at his midday meal. These can either be from the jar or freshly prepared in the blender or food processor.

■ Take note that it is a good idea when first starting solids that you introduce only one new solid at a time—one about every 4 to 5 days. If your baby has an allergy to a certain food or that food just doesn't agree with him, you will be able to easily identify it by introducing one new food at a time.

Some Meal Suggestions

STRAINED VEGETABLES, POTATOES, AND MEAT

Once your child has tried and tolerated the above ingredients, then you can make a cooked meal from fresh ingredients and serve this mixture at lunch or dinner.

1 potato, about 1.8 ounces (50 g)
3.5 ounces (100 g) carrots
1 ounce (30 g) lean ground or finely chopped lamb, beef, poultry, or pork
3 tablespoons water
1 teaspoon butter

Boil the potato after skinning. • Meanwhile, peel and finely dice the carrots. Steam in a pot for about 15 minutes, along with the meat and the water. Add more water as needed. • Peel and dice the potato and add it to the pot, along with the fat. Using a blender or food processor, puree briefly. If necessary, thin with additional boiled water.

MEALS FROM THE FREEZER

Making the baby's noon meal takes a bit of time and, because of the small amounts, the mixture is not easy to prepare. It is a good idea to cook ahead for the entire month, freezing individual portions in freezer bags.

For 30 portions:
32 ounces (900 g) lean meat
2 cups (0.5 l) water
1 pinch fennel seeds
3.25 pounds (1.5 kg) potatoes
6.5 pounds (3 kg) carrots

After thawing, add to each portion:
1 teaspoon butter

In a pressure cooker (at setting 1), cook the meat with the water and the fennel seeds for about 45 minutes. • Meanwhile, wash the potatoes well, then peel and cook them in a regular pot. Wash, peel, and dice the carrots. • When the meat is done, remove it from the broth, add the diced carrots, and cook in the pressure cooker (at setting 1) for about six minutes. • Dice the meat, then puree in batches in the blender with a little broth and some carrots. • Peel the hot potatoes and mash them finely—you can also put them in the blender for a younger baby. Mix the mashed potatoes with the pureed carrots and meat. Put portions of about 7 ounces (200 g) each (somewhat more or less, depending on the child's age and appetite) into freezer bags and place them in your freezer. If you do not use a pressure cooker, you will need longer cooking times.

■ At mealtime, heat one portion in a double boiler over hot water, then mix with 1 teaspoon of butter.

Remember to check the temperature of the food before serving it to your child.

Important!

Don't taste the pureed foods you make for your child; that way you won't even think of "seasoning to taste." Your baby cannot tolerate salt yet. For his sensitive taste buds, the mild aroma of milk, cereal, and fruit is completely adequate!

Sample Meals for the Fifth and Sixth Months

Breakfast:
2 tablespoons iron-fortified cereal mixed with 2 ounces of fruit juice breast milk or 6 to 8 ounces of formula

Lunch:
2 to 3 tablespoons of pureed fruit breast milk or 6 to 8 ounces of formula

Afternoon Snack:
2 ounces of juice

Dinner:
2 tablespoons pureed fruit 2 tablespoons infant cereal 6 to 8 ounces of formula or breast milk

Bedtime Snack:
breast milk or 6 to 8 ounces of formula

Sample Meals for Six to Eight Months

Breakfast:
breast milk or 6 to 8 ounces of formula 4 to 6 tablespoons iron-fortified cereal 2 tablespoons of fruit

Lunch:
6 to 8 ounces of formula or breast milk 2 to 3 tablespoons of vegetables 1 to 2 tablespoons of pureed meat or yogurt

Afternoon Snack:
4 ounces of juice in a cup finger foods: Cheerios, graham crackers, or teething biscuits such as arrowroot cookies or Zweiback

The first real strained food should be served at lunch. Cooking more than you need and freezing it for later use will save time.

Dinner:

6 to 8 ounces of formula or breast milk
2 to 3 tablespoons of vegetables
1 tablespoon of pureed meat
2 tablespoons of fruit

Bedtime Snack:

breast milk or 6 to 8 ounces of formula

Cereal with milk and juice, an evening menu item.

■ Note that your baby may drop his fourth feeding around this time—and therefore will increase his solid intake.

Sample Meals for Eight to Twelve Months

Breakfast:

4 to 6 ounces of formula or breast milk
$^1/_4$ to $^1/_2$ cup cereal—infant cereals or plain hot cereals

Ripe soft fruits—pears, bananas, peaches, cantaloupe (mashed to chunky consistency closer to eight months—small slices or cubes closer to one year)

Morning Snack:

4 to 6 ounces of fruit juice
Diced cheese

Lunch:

4 to 6 ounces of formula or breast milk (offer formula from a cup)
$^1/_4$ to $^1/_2$ cup of vegetables—from the jar or freshly prepared, soft vegetables— white or sweet potato without the skin, very soft or mashed carrots, mashed peas, cooked, finely chopped spinach
$^1/_4$ cup of yogurt or hard-cooked egg yolk

Afternoon Snack:

4 to 6 ounces of fruit juice or water
Crackers or a soft bagel

Dinner:

$^1/_4$ to $^1/_2$ cup diced or chopped turkey or chicken, or a soft meatball
$^1/_4$ to $^1/_2$ cup noodles or rice
$^1/_4$ to $^1/_2$ cup vegetables
4 to 6 ounces of formula or breast milk

Bedtime:

6 to 8 ounces of formula or breast milk

■ Egg whites can be introduced between 9 and 12 months of age—ask your doctor.

When the Baby Is Teething

. . . he will need something hard to chew on. You have several options to help your baby with his teething discomfort: teething toast, cold bagels, a teething ring (you can also refrigerate this), teething anesthetic gels or ointments (available over-the-counter), or massaging the gums with one of your fingers. Offering your teething baby a cold chewing object probably works the best of all the options. The cold will help to numb the sore gums. The gels for the gums work at relieving discomfort, but their effects don't last very long.

Once the teeth begin to break through, it's a good time to start thinking about thickening his solids—making them a little more on the lumpy rather than the smooth side. Starting to thicken his food at this time will help you later with the transition to table foods that have even more texture.

THE FIRST TEETH

The first teeth will appear, on average, between the sixth and the ninth month (for some children earlier, and for some later). The first teeth to erupt are usually the two center bottom teeth. After these have appeared, the next will come 1 to 2 months later—the four center upper teeth. The next teeth that will come about 1 month later are the two lower lateral incisors (next to the central teeth). Next will be the first molars, followed by the canine teeth. The second-year molars will come somewhere between 20 and 24 months. Remember that there can be wide variation in the timing of the appearance of teeth from child to child, so don't worry if your friend's or neighbor's child has teeth before yours—this variation is normal. By the age of $2^1/2$ years, your child will have 20 teeth.

Usually the first sign of teething is increased drooling. Often you will not notice anything until the little tip of a tooth is already visible. Sometimes, however, the gums are reddened and swollen, and your baby is irritable and has decreased appetite. Teething does not cause fever! If your baby's temperature is 100.5 degrees Fahrenheit or higher, and he seems ill, consult your doctor. Loose stools with teething is an area of controversy. Many mothers will insist that every time their baby is cutting a tooth, he has loose stools. Many physicians, on the other hand, will insist that this phenomenon does not occur. So how do you sort all this out? If your baby is having frequent watery stools or vomiting, this is probably a viral "stomach bug," and you should consult your pediatric provider.

Important!

Do not use carrots or apple slices for teething. Once your child has a couple of central incisors, he can bite off small pieces and is *then at risk of choking. It is not a good idea, in general, to leave your teething infant unsupervised with a teething object.*

Learning to Eat—It's Not Automatic

Your baby is able to suck within a few minutes after birth, and actually has been sucking since about 33 to 34 weeks of gestation. But eating with a spoon, biting, chewing, and drinking from a cup are things he has to learn with your help. And sometimes that is not an easy task.

From the Breast to the Bottle

Breastfed babies frequently have a hard time with the bottle. Often they

would rather do without than take the artificial nipple into their mouth.

You may have decided to introduce a bottle early in your baby's life, either to give yourself time for errands or for working, or to allow the baby's father to participate more directly in the feeding routine. If this is the case, it is a good idea not to introduce the bottle until after your baby is 2 weeks old. It is easier for your baby to drink from a bottle than your breast, and therefore, if given the choice he will choose the bottle. So it is important to establish breastfeeding before introducing that first bottle. You will find that many pediatric providers and lactation consultants are strongly against any bottles until you are starting to wean from breastfeeding. You and your husband will need to discuss this issue, and come to a decision based on your particular situation and desires. Your baby will be fine either way!

At first, it's better not to let your child hold the cup himself; let him sit on your lap to drink. Once he can sit without falling over, he can try to manage the cup alone.

Some tips at making the transition from breast to bottle:

■ Most babies who are weaned after the age of eight months will get enough nourishment from solid foods and fluids from a cup—formula, juices, and water.

■ Wean your baby from the breast gradually. If you wean too quickly, you will be uncomfortable, and some breastfeeding babies take a little time to catch on to the bottle or cup—which will prolong the weaning process.

■ You can begin by replacing the lunchtime breastfeeding with a cup of formula. You may have a little discomfort and feeling of fullness at this time of day, but this will pass in just a couple of days.

■ Next, you can offer solids and formula at the beginning of the meal, and end the meal with breastfeeding.

■ After a couple of weeks you will probably be breastfeeding only at "comfort times"—early morning and just before bed.

■ Remember that you can also use bottles for the transition between breast to cup now or for younger babies. Some babies take several months before they are getting enough fluid from a cup alone.

■ Expect setbacks: When your baby is teething, has a cold, or if you are traveling, he may "ask" for more frequent breastfeeding.

Appearances are deceptive: Feedings go this smoothly in the beginning only if Daddy is using diversionary tactics. Normally, the first few tries with the spoon aren't this simple ...

Weaning from the Bottle to the Cup

Most pediatric providers will recommend weaning from the bottle to the cup at around 1 year of age. This is mainly because of the risk of bottle caries: Juice or milk pooling around the teeth will cause the incoming teeth to decay. This can occur if a toddler constantly has a bottle of juice or milk hanging out of his mouth. And the longer you wait to change from bottle to cup, in many cases, the harder it is. Don't forget, also, that lying flat, or sleeping with a bottle in the mouth can contribute to middle ear infections.

Tips on weaning from the bottle:

■ Start by replacing the lunchtime bottle with a sippy cup; it is best to *introduce* the cup between 5 and 8 months of age—even if it's just a couple of sips to start off with.

■ After this has been successful, you can replace the snack-time bottle with a cup.

■ Feed your toddler a bottle only when he's sitting down or sitting on your lap. This is the time he has become very mobile and interested in exploring his surroundings: It's not a good idea to let him roam with a bottle in his mouth, as previously stated.

■ In the beginning, use the bottle for milk. Give juice and water only in the cup. As your child uses the cup more and more, try to make the bottle less interesting by using only water in it.

Learning to Eat from a Spoon

Before the fourth month, your baby won't be able to do anything with a spoon except suck on it, perhaps. His sucking reflex is still so strong that the motions of chewing and swallowing never even occur. In addition, after the age of 4 months, the tongue-thrust reflex is lost. Earlier than this age, if your baby is offered solids, he will extrude most of it out of his mouth with his tongue. So now is the right time to start using the spoon for feeding solids.

HIGH CHAIRS FOR YOUNG TABLE COMPANIONS

You can choose among chair-and-table combinations, high chairs that grow along with the child, and simple high chairs with a removable tray. Before you buy, check consumer magazines for comparison shopping. Look for high chairs manufactured after 1997 to meet all safety standards set forth by the Juvenile Products Manufacturers Association and, therefore, be certified.

■ *The combination high chairs can be quickly converted to a child's chair and table. Drawbacks: They are heavy and clunky. Also, the chair is so small that your child can't sit at the table with you later on. At most you will get some use out of it in the nursery for the first three years. Make sure that a foot rail is attached to the chair itself.*

■ *High chairs that grow with the child are great, especially for small children at the family table, because they can be pushed up close to the edge of the table. The drawbacks: They are uncomfortable for very young children, give little support, and rarely have an integrated tray.*

■ *Plain high chairs without all the extras are ideal for small apartments. Generally they fold up and can travel from one room to another.*

Making It Work

■ Make your first attempt at using a spoon when your baby has already taken some breast milk or formula and is half full. A hungry baby will reject a spoon very angrily!

■ For the first few attempts, use slightly sweet strained carrots or pureed fruits.

■ Use a plastic spoon—it is warmer and softer than a metal one. Choose one that is narrow and shallow, so that it fits nicely into the baby's mouth.

If the Baby Goes on Strike

■ If your child refuses solid food, it may be because of the unfamiliar consistency. You can abandon that meal, and try again later, or tomorrow. Don't get discouraged—this is more common than you may think. He will eventually love his cereal and vegetables!

■ Patience is very important! Don't start this experiment unless you are relaxed and alert!

■ Never make the mistake of offering your baby different "menus" all the time. This will confuse him. And it is always a good idea to introduce one new food at a time—every 4 to 5 days.

■ He may refuse the spoon not because he dislikes the taste, but because the solid food and the utensil simply are unfamiliar.

Eating at the table with the "big folks" stimulates the baby's appetite and puts him in a good mood.

You Eat at the Same Time!

Some babies can sit quite easily in a chair by the end of the first year—others need a little longer. Put him in a booster seat at the table, or pull the high chair up next to the table. A baby who can sit by himself also wants to do what the adults are doing. Let your child take part in your meals. They will not always coincide with his mealtimes, and certainly he is not yet able to have everything you are eating—but a lot will be gained anyway. Your child will feel that he belongs and learn quite a lot just from observing. The lesson will be easier if you make sure that spills don't matter.

Tips for Making Eating Fun

■ If your floor is carpeted or hard to clean, buy heavy-duty, transparent plastic sheeting from a roll (available in department stores or home furnishings centers) and cover the floor under your child's high chair. It will hardly be noticeable, and it will protect the floor or carpet from spills and stains.

■ Another alternative is a smaller, thin plastic mat that you can place directly under the high chair. These are bright and colorful, and are available in most toy stores. After a messy meal, just bring the four corners together and empty the crumbs into the garbage or in the backyard.

■ A bib that covers the baby's arms and extends over his lap is a necessity. If you are so inclined, and have the time, you can easily sew such "capes" out of old towels. Otherwise, they are available in supermarkets, baby stores, toy stores, and baby catalogs.

■ Plates and cups made of plastic are ideal for babies who feed themselves. So-called training plates that don't tip over easily and have a curved rim are really quite practical.

■ Spoons with a curved or angled handle are helpful now as well: Your baby's arm is still so short that it can't reach "around the corner."

■ Give your baby finger foods that he can manage on his own. Babies enjoy feeding themselves. True, the end result often is an indefinable squashy mass, but your child will be developing a feeling for biting and chewing—and enjoying his meal as well!

Important!

Never leave your child alone when he is eating! It is always possible that he will swallow an especially large morsel the wrong way and be unable to get air. Then quick intervention on your part is called for: Immediately take him out of the chair, hold him in a head-down position, and with the base of your palm give several forceful back blows aimed in between his shoulder blades to dislodge the bite. For more on CPR, see page 250.

Feeding Time Options:

1 *Feeding on your lap*

2 *Feeding in the infant seat*

3 *Sitting at the table*

4 *High chairs for young table companions*

Feeding on Your Lap

1 An apron for you and a bib for the baby are definitely necessary at the outset—strained carrots leave stubborn spots!

2 When feeding your baby, always hold him on your lap. If you are right-handed, put your child at your left, so that he looks to his right and his right arm is pressed to your side. Put your left arm around him and keep a firm hold on his free left arm. This is the only way you can fend off attacks on the solid foods— since babies truly want to "grasp" everything, and that means that a portion may occasionally go down the front of his mama's clothes.

3 Now you can use your free hand to feed the baby.

Feeding in the Infant Seat

■ Naturally you can feed your child in his infant seat if that seems more practical to you.

■ This is best for younger babies—4 to 6 months of age.

■ Do not put the seat on a counter or table—the risk of falling is too great!

■ If you choose this method, you should place the seat on the floor and sit next to your baby to feed him. This will also prevent you from leaning over while feeding.

Sitting at the Table

■ Once your baby can sit fairly well by himself—between 6 and 7 months— you can let him join you at the table in his high chair (more about this in the box on page 140). This will prepare him for joining the family at mealtime later on. In a high chair, he will have his hands free, and will progress from eating with his fingers to using a spoon nicely.

Helpful Tips When Shopping for a High Chair:

■ Look for a chair with wheels—so that you can move from room to room easily without lifting a heavy piece of furniture, but also look for a stable chair that will not tip over.

■ The chair should be equipped with a safety strap—and you should always use this when your child is in his chair.

■ Look for a removable, washable tray that locks into place when your child is in the chair and is operable with one hand.

■ Washable vinyl padding also makes clean-up time easier and is more comfortable than a wooden seat.

Help for the Entire Family

A baby literally turns the entire family upside down. The roles are redistributed, and everyone first has to find out what his new place is to be. The following pages will tell you how to involve the baby's father, siblings, and grandparents in the events, how to solve problems in your marital relationship, and how you can "survive" as a woman, apart from being a mother.

BECOMING A FAMILY

. . . is like embarking upon a journey to another country.

Especially far-reaching is the change that occurs after the birth of the first child,

for it makes a couple into parents, parents into grandparents,

a husband into a father, and a wife into a mother.

An entire family is born. After this "cataclysm," you first

have to find a balance that is fair to everyone.

That's not always easy!

The new roles often are weighted with enormous expectations. Your own childhood memories resurface and may cause emotional havoc. If problems are swept under the rug now, it can affect the entire family. But if you confront your feelings and take advantage of the chance to experience and share your wants, desires, and fears, the "birth of the family" will be a real new beginning for you.

This is also true for the second, third, and fourth children and for stepfamilies with their first baby together. At first, the family is thrown off balance by the new arrival. But that is the prerequisite for achieving a new togetherness. After all, when something new comes into being, something old has to come to an end.

The changes are greatest for the mother. She carried the baby, gave birth to him, and is able to breastfeed him. Where women's liberation prevailed before, she now may feel strapped back into the traditional role of wife and mother.

The father is also undergoing changes at this time. If the mother is not returning to work, he has to figure out how to provide for a larger family by himself. Give him the opportunity to express his wants, desires, and fears, also.

And finally, you still have to sustain the partnership and love that created your new baby—and in the beginning, expect the baby to place some strain on that relationship.

Just Parents, No Longer a Couple?

After the birth of your child, you remain husband and wife. One day your child will go out on his own—but the marriage partners have chosen a joint path through life. If you are starting to call each other Daddy and Mommy now, your relationship will become limited to parenthood. And over the long run, this is no basis for a marriage.

You need to agree that these names are reserved for use by your child—and for your own parents. Interpret your behavior as a warning signal that it is time to do something for one another again. This is a summons to see yourselves as a couple again, to talk about your own worries and wishes—quite apart from "Baby & Co."

Togetherness Makes You Strong

A baby cannot improve or patch up a relationship—nor can he ruin it. In this period of the utmost stress, problems that a couple thus far have successfully repressed make an appearance. In other words, a difficult partnership may become even more trying now, and without proper communication, it may shatter. A good relationship, on the other hand, will be strained but will emerge strengthened from the conflicts. The basis of a harmonious relationship is respect, honesty, and trust. If you talked openly about your expectations and fears before the birth, you can go right on doing so when the baby is there.

If the father, however, lacks the basic readiness to be a father, the relationship is in trouble. A husband who refuses any and all responsibility for the baby and takes no interest in the child is revoking the entire basis of the partnership. A mother left completely on her own will at some point come to truly prefer raising the child by herself than living with a man who shares and accepts only a fraction of her life.

Avoiding Conflicts

As a mother, you need your husband's support in every respect. It is essential that you make it clear to him how important he is to you.

■ Don't join a mother's group that leaves the father out in the cold. Place your confidence in him. And trust him to be able to deal with the child the two of you have produced.

■ Don't relegate the father to the role of someone who slavishly carries out your orders, who fills the role of someone who just hands you the bottle, brings the rompers, and buys diapers. Discuss with him all the decisions,

147

worries, and deliberations that have to do with the baby.

■ He may be in need of some encouragement or a little push; this takes a bit of diplomacy on your part.

■ Don't hesitate to show weakness in your role as mother, because a supermom will discourage any father.

The First Time "Afterward"

Two-thirds of all women have slight injuries after the delivery—from internal tears in the mucus membranes to an episiotomy. Every mother, however, has a large internal wound inside the uterus that gives rise to the discharge known as lochia (see page 26). In early times the discharge was considered highly infectious and was stigmatized, almost superstitiously, as unclean. In actuality, lochia is no different from other matter normally discharged from wounds. Theoretically, there is no objection to sexual intercourse, provided the man uses a condom. Without such protection, there is too great a risk of infection for the woman, because the mucus membrane is still very sensitive, and there are cracks and tears in it.

The taboo formerly placed on sex after childbirth—one that is common in other cultures as well—has the deeper purpose of giving the mother time. Time to heal, time to become close to her baby, time to reflect. Most men instinctively honor this period of protection. They wait for their wife to give the first sign. It is certainly nicest for a woman after delivery if her husband treats her tenderly and lovingly, without letting his attentions immediately lead to sexual demands.

Birth Control after Childbirth

The erroneous belief that breastfeeding is a reliable way to prevent ovulation has fathered many a child. It is indeed true that frequent nursing at intervals of fewer than four hours prevents ovulation by virtue of the regular secretion of hormones—but it is not a reliable means of contraception. Once the intervals between breastfeedings lengthen, conception can occur. If you are breastfeeding, you still need to practice birth control (and if you aren't, it is all the more necessary).

Your Options
■ *Condoms* are the male's contribution to contraception.

■ A low-dosage *minipill* containing the corpus luteum hormone is also a reliable means (discuss it with your obstetrician). It diminishes milk production for only one or two days, and then the situation returns to normal. In addition, almost none of the hormones are passed into the milk.

■ The *diaphragm* is less reliable, and it may also be uncomfortable to insert.

Problems with Sex

Even if the lochia has subsided and every precaution has been taken to prevent another pregnancy, there often are problems in bed.

■ Sometimes the episiotomy site is not completely healed yet. Instead of clenching your teeth, go to the doctor: An episiotomy that continues to cause pain should be investigated by your obstetrician.

■ A brand-new mother may have trouble feeling at home in her altered body. She may think that she is unattractive, and would like to go into hiding.

■ Many women feel drained, completely exhausted by pregnancy, childbirth, breastfeeding, and the need to be on 24-hour duty. The constant physical demands leave little room for sexual appetite. Once a woman can get more sleep at night, her sex drive usually reasserts itself.

■ For some women, the apathy has a deeper cause. They are disappointed at their husband's lack of cooperation or they feel abandoned and exploited. Here, only honesty and open discussion can help, perhaps with counseling as well.

■ A delivery that was a traumatic experience can trigger a profound aversion to penetration of any kind. Without the help of a sex therapist or a self-help group, couples often are unable to solve this problem satisfactorily. Ask your obstetrician for the appropriate places to contact.

The most important thing during the "aftermath" is patience: The baby grew inside his mother's body for nine months. Your mind may need at least that long to regenerate. Deal carefully with each other in your relationship as a couple. Show each other tenderness and warmth, and then your sexual relationship usually will return to normal on its own.

SHOULD WE PUT THE BABY IN OUR BED?

Probably not. This decision is not at all easy, because babies often sleep extremely well in their parents' bed and develop in a highly desirable way. Besides, if you are getting up frequently to comfort your child, at some point you may give up and place the little squaller into your own warm nest.

But there is a reason for concern as well: What if the child rolls off the bed? Will your bed ever belong to you again? You, as parents, need to discuss these reservations with each other openly.

If you continue to let your growing child sleep in your bed, your fears could come true. But if you always put him to bed in his own room first every evening, he will gradually come to feel at home there, even if there are a few "relapses" later.

Finding Time for Each Other, Despite the Baby

A relationship needs quality time to stay strong. If all you share is duties and the daily routine, your marriage will suffer. Wonderful hours together, on the other hand, have a positive effect: The difficult times will seem less difficult if good times are inter-mixed with them. In addition, problems can be discussed much more openly and easily when one can travel away and look at them objectively, rather than trying to always solve things in the heat of the moment. This doesn't necessarily have to take place in the first few months, but after half a year, you should be able to try it.

Leisure Time as a Couple

■ The prerequisites for an evening without the baby are committed grand-parents, friends, or a reliable baby-sitter (see page 262). Maybe you can arrange to trade baby-sitting with friends who also have a baby. Where there's a will, there's a way!

■ Don't wait for fate to be kind. You will make an evening together a reality only if you set a definite date. It is best to make the evening out a regular monthly event: The baby-sitter, and later on your child, can get in the habit.

■ Especially in the first year, you can cultivate togetherness as a couple without leaving your baby. Walks will give you time for talking, and a bicycle

EXTRA-TIP

A weekend without the baby can give you the strength to keep going for months. While you are breastfeeding, this is not possible, of course, and during the first four months, it is not a good idea to leave your baby for this length of time. But during the second six months, you can easily try to arrange some time away. If your baby's grand-parents live nearby, this is a good choice. It's a good idea to have him looked after at home, in familiar sur-roundings. Important: Leave a list with the baby's peculiarities, likes, dislikes, and familiar rituals—and, of course, your telephone number.

trip will do the same (usually reserved for children who can sit on their own).

■ For a long time to come, the evening meal will be the one you can eat with-out having your child present. Even if you're only having sandwiches, sit down at the table to eat in peace and quiet, and use this time to relax and chat together. In front of the television set, you'll never get any closer to one another.

Togetherness Isn't Always Possible

Even as a couple, it is important to cul-tivate your own individual friendships and hobbies. This doesn't change with the birth of your child. Naturally, a friendship that both partners share has the best chance of enduring. But for solely practical reasons, you need to get out and do some things alone as well. If you have no baby-sitter, at least one of you can occasionally go to a movie with friends. And if sports are important to you, you can take turns minding the baby, so that both of you can participate.

If only one of you always gets out of the house, that's not good. But it's just as unhealthy to make this your rule: If I can't go out, you have to stay home, too.

The Father's Role

No role has undergone as much change in the past few decades as that of the father. Today most men are distinctly more involved with their family than their fathers and grandfathers had been. Correspondingly, the demands

FAMILY LIFE DOESN'T HAVE TO TAKE OVER

Observers of sociological trends use the term "cocooning" for the tendency to withdraw into one's own four walls and spin a "protective web." This tendency is never greater than after the birth of your first child.

From lack of time and sheer exhaustion, contacts to the outside world are neglected. Customary recreational activities with old friends are discontinued for practical reasons. Interests change after the birth of the child—couples without children and singles often pull back. In the end, then, the roof may fall in on the new parents in their isolation. This doesn't have to happen.

For one thing, new relationships can also develop through the baby:

■ Baby care and birth preparation courses offer initial opportunities to get acquainted.

■ Nursing support groups, playgrounds, and mother-and-child groups are real "stock exchanges" for contacts. If you read the classifieds, you will find ads for baby play groups, baby-sitting exchanges, and discussion groups.

■ Mothers can give each other an enormous amount of help and support—both practical and moral. The exchange of information in these informal circles is very helpful: You will find experts on any and all baby-related topics, names of baby-sitters, and the latest information on the kindergarten situation. And there is no reason such a contact can't develop into a real friendship, if the mothers take a liking to each other.

■ You can do something to help existing relationships as well. As a rule, you will not lose really good, old friends. It is important that both sides understand the changes in the situation. Don't act as if everything were still the same. Instead, give some thought to the things you still have in common. Don't expect a superhuman level of understanding from your friends without children; try to remember how you once felt about brand-new parents.

made on new fathers have changed as well: Participation in birth preparation

The "New Father"—not afraid of physical contact in dealing with the baby.

and baby-care courses, support in the delivery room, and job leave after the delivery are almost a "must." Some fathers-to-be feel overwhelmed by their partner's level of expectations. Alternatively, unreasonable expectations may be self-inflicted by the father who is trying to overachieve and be "superdad." More likely, though, the father doesn't know what he should expect. In our society, women tend to have spent more time considering their eventual roles as wives and mothers than men have spent considering their roles of husband and father.

The Search for New Role Models

A distinguishing feature of "modern" society has been the changing nature of gender-based roles—to the point of "role reversal" in some families. As more women pursue careers outside of the home, fathers and day-care centers fill the remaining void. Day-care providers are not capable of providing the level of attention and loving that has been provided by mothers for generations. Fathers, on the other hand, are equally capable of providing what has formerly been referred to as "mothering." However, while role models for women in the workplace fill the television, movie screens, society pages, and local social networks, the achievements of "Mr. Moms" do not receive equal press.

Don't Be Afraid of Being a Father

There is no reason to fear one's new role as a modern father. New research shows that men can instinctively behave just as "maternally" as women. In experiments, men touched children in the same way as women, returned their smiles, spoke to them using similar sounds, and fed them just as sympathetically as their mothers. When blindfolded, new fathers recognized their baby as easily as the mothers. In other words, being a father is something that really doesn't have to be learned. You'd be surprised to learn how many "Mr. Moms" there are out there today, and enjoying it!

Do It Yourself

Like every other relationship, the relationship between father and child depends on what you invest in it.

In the first months, especially if you are at work all day, the chores and tasks of daily living will need to be divided up. Each household and couple is different, but, for example, you might stop at the grocery store and the dry cleaners on your way home from work—while your wife has kept the house in order and taken care of the baby. Then you may want to trade "jobs" in the evening—you have some quality time with the baby, bath and diaper-changing included, while your wife prepares dinner. These arrangements should be discussed—all parties should feel they are getting a fair deal.

Spending time with your baby in the evening or on the weekend will help to make you feel more comfortable with the task of care-taking, and will surely give you great satisfaction and pleasure as well. Being alone with your baby from time to time will deepen your relationship. Don't say, "My time will come when the kid can walk and talk." Your time as a father begins when the baby is born. If you don't build a relationship with your baby now, it will become increasingly difficult later on.

By paying attention to your child, you basically have nothing to lose, but a lot to gain.

Tips for Fathers

■ Let your wife get out of the house for a few hours, or take the baby on a little outing yourself. Your wife will be able to accept your help if she has the feeling that you know how to handle your child. And you will have a completely different kind of relationship with the baby when you are alone with him.

■ Basically, you should be able to diaper and dress your child. For tips

——ESPECIALLY FOR FATHERS——

You offer your child something fundamentally different from what his mother can offer: your deep voice, your physical differences, and very different patterns of behavior.

As a rule, fathers are more animated in playing with their child and place more emphasis on daring—they tend to be a little less protective than mothers at times. The words, phrases, and intonations that you use in speaking to your child, your movements, and even how you hold your infant are very important to your baby as he develops knowledge about his surrounding world through a multitude of different experiences.

"Raising" children is not just a woman's job; it is a joint venture for husband and wife.

This kind of father not only is different—he feels different, too!

and information on these topics, see the sections beginning on pages 46 and 60. You should be able to pick him up and lay him down (see pages 64 and 71). When he is old enough for solid foods (see page 129) or a bottle (see page 126), you should take over one of the feedings. This regularity will allow a close relationship to grow and will give your wife a break for a period of time that she can count on to do something for herself—like take a walk, a bath, or go shopping.

■ Baby carriers (see page 86) are justifiably popular with fathers: The carriers allow them to be just as mobile as usual; the light weight is not a problem;

and fathers get close physical contact in a very practical fashion. In a carriage or stroller, the baby is at a distance, and some fathers simply feel ill at ease pushing such a conveyance. Carriers worn on the front of the body are best. You will have to adjust the carrier to fit. It is a good idea also to have a bag to carry incidentals (often referred to as a baby or diaper bag).

■ If you come home early enough in the evening after your day at work, you can take over the job of giving the baby his bath (see page 53). It will be a relaxing change from whatever labor you perform during the day. And, at the end of a long day, it will be a great relief for your wife!

Being a Mother— Staying a Woman

The picture of the happy mother with her baby—is it still a true one? I think it is. It is wonderful to step out of your usual life for a while into this completely new existence, and despite all the difficulties and undeniable burdens, it also has its positive sides. Suddenly you are forced to withdraw to a calmer place, to "drop out"—for the baby's sake—and that can be beneficial. Having a baby, after all, means far more than stress and fatigue. It is a meaningful experience to see how happy your child is to see you enter the room, how intensely he reacts to you. In addition, it can be exciting to see the world freshly from a child's perspective. It is fun to decorate the nursery and make a fresh start in life with the baby.

In the future you will learn the great art of doing justice to both your roles. You may see how one enriches the other. You will see that your baby not only draws on your strength, but replenishes it when you enjoy the time you spend together. On the other hand, you will pursue your career or perform your other duties much more effectively when you consciously employ your family life as a counter-balance.

Don't forget, the time spent with your baby and, later, your toddler, is only a fraction of your life; it passes very quickly. It is an intense, marvelous time, one you should enjoy to the fullest.

Maternal Feelings Have to Develop

The joys of motherhood and maternal feelings don't appear automatically when your child is delivered. Even during pregnancy, not all women feel the same. While one may float in a sea of bliss and communicate extensively with the baby in her belly, another may have an uncanny feeling that she is no longer alone but is carrying a silent partner around inside. Once the baby is born, he is no longer just an abstract fullness in your abdomen. Once you can see and cuddle him, it is easier for maternal feelings to develop. But even then, the feelings may not come immediately.

Many mothers are both disappointed and shocked when they feel very little upon first seeing their child after delivery. They may feel guilty that their need for rest is greater than their curiosity about their baby. Usually they don't dare to talk about it, since the absolute nature of the mother–child relationship is an institution. In fact, while it is a particularly strong relationship, it must develop like any other relationship. And, importantly, as it grows in strength, other relationships and other aspects of your life do not need to shrink. It is no longer true that the qualities of renunciation, sacrifice, and subordination are expected of women when they have children. As a rule, young mothers are just as well-educated as the fathers. They attend the same schools, universities, and training courses. They have to learn to hold their own in the working world where the qualities they need to succeed are not exactly maternal ones. Being a mother without surrendering one's own personality is part of being a "good" mother as much or more so than is the concept of self-sacrifice.

Now that most women have only one or two children, the birth process itself is taking on immense significance. Thus the trend toward a gentle delivery controlled by the woman herself is positive, but expectations of a natural, "happy" birth where everything goes right are increasing to unrealistic levels. There are mothers who experience a real crisis after a C-section because they had focused so completely on a natural delivery.

All beginnings are difficult. The first few months are a time of intensive learning for both baby and mother.

Irreconcilable Interests: Child and Career?

It has become much easier for women to maintain a career and family at the same time. Today it is rare to hear of a woman losing her job or being demoted after starting her family. However, there are many things to arrange if you are going to both work and raise a family. If you work full-time, you will need to find a good day-care or in-house child-care provider for your child. Many options exist, and most parents research the possibilities very thoroughly before choosing. Options include: home or family day-care; day-care centers; on-site day-care at the workplace; nursery schools that take young children; in-home help—by the day or live-in. Many women today work part-time, but they still need to find help for the days they are at work.

Some women may choose to devote themselves entirely to their child during the initial period. Raising children can be more satisfying, though more exhausting, than many occupations. Often, however, the mother feels a lack of independence and recognition or a loss of perspective. Each woman needs to make a decision—best made as a family—about what the best options are for herself as well as for her new family.

Difficult: Putting the Plan Into Action

Certainly it is a good idea to stay home, if possible, the first four months. But after that, there is no reason not to work. Unfortunately, finding child care before kindergarten age is not easy. If you have a 40-hour-a-week job, perhaps your husband can spend half a day with the baby. One thing is clear: Having mothers of young children in the workforce still is not something we take for granted. Nevertheless, you have a chance to make this wish a reality if you are firmly convinced—and if your spouse shares this decision jointly. There are a number of ways to get household help and relieve some of the burden (see page 255).

You cannot leave this to chance, however; as the mother of a baby, you have to carefully plan your involvement in the working world. The solution always has to suit your particular needs: You have to come up with some practical ideas. But where there is a will, there is a way. I myself wrote my doctoral dissertation before and after the birth of my first child, and I accepted my first position when our baby was four months old. By the time our second and third children were born, I was self-employed, and therefore kept on working—but at home. Without my husband's support, that would have been impossible. It was an exhausting time, but the children always got their fair share, and my efforts paid off. In retrospect, I would approach the initial period after birth with more composure: The main thing is to keep one foot in the door where your career is concerned. Sooner than you think, your child will be leaving you more free time again. Don't put too much pressure on yourself—but keep your objectives firmly in view.

"Stay-At-Home Mom": A Discontinued Model?

It has become increasingly difficult to survive financially with one income. Many young families cannot afford to do without the second income for long. The repercussions of losing this second income needs to be evaluated by you and your spouse. What will the effect be? Will you be unable to survive economically? Will you have to cut out luxury items like vacations, shopping trips, or dinners out? You can make compromises—you may decide to stay at home for 1 or 2 years and then return to work. You may want to return to work part-time for a while—maybe until your youngest starts school. An option may be working out of the house—so that you are home most of the time, but still earning a salary. It's best to sit down with your spouse and discuss all the available options, and make sure you're happy with the one chosen.

Stay-At-Home Mom—a Full-time Job

If you have more than one child and take your responsibilities as mother, wife, and housewife seriously, you basically are operating at full capacity. That's a full-time job! After all, the space within which children can move freely is becoming smaller all the time. Whether we like it or not, everything, from hobbies to free time to school and friendships, is usually organized by mothers—in addition to running the household, of course. Honorary posts, all connected with the children and the community, descend upon these women. If a mother can do all that with circumspection and enthusiasm, that's great. Anyone who chooses this path should have all the support and respect our society can bestow. In many instances, however, the men who reap the benefits of this decision for years on end often cease to take their wives, whose lives are so very different, altogether seriously, when all is said and done. For this reason it is important not to lose sight of the need for continuing education and a return to the workforce later on. You are there for your family, and at the same time you try to cultivate a small sphere just for yourself. With this perspective, you can really enjoy time at home.

Siblings and Grandparents

Siblings: Between Love and Jealousy

The feelings parents have for their older child are very contradictory: On the one hand, they want her to have brothers and sisters so that she doesn't grow up alone. For many parents, this may even be their chief motivation to have a second child. They think growing up in the company of other children near the same age is desirable. This can lead to your telling great things to your firstborn about a playmate, whom she then will await longingly. Disappointments after the baby's birth will thus be inevitable. On the other hand, parents often feel profound sympathy for their firstborn. They bear in mind what the child will lose, remember unpleasant experiences from their own childhood, and wait for jealousy to make an appearance. Through thoughtless remarks, the older sibling is virtually pushed into a keen sense of his dethronement.

And the children themselves? Even in the first weeks, babies' reactions to children and to adults are different. They seem to have a complete communication system of their own with children, especially siblings—and vice versa. In principle, children who are loved themselves are prepared to love their little brother or sister as well. Conflicts usually appear later, when the baby starts to crawl and interfere with the older child's spheres of interest.

Making the Situation Easier for Older Children

Put your trust in this positive feeling, and avoid the following mistakes:

■ Don't arouse your young child's hopes of getting a playmate. Instead, visit friends with newborns, possibly parents of your child's kindergarten friends. Help her understand how helpless the baby is, and how appealing as well.

■ Don't overburden your child with the duties of looking after and helping the baby. She would quickly feel discriminated against and exploited. On the other hand, do trust her to handle the baby. That is the only way she can develop her own relationship with her sibling.

■ While you are breastfeeding, her father or someone else close to the older sibling, such as a grandparent, is particularly important. Someone should have time just for the needs of your older son or daughter.

A great many older brothers and sisters are often fascinated by the baby—and a real help with him. Make sure the older sibling continues to get his or her fair share of attention.

■ Reserve certain privileges for your older child: a little chair next to the place where you nurse the baby, a set time for being read to, a time to snuggle in the evening before going to bed. The older child often has a hard time seeing why the baby sleeps in your bedroom while she has to stay in the nursery or in her own bedroom. It may be difficult, but you should attempt to explain to her that the baby needs frequent feedings at this age for proper nutrition and that it won't last forever. Be patient; your older child will get used to the current set-up.

■ A simple, but time-tested solution is the custom of presenting the older child with a lovely gift when the baby is born—on behalf of the new arrival.

Grandparents Today

Our image of grandparents has changed: Young, active, often involved in their careers, they usually are less available than in earlier times. Moreover, they frequently live in another town. On the one hand this is a pity, and the new parents often regret the lack of grandparents' help and support in everyday matters. But this slight distance often creates an opportunity as well.

In many cases, grandparents, particularly grandmothers, interfere with the children's upbringing, and are critical of everything you do or don't do. They are constantly on the new parents' backs because they identify too closely with their grandchildren's lives. There is trouble ahead. Sometimes the situation is aggravated by conflict over roles as well: The mother or mother-in-law cannot understand that the new mother wants to organize her life in a way that breaks with established tradition.

Conflicts in the new mother's own childhood and her relationship with her own mother add fuel to the fire. On the other hand, respect and understanding for the achievements of our own parents usually increase when we have to take care of a baby ourselves.

Good for Parents and Children Alike: Tolerance

The basic rule for grandparents is to practice tolerance. It is better to pull

> **EXTRA-TIP**
>
> *If the grandparents live far away, you can bolster their relationship with their grandchild by sending them videos or photos of your child in action at regular intervals.*

back a little and be silent than to overwhelm the new parents with help. Grandparents can play an enormous supporting role in their grandchildren's upbringing, and they can lighten many a load and enrich many a life—if they are in accord with the younger generation and if they refrain from tying their assistance to certain conditions.

For their efforts to succeed, however, they also need children who, equally tolerant, know how to accept and appreciate this assistance, and who realize that grandparents have something very special to pass along to their grandchildren: They love their grandchildren like their own children; they usually are in a quieter phase of life; from the distance of their age they view the children with greater serenity and imperturbability; and they impart a sense of continuity and dependability in a restless, ever-changing world. How wonderful, if there are still grandparents like that!

WHAT WILL HELP THE MOTHER?

"As long as I had a big belly I was waited on hand and foot.

Careful treatment and consideration for the mother-to-be were the dictates of the hour.

Once the baby was born, all this thoughtfulness was directed at him. I was supposed to

feel happy and perform my duties. Yet my need for help and support—

at least moral support—was greater than ever."

Does this complaint sound familiar to you? The birth of your first child in particular is an enormous turning point in your life: The experience of birth has shaken you to your very foundation. You no longer have control over your time; your independence is history. You get too little sleep and are probably exhausted from the huge hormonal change and tending to the needs of your newborn. Nothing is the way it used to be, and in this altered situation you have to get your bearings again.

Allow yourself to feel weak, weepy, and hypersensitive—you're entitled to do so. During this time you need, above all, support, help, warmth, and understanding from those around you. It is great if you get those things. But don't count on it. Take care of yourself, and don't be reluctant to think about yourself, too.

In one area, however, you have to be strict with yourself: Daily exercise is a must in the first six weeks, to help you get in shape again! This is the time when the body is best prepared to regenerate; later on, the same expenditure of effort will be far less effective. Besides, after the initial exhaustion, it is fun to return to the gym, pool, track, or bicycle again. To help you do so, this chapter presents exercises to firm your breasts and combat varicose veins, tips on skin and hair care, and tried-and-true physical fitness exercises. Pick and choose whatever will help and benefit you.

In the last analysis, your family will also profit if you feel at ease with yourself and your place in the world.

Getting the Psyche on an Even Keel

The nine months of pregnancy, the tumult of childbirth, and then the appearance of your baby leave you a changed person. As an old saying so aptly puts it: "You're like a felled tree." Women react very differently to the experience of giving birth—some women, when looking back, feel that their delivery was natural and under their control; others experience the event and everything connected with it as a shock. For these reasons, it is very important to talk about the birth with loved ones around you.

Assimilating the Birth Experience

In the initial aftermath, your thoughts will revolve repeatedly around this decisive event. The more you can talk about it, the better. It is nice if you can swap stories with both grandmothers, a sister, or a sister-in-law: They share your interest. But friends who are pregnant (watch out, don't scare them!) or already have children also are patient listeners. The best audience, however, is your husband—especially if he was present in the delivery room. If your experiences were very negative, talking to other women in a similar position or to a therapist may help you.

After giving birth, many women experience euphoria. This helps with the establishment of contact, the start of the bonding process between mother and child (see page 14). On the second or third day, this emotional high will change into hypersensitivity, even into depression (see page 34). This unstable emotional state will persist throughout the first few months: The more support you get and the better you cope with the new situation, the more emotionally stable you will become. This is completely normal; it is no reason to feel that you're a bad mother.

Reorientation Is Needed Now

It is not "only" hormones that can trigger an emotional downer. Life with the baby, may be quite different from what you had imagined. You may be just becoming aware that you have a lifelong responsibility. And your child's dependence on you may be a burden; after all, you are not used to being on 24-hour call for a helpless creature. The memory of your own mother may be giving you trouble, as well as your idealized notions of motherhood and maternal feeling. The anxieties you have are likely to be exacerbated, if anything, by those around you. Once you become a mother, the curtain seems to fall: From now on, your future is exclusively your child. Or so society suggests— and perhaps you are afraid that it's true.

Being a Mother Doesn't Mean Giving Up Your Self

Don't let yourself be driven into a corner! As a mother, you still can retain your own personality, along with your strength and independence. "I am what I am"—this simple sentence applies to mothers as well. Even if pregnancy, childbirth, and breastfeeding seem to dissolve the boundary between you and your child. For some women, this is frightening. But when you gave birth, you reached your limits and survived, and this experience made you strong. Take a look at mothers with older children:

You will see that as time passes, they regain much of their independence. This may well explain why mothers often enjoy children born later with special intensity. They know that the period of close and exhausting attachment is limited in duration. Looking at things from this point of view may give you encouragement, even though it is all highly theoretical for the time being. For more on coping with your new role as mother, see page 154.

Important!

During the first months, you may have a feeling of unreality—that, too, is normal. The change is simply too great. The rhythm of your life is offbeat; it is being determined by your child at the moment. Be patient here as well. It may take a year for you to regain your composure fully. Give yourself all the time you need.

Your Body Needs Time

At the end of your pregnancy there is nothing you want more than to get rid of your big belly at long last. So, you are likely to be disappointed at first after the delivery. True, you are now carrying your baby in your arms, but for some reason the belly is still there! During the first few days you lose pound after pound, but it is primarily stored-up fluid. The fat reserves that built up, especially around your waist, are still present. This is why you cannot get

into the pair of jeans that fit you nine months ago! In addition, your milk is coming in: You acquire imposing breasts that remain so as long as you continue to breastfeed. A C-section or an episiotomy may have left their scars, or you may have tiny tissue tears, red at first—stretch marks, or striae—on your abdomen, hips, or breasts. In other words, your body has changed.

It will take some time to get your figure back. But it can be done! Don't get discouraged. After all, your belly grew for nine months along with the baby, and it needs at least that much time to return to its former shape. The stretch marks will fade, but only after a year. Your breasts, too, need a few more months to regain their contours after the baby is weaned.

Interpret the following tips for taking care of your overtaxed body as suggestions for being kind to yourself, ways of helping yourself return to glowing health, rather than as compulsory measures. It will simply do you good to look after yourself as well as the baby, to have a space where you can withdraw to rebuild your strength. Don't put too much pressure on yourself, but don't put off getting in shape as this will just make it harder in the long run.

What Will Help Your Breasts

During the pregnancy and nursing, your breast measurements will increase substantially—a physical strain you can offset through proper care.

■ Even if you got by without one before, while breastfeeding wear a bra that provides excellent support. This will keep the tissue from stretching too much.

■ Do without cold showers. They could affect milk production. Vigorous massage also is not suitable, because your skin, already stretched, might take it badly.

■ Rub your breasts every day with an unscented lotion (perfume residue has been found in breast milk). Breast milk itself also has a beneficial effect.

■ Good posture makes you look more attractive.

■ Isometric exercises, low-impact aerobics, and swimming are all things you can do during the breastfeeding period. Always make sure to engage in these activities right after nursing, when your breasts weigh less and the milk does not let down so readily.

ACCEPTING CHANGES

In a reader survey conducted by a parents' magazine in 1994, one-third of the brand-new fathers said they found their wives more attractive and more feminine than before— and slightly more than half found their spouse just as attractive as before. The women were much harder on themselves: One of every two was unhappy with her weight; only one of every seven thought herself prettier than before; and one of every six was completely unable to come to terms with the changes in her body. So we ourselves have to change our attitude! You need to understand that your body is not static but continues to change throughout your life. Don't look at it with the critical eyes of a model agency. After the delivery, give yourself a break, as a woman as well.

Isometric Exercises

In these exercises, the breast muscles are tensed against an opposing force and then relaxed. This strengthens them on a lasting basis and shapes the pectoral muscles. The breasts themselves contain no muscular tissue, so the exercises do not make them firmer.

1 Sit back on your heels. Place your hands together in front of you in prayer position, push them together with all your might, hold for five seconds—and relax again. Repeat this exercise 5 times.

2 Put your hands over your head and do five repetitions of the exercise described above.

3 Stretch your arms behind your head as far as possible, and repeat the exercise 5 times.

4 Stand with your legs apart and knees slightly bent. Stretch your arms out to the sides and roll your shoulders forward and back, moving them from the shoulder joint. Repeat the exercise 10 times.

5 Finally, make small circles with your outstretched arms—10 times— without moving your upper body.

And After Weaning?

Once your breasts stop producing milk, the milk glands will recede. This causes the tissue to shrink, since it lacks fatty and connective tissues, which were displaced earlier by the growing glandular ducts. The skin is slower to shrink. As a result, your breasts are flaccid and smaller than before. But don't despair: Usually they return to their previous state over the course of the first year. Regular exercise and care are the only ways to help the process along; neither special creams nor hormones are effective.

Does Nursing Really Ruin Your Breasts?

There are mothers who are reluctant to breastfeed for this reason. Sometimes they are also motivated by pressure from their husband. But pregnancy itself changes the breasts, and the normal aging process will leave its traces anyway, particularly on the breasts. The additional strain due to nursing makes no appreciable difference. Women with strong connective tissue have no cause for concern in any event. Pregnancy and nursing may help us attain a better relationship with our body and stop measuring ourselves exclusively by the customary standards of youth.

Miracle Worker: Postpartum Exercises

Never again will your body be so ready to rid itself of stored fluids, reduce cushions of fat, and build up loosened muscle groups as in the first few weeks after delivery. Often, however, finding time for this is difficult in this exhausting initial period. Give it a try, nevertheless. If you don't succeed right off the bat, don't give up. Pick and choose what matters most to you, and start the program at a time when you have a little breathing space. There's so much available today in terms of health clubs, weight-loss centers, videos, and books. Look at what's out there and pick something that will fit your lifestyle and one you'll enjoy!

What's Going on in Your Belly

Your uterus performs an enormous feat not only during, but after childbirth as well. Within the first week , it returns almost to its normal size after a 100-fold increase (see page 26). At the same time, the layer of muscle that separated over the growing abdomen to form a long opening—termed *rectus diastasis*—slowly closes again. In addition, you are losing weight by the pound.

Training the Muscles of the Pelvic Floor and the Abdomen

From the first day on, you should exercise the diagonal muscles of the pelvic floor. Strengthening the abdominal muscles will enable the diastasis to close again and the abdominal wall to become firm. Exercising the pelvic floor is also important. Pregnancy and childbirth may cause the muscles of the pelvic floor to become loose, and without an exercise program you may be at risk for uterine descent (falling of the womb), which is somewhat rare, and bladder problems.

■ In the hospital, the nurse will show you the exercises and come by every day to help you. Doing the exercises consistently is extremely effective at this time. The four most important basic exercises for the first few weeks are presented on the following pages.

■ If you want to do even more, you can go through a set routine of exercises with a cassette or videotape every day. This has advantages: You aren't tempted to shorten the exercise program because there is someone assisting you—either by voice or on the video—so that you can concentrate completely on the exercises, and the music makes it fun. In my house, the bigger children exercised along with me, with great enthusiasm!

■ Do your exercises after you nurse the baby. Usually he is quiet then, and

> ## BE CAREFUL WHEN YOU LIFT AND CARRY!
>
> *Under the influence of hormones, our tissue, especially that of the pelvic floor, is particularly soft and pliable before and after delivery. This makes giving birth easier, but it also renders these muscles less able to withstand strain.*
>
> ■ *Anything—other than the baby—that weighs more than 11 pounds (5 kg) is off limits in the first weeks.*
>
> ■ *Don't pick up small children. To cuddle, have them sit on the sofa with you or on your lap, or kneel down beside them.*
>
> ■ *Every time you lift something, even fairly light objects, also lift the pelvic floor to level 3 (see exercises, page 169) and hold it there!*
>
> ■ *It is best to hold babies in a fabric front carrier; this will cause the least amount of strain.*

your breasts won't feel uncomfortable or leak either.

■ Try to exercise daily the first six weeks. That's what it takes to get your old figure back after giving birth.

Important!
Vigorous athletic activity before nursing increases the lactate content of the milk: It tastes less sweet. This causes some babies to lose their appetite. While you continue to breastfeed, take things slow and easy.

The Four Most Important Postpartum Exercises

Do these exercises on a hard surface. It is best to do them on the rug or on a padded exercise mat. The program is short, but to the point: If you can manage to get through it every morning and evening, it will be especially effective.

To Combat Rectus Diastasis

1 Lie flat on your back with your knees bent.

2 Pull your navel firmly toward the surface beneath you. Imagine that you're making your abdomen very tiny.

3 Hold the tension for one minute—then release.

4 Repeat the exercise 5 times.

For the Diagonal Abdominal Muscles

1 Assume the basic position as in the first exercise, with your hands under the back of your head.

2 Pull your navel in, while at the same time bringing your right elbow to meet your left knee.

3 Relax—then do the exercise with the left elbow and the right knee.

4 Repeat two more times.

For the Pelvic Floor

1 Assume the basic position as in exercise 2.

2 Lift only your bottom off the mat, leaving your upper back, shoulders, and feet on the ground. Hold this position for 5 seconds, then lower it again.

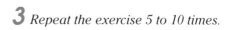

3 Repeat the exercise 5 to 10 times.

Split-Second Pelvic Floor Exercise for In Between Times

■ Whether you are sitting or standing, at odd moments during the day, you should consciously tense your pelvic floor muscles. Raise the pelvic floor, as you were taught in birth preparation class, into the air in several stages: Level 1–2–3–4. Then relax again.

Important!

If you have a severe rectus diastasis that still "gapes" even two weeks after delivery, your physician should advise you.

The Best Way to Prevent Back Pain

Pregnancy already has placed a great amount of strain on your spinal column. Life with small children is physically taxing, and it puts additional stress on the intervertebral discs in your back, especially if you don't maintain correct posture at all times. Back pain is the result. Here are a few tips for making your daily routine with your baby and small child ergonomically correct:

■ The changing table should be high enough that you have no need to bend over. It is best to raise one foot slightly higher than the other from time to time (keep a footstool next to the changing table) and to use one elbow for support.

■ When nursing, make sure you are in a relaxed position: Keep your feet on the floor or on a footstool, slightly spread; use your elbows for support on each side; and sit straight—your neck and your bottom should be in a straight line. A cushion at the small of your back will help. Deep armchairs are more comfortable with a wedge-shaped cushion on the seat, sloping upward toward the chair back.

■ At first, make sure your child's bed is at the topmost height setting. Only later on does the surface need to be close to the floor, for safety reasons.

■ When you lift a child to carry him, bend your knees, keep your upper body upright, and go from a squat into a standing position. Use the same technique to lift any heavy object.

■ When you have to stand while holding your child, it is best to place him on one hip (see page 67). Try to keep one leg higher than the other—on a staircase landing, a curbstone, or a footstool.

■ By the way, strengthening your abdominal muscles (see page 168) also reduces the strain on your back!

What About Varicose Veins?

After the delivery, you are not protected against varicose veins. The tissue is still soft, and the veins can dilate abnormally even after the extra weight of the baby is gone. This is why you need to wear support hose consistently during the first weeks. Instead of just sitting, it is better to put your feet up. Get in as much walking as possible. Here are two more exercises, especially for varicose veins:

1 *Lie on a hard surface. Keeping your legs straight, lift them one at a time and move your foot in a circle.*

2 *Don't do the following exercise until your abdominal muscles are strong again. Lie down, as in the previous exercise. Then pedal, with your legs perpendicular to your body—for two minutes at first, then up to five minutes.*

Sports and Baby—(Not) a Problem

While you are breastfeeding, it is best to exercise moderately. This will boost your milk production and heighten your physical well-being.

Through exercise you can recover your body and help your muscles become firm once more. In addition, exercise is a wonderful stress reliever.

Getting in Shape

■ *Swimming* is especially beneficial at this time. However, you need to wait until the discharge of lochia (see page 26) has subsided. The warmer the water in the pool, the better. The backstroke, incidentally, is particularly good for your breasts, pelvic floor and back. And the baby? It is best to leave him with a baby-sitter or your spouse (see page 262) while you swim. If the baby is present, you won't be able to concentrate on swimming.

■ *Jogging* outdoors will get your circulation going. You can't carry the baby along like a mama kangaroo, however. "Baby joggers" are now available and very popular for jogging mothers and fathers. Note though, that these are not appropriate until your child has good head control and can sit up on his own—after 6 months.

■ *Going for a walk* with the carriage or stroller or hiking with the baby in a front or back carrier is the simplest form of sport—and it benefits your child.

■ *Biking* is fun, and promotes overall fitness. But where to put the baby? We had a bike trailer into which our baby's car seat fit perfectly. That way we could take bike trips as a family, even with the baby—a great pleasure for older siblings as well. This type of recreational activity should be reserved for areas *without cars*. Make sure that you have adequate protection from cold weather or from the sun (see page 82). You should *not* ride a bicycle with the baby on your back. Once your baby can sit up well, sometime during his second six months, you can have a child seat mounted on the back of the bike. Pay close attention to the backrest, leg guards, and safety belt. Remember, only ride on roads *without cars*! If this is too difficult to arrange, you might consider buying a stationary bicycle, which you can set up in the yard or in the house, right next to the baby carriage.

■ *Gymnastics, dance, stretching exercises, and moderate body building* are all beneficial, especially if they contribute to your physical regeneration. Aerobics, hip-hop, and jazz dancing, however, are simply too strenuous for the first few months. Some health clubs have low-impact aerobics classes: You should check with your health club for a description of the class.

What Your Skin Needs

During pregnancy, your skin is especially lovely because of your hormonal state and water storage. During this time, which is devoted to processes of growth and synthesis, your hair also grows extremely thick and luxuriant. Also, an expectant mother usually watches her diet more closely, and that benefits her physical appearance.

After delivery, the skin gets rid of the stored water, and lack of sleep and irregular meals take things a step further. Naturally, you have very little time now to take care of yourself. Take advantage of odd moments whenever possible: while you're showering or breastfeeding or before you go to bed. It's long-term results, rather than any instantaneous impact, that you're after.

Care That Does You Good

■ Drink one "beauty drink" every day:

VITAMIN COCKTAIL

Mix together 1 quart (1l) of carrot juice, 1 quart (1l) of orange juice, 1 teaspoon of wheat germ, 1 teaspoon of honey, and 2 teaspoons of brewer's yeast flakes (available in health food stores).

Sip while breastfeeding.

■ Always keep fresh fruits and vegetables in the house, and eat them raw whenever you get a chance (for varieties that are good for nursing mothers, see page 113).

■ Massage your body with a loofah glove (a soft, natural, porous sponge) before or during showering to stimulate circulation: Skip your breasts, and go easy on your still tender abdomen.

■ Take alternating hot and cold showers. Don't let the cold water run on your breasts, however.

■ If your skin is dry, massage it daily with 10 percent lavender oil and oil of melissa (balm)—the scent also has a calming effect.

■ If your facial skin is tired and slack, try applying a mask every two weeks. Either buy one at a health food store, or make your own. Mix one package of baker's yeast with milk until it reaches a spreadable consistency, brush on your face, and rub off with your hands when dry. Rinse with lukewarm water.

EXTRA-TIP

You're at your most relaxed when nursing. Once or twice a week, apply a mask before beginning breastfeeding—not too white, though; it may scare the baby. Try products from the health food store; they are affordable and less heavily perfumed. Here's a recipe for making a mask yourself:

Mix 3 tablespoons wheat germ oil (available in pharmacies or health food stores) with 1 1/2 tablespoons brewer's yeast, 3 tablespoons oatmeal, and 1/2 teaspoon carrot juice, and apply to your face—making sure to skip the area around your eyes. Let it take effect while you nurse, and after the feeding wash it off with lukewarm water. In a pinch, you also can apply a slightly thicker layer of your regular cream as a mask.

Hair Needs Special Care

Your hair, too, will suffer from the hormonal swing. Especially while the baby is being weaned, hair loss is often dramatic. There is no way to prevent that, and no reason to worry. Once the transition is complete, your hair will grow back just as full and thick as ever. The beauty drink we recommend (see page 171) is also good for your hair.

■ Eat millet frequently. Millet flour is an excellent thickener for sauces and gravies! Millet noodles are available in health/organic food stores, and millet can be substituted for wheat flour in baking recipes and pancakes. You can obtain millet flour by grinding grains of millet in your high-speed blender or food processor at home.

■ The following will work too: Mix gelatin (available in supermarkets or pharmacies) into your barley malt coffee or into a glass of lowfat milk.

■ How to take good care of your hair: Always rub special hair oil for split ends onto the dry tips after you have washed your hair and let your hair air dry.

■ An occasional acidic rinse adds shine. Add 2 tablespoons cider vinegar to a bowl of water, pour over freshly washed hair, and rinse with plain water.

A short haircut will make the hair loss less dramatic. If your hair is longer than shoulder length, don't cut it yet: You can put it up for an attractive look if there's no time for a shampoo.

And Your Weight?

During the first few days after childbirth, the initial pounds will fall off quickly because of fluid loss. But if you are breastfeeding, you should not aggressively try to lose weight. If the fatty tissue melts away, environmental toxins stored there find their way into your breast milk. Exercise consistently instead of dieting, and get plenty of physical activity; then your contours will become firmer, even without weight loss. When you are breastfeeding once a day, you can start your weight-loss campaign—if you really have gained some poundage. During the hormonal readjustment, the body loses fatty tissue more readily. But don't torture yourself with a crash diet or a strict regimen. During these unsettled times, you won't be able to stick to it anyway. It is better to follow simple rules; then success will come easier.

Making the Pounds Disappear

■ Cut down on fats. According to the latest studies, this is the most effective way to lose weight. Give preference to 1 or 2 percent milk and dairy products, eat lowfat cheese (35 percent fat), don't use spreads on bread, eat fish, choose lean meats over fattier ones. And avoid foods with a high percentage of concealed fat: chocolate, cakes and pastries, nuts, snack foods, sausages that are not low in fat, and ready-to-serve meals.

■ Eat plenty of fruits and vegetables, as often as possible. You will want to do so anyway, after having been so careful while you were breastfeeding.

■ If you snack, eat popcorn or bread sticks.

■ Don't wait until you are ravenous. Instead, eat some fruit or vegetables or yogurt in between meals.

■ Don't hoard supplies of chocolate or other foods that are high in fat. Make sure you always have fruit, vegetables, and yogurt on hand at home.

■ Drink mineral water or diluted fruit juice. Try tea or coffee with only 1 teaspoon of sugar or none. Use milk, not cream. Sodas and other beverages often conceal large amounts of calories.

Relax—But How?

In the first months with the baby, you'll often feel as though every bone in your body were aching. Every time I heard water run out of the faucet, I thought I was hearing my baby cry. Being able to relax is also a problem of time—for ways to find time for yourself, see the section beginning on page 254.

If possible, nurse while you are lying down. Then you can stay there for an extra five precious minutes until you have to burp and diaper the baby. If your husband, mother or mother-in-law, or a friend is there, stay there for 15 minutes, drink some fluids, and leave the diapering and care of your child to someone else. If you can't calm down, do the breathing exercises you learned in your childbirth class.

Relaxing Breathing Exercises

Here's a little breathing exercise, a therapy that you surely remember from your childbirth class:

While Lying Down

1 Lie down on your back, with your hands resting on your abdomen.

2 Do deep abdominal breathing, while trying to "breathe your hands away," until you no longer feel your hands.

3 It is important to breathe out deeply.

While Seated

This includes while at the playground, at your desk, or on the train or plane.

1 With your legs spread, your back bent, and your elbows leaning on your knees, assume the "horse cab driver's position."

2 Now inhale deeply, using your back muscles, while pulling your shoulders back and straightening your back.

3 When you exhale, let your shoulders drop and bend your back again.

And Still More Relaxation

■ Wonderful music for relaxation and instructions on biofeedback are available on cassettes and CDs. A private tip: Psychomotor exercises will help your body return to its prepregnancy state.

■ Try to make a conscious effort to relax from time to time, whether it be while nursing, feeding the baby, or driving the car. Your mouth and the surrounding area are good indicators of your overall tension level. Is your tongue soft and relaxed inside your mouth? Are your teeth clenched? Are your chin muscles relaxed?

■ Sleep when the baby sleeps. Don't stick to your usual schedule. Turn the telephone off and the answering machine on! You can return the calls later.

Getting More Sleep

The greatest problem undoubtedly is the lack of uninterrupted sleep at night. While you are breastfeeding, you probably won't manage to sleep through the night. But you can make the nightly disruptions a little easier to take:

■ Have your child sleep in your bedroom; then you don't have so far to go.

■ Don't turn night into day. Except for feeding and changing, nothing else should be going on between midnight and early morning!

■ Maybe your husband will take on the job of changing the baby; then you can continue to sleep even while nursing. And if he can't manage that all the time, at least you can arrange a "night of relaxation" on an occasional basis.

■ If you are completely at the end of your rope, perhaps your husband can manage to keep the baby contented for a couple of hours with a bottle of water and some rocking—six hours of unbroken sleep will give you strength for the entire week!

Finding Time for Yourself

For women who are used to working independently and with great concentration, the new life with baby is particularly hard to take. Apparently unstructured, each new day descends upon the despairing mother—there is not the slightest organization. You have to cast off your previous patterns of thinking and become less rigid; then you will gradually find ways to add more structure to your life—of a flexible kind!

■ Quite soon you will see that your baby is especially peaceful at a certain time of the day. Don't try to get all your housework done then; make that "your" time—whether you use it for reading, exercising, talking on the phone, or eating. Then you are more apt to be able to cope with all your chores.

■ If grandparents or godparents help with the baby, don't feel guilty about using this free time for yourself. Talk about it, and make it clear that this is helping you get back on your feet. Your recovery is just as necessary and legitimate as the performance of your responsibilities as a new mother.

■ Get in the habit of using even short periods of time for yourself. This will stand you in good stead as long as you have children living at home. Don't say, "It's no use any more." Just do it, and I mean right now! In each of this book's sections on health care and personal grooming, you will find suggestions for "quick solutions."

■ Be flexible: Schedule as few fixed appointments in your day as possible. Don't make plans for all the things you want to get done. Set rough, rather than precise, goals for the week, and make use of opportune moments.

■ When your husband is busy with the baby, you are dispensable. And when you are doing your exercises, your husband has to look after the baby—and he may find that it's fun!

HOW YOUR BABY DEVELOPS

It is amazing what developmental progress your child makes during his first year of life. The helpless little creature turns into a self-assured child who is in the process of becoming acquainted with the world. In this chapter, we want to help you understand your baby's stages of development and accompany him through them sympathetically.

PROGRESSING BY LEAPS AND BOUNDS THE FIRST YEAR

During the first year your child acquires the basic abilities he needs to live and to survive:

He learns to eat and drink, to take things and give them back again,

to sit upright, and to move his body in order to get someplace.

In the following chapter, we are concerned primarily with the development

of these physical abilities in your baby.

Your child's development does not proceed in a straight line and according to a set schedule. For this reason, our "What Your Baby Can Do Now" sections are not meant to be interpreted too strictly. The differences between individual children are great—and become greater as they grow older. But every developmental advance is linked in a great variety of ways to other abilities. Consequently there is a certain process of maturation that can be constructed for each child. You will find it easier to understand and encourage your baby if you are familiar with this process and are able to encourage it.

A baby cannot be trained as we train a dog, naturally, nor can he be made into an infant prodigy. Your baby himself will determine his own personal rate of development. However, you can offer him the best possible conditions for reaching his potential. To succeed, you need to give him plenty of love, attention, and time.

For each phase of development, we present—under the heading "What Stimulates Your Baby"—suggestions for appropriate toys, games, and activities that you can share with your child. The stimuli and ideas you provide your baby should be simple, full of contrast, and not hurried. Also, they should be repeated frequently. You can let your child guide you; then games and dialogues will develop automatically.

Don't forget: Your child wants to learn to control his body and to comprehend and master his surroundings. Even with no particular encouragement, most children learn to walk, eat, talk, and play. Place your trust in this desire to learn, and don't put pressure on yourself and your baby to perform.

Which Toys?

Babies become acquainted with the world around them through their toys as well. The different shapes, colors, and materials stimulate their senses. A baby simply enjoys discovering things himself and being surprised by his experiences. Repetitions increase the learning effect.

Important: The toys should suit the baby's phase of development. Only then can he really get anywhere with them, and only then can his playing turn into a learning experience. You will find age-appropriate recommendations in the discussion that follows.

But don't do too much of a good thing. Don't inundate your child with too many different objects. The baby first has to be able to comprehend something in his own time, before he feels inclined to make new discoveries.

TOYS: SAFETY COMES FIRST

For safety reasons, you need to keep the following in mind:

■ *Pearl or beaded necklaces, ribbons, braid, and lace are unsuitable for babies. A baby could easily get entangled in them and choke.*

■ *Small objects that the baby could swallow, such as marbles, beads, barrettes, and Lego blocks are also dangerous: Your child will put everything into his mouth—and that covers quite a wide range!*

■ *Foam rubber parts, modeling clay, animal figures made of wobbly substances, papier-mâché figures, and other things the baby can tear pieces from are dangerous. The material has to withstand the baby's teeth!*

■ *Paints and varnishes for babies' toys have to be nontoxic and colorfast; after all, everything finds its way into the baby's mouth! Ask about these features and read the box carefully before purchasing a toy.*

■ *The toy should have no sharp corners or edges, rough surfaces, or sharp points. Run your hand over it to make sure.*

■ *Most toy manufacturers have labels on the box indicating the appropriate age for that particular toy.*

■ *Make sure that stuffed animals are washable—and don't have easily removable parts such as eyes or nose.*

■ *In your household, you will come across a great many objects that make good playthings for your baby, particularly when he is a little older. His toys don't always have to be expensive: Pots and pans, plastic containers, wooden spoons, and the like will elicit an equally enthusiastic response.*

Your Baby: One to Four Months

Over the course of the first four months, your child will grow by almost 25 percent of his length at birth and almost double his birth weight! His skin now is rosy and firm, his body rounded and plump.

His movements become more deliberate; he reaches out for toys, holds his head up, makes noises—and smiles at you. This development is made possible by the interplay of all his sensory capacities.

Nevertheless, your baby is still an infant, and under the age of four months it is too early for him to try eating from a spoon.

Usually he will have established a certain rhythm of waking and sleeping by the fourth month—he may even be sleeping through the night.

What Your Baby Can Do Now

Seeing and Hearing

A newborn can focus on objects about 8 to 14 inches from his face—the distance from the bridge of his nose to your face while breastfeeding. Objects further away than this will appear blurred to a newborn. In the first several months, your baby lacks complete control over his eye muscles and he may appear cross-eyed. This is normal. If you notice this still after 4 months of age, or if one or both eyes appear "fixed" inward, you should alert your doctor.

By the end of the first month, a baby can follow an object to the midline. By the second month, he can recognize his parents. By the third month, he can respond to your facial expressions. And by the fourth month, he can follow an object through a 180 degree horizontal arc.

Babies can hear even when they are in the womb. Babies are soothed by calming voices and startled by loud

Nobody can (or wants to) resist your baby's smile . . .

noises. A newborn will become alert in response to voices around him and will react to a loud noise with a startle or "Moro reflex"—an extension, then flexion of the arms ending with a cry. In the first several months of life, a baby will respond to new sounds with eye widening and changes in activity level. Between the ages of 2 and 3 months, he will turn toward the direction of where a sound is coming from. Your child will respond with raised arms when you say "up" between the age of 6 and 9 months. Between 9 and 12 months, he will begin following one-step verbal commands.

At the age of four months, your baby will grip his toys firmly—and not let go.

Movements Become Better Coordinated

His motor development proceeds in an analogous fashion. Many of his early reflexes (see page 21) disappear. The child's entire body elongates and becomes more relaxed. At two months, his fists open more and more; he can take hold of things and move them, but cannot yet let go. Your baby can lift his head for only seconds at a time. During the third month he learns to move individual limbs without moving his entire body. This enables him to turn onto one side and to grab for things much more successfully. At the end of the fourth month, he reaches for objects very deliberately, but does not grip them firmly. This movement is made easier for him by the improved control of his body: Now he lifts his head about 90 degrees and holds it up when you set him down.

What Stimulates Your Baby

Your child is still rather clumsy. But at the end of the fourth month, he is already able to classify his surroundings and do something with his hands. His body, too, becomes somewhat more flexible, but he still can do little to change his position. Somewhere between 3 and 5 months, he will begin to roll over. You should emphasize games in which you take the active role: Put a toy in your child's hand, massage his body gently, or hold him while you swim.

He still needs a relatively large amount of peace and quiet, as well as sleep, in order to process all the new information.

Test your baby's hearing from time to time to make sure there are no problems. Make a noise from a position close to your child, but he shouldn't see or feel you. In early infancy, he will respond with a startle reflex, at about 3 months with blinking of the eyes, and around 4 months by turning his head toward the origin of the noise. From the third month on, the noise can be as slight as the rattling of his key-ring teether. If your baby fails to respond you should try again a little later. Some babies become used to sounds around them—especially if they are in a busy, bustling household. This is called extinction. Try to look for other responses to sounds: Does he calm when spoken softly to? Does he startle to a new, unfamiliar noise? If your baby fails to react, you should consult your pediatric provider. If your suspicion is confirmed, you will be referred for formal audiology testing and a consultation with an otolaryngologist (ear, nose, and throat doctor).

Grasping and Holding

Up until about 6 months of age, your child plays best while lying on his back, because in this position he has the widest angle of view and plenty of freedom to move his arms. Usually he will still be lying in his crib. His technique of gripping becomes increasingly

better: He begins to grasp things, both physically and intellectually.

In the second month, when you put a toy in his hand he is able to hold it firmly. Best are *lightweight toys* that make noises, such as a rattle, a plush animal that jingles, or a ring-shaped noisemaker. In the third month, you can hang a *"play-trapeze"* or mobile in the crib, so that he can reach and touch it while lying on his back. (Note: It should not have removable parts that he can pull off and swallow.) This is fun for him because he can reach out for it, set it spinning, and produce sounds and movements. In the fourth month, your baby wants to really take hold of things. Attach a *toy bar* or *activity arch* to his crib. Choose a model that can be easily grasped and does not move away when touched. Your baby now can produce sounds from *stuffed animals that squeak.*

Music That Soothes Your Child

As his hearing develops, your child also becomes increasingly receptive to music. A music box inside a soft, cuddly pouch thus should be part of your baby's "basic equipment." You can incorporate its melody into your daily routine so that it becomes a little ritual. Perhaps you can play it when the baby goes to bed or when you burp him. The repetition of the melody adds some structure to the baby's daily schedule. Your baby will also enjoy a special "on the road" melody for outings in the car or baby carriage. But nothing is nicer for your child than hearing your voice. *Sing* songs to him, whatever the situation demands: happy, soothing, or comforting songs. If you limit yourself to a small repertoire, your baby will recognize the songs again and again, and that accounts for a good part of their effectiveness.

A Good Time for Baby Massage

Frederic Leboyer, an obstetrician-gynecologist, has made this ancient Indian art popular in Europe. The gentle, sympathetic stroking stimulates the muscles and the circulation and, at the same time, helps the baby relax. With a little practice, you can calm your child with your hand movements or even massage away his tummy-ache. Particularly now, when he is beginning to grow in length and gain more control over his movements, massage will help your baby become more aware of his own body.

Important!
Don't start massage unless you really can set aside 15 minutes for this purpose every day. Your baby learns primarily through repetition.

■ It is best to get a book with instructions on massage.
■ Learn the movements by heart ahead of time, so that you can concentrate completely on your child.

■ The contact is most intimate if you lay the baby on your thighs. First, sit down on the floor, with your back resting against some kind of support.
■ You can also do the massage on the changing table or on the floor.

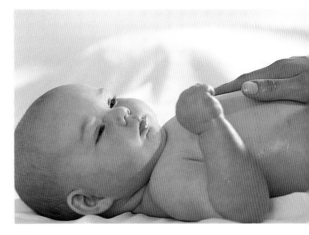

Massage is a way of communicating with your child without using words.

■ Your child should be naked. Make sure the room temperature is in the range of 75 degrees Fahrenheit (same as for the bath). In summer, it is wonderful to do the massage out-of-doors, but make sure you are protected against the wind and not in direct sunlight.
■ Many babies react to the unaccustomed nakedness or the first massage strokes by producing a spontaneous stream of urine. To keep the puddle from inundating your lap, secure your baby with a cotton or disposable diaper. You also can place a thick towel under him.

■ Rub a neutral baby oil (ordinary mineral oil, unscented if possible) or a special baby massage oil between your palms until they are quite warm; then your touch will be especially pleasant for your baby.

■ If your baby isn't enjoying it, don't give up right away. He may be tired or hungry, or his tummy may be full. Perhaps he is reacting with fright to the unfamiliar situation. Keep stroking him, sing his favorite song, and talk to him; then he will soon relax. If your child continues to be cross, take a break, pick him up, and try again later.

How Healthy Is Swimming for a Baby?

Your child can't really learn to swim until he is three years old. Where babies are concerned, swimming has more to do with moving in the water—and being together with their parents. The buoyancy of the water allows the infant, who "on dry land" is still quite clumsy, to move much more freely. Don't expect a swimming class for babies to produce infant prodigies or enormous leaps of development.

If you want to take a baby course with your child, you should start before the third month. At that stage, the child still possesses the "respiratory protection reflex": When his mouth and nose are in the water, his breathing is blocked. This keeps water from getting into his lungs. In the course, your child practices using this reflex and thus retains it—a clear advantage later on, when he learns to swim properly. Besides, swimming together is fun!

If your child has a tendency to develop respiratory infections, however, it is better not to try swimming just yet.

Important!

Prerequisites for swimming with your child:

■ *The baby has to be in good health and have open respiratory passages. He should be able to hold his head up. His swallowing, sneezing, and coughing reflexes have to function.*

■ *The water temperature should be at least 91.4 degrees Fahrenheit (33°C) and the water itself should be "drinking water quality." Don't spend more than 20 minutes in the water.*

Now the baby can have a fine time playing peek-a-boo with the bath towel (see page 187).

Your Baby: Four to Eight Months

Your baby is no longer growing as quickly as in the first months, and his weight is also increasing at a slower rate. On the other hand, he is becoming increasingly active: At eight months he has good control of his head; he rolls all around the room if there is enough space to do so; he can sit unaided, and he is beginning to pull himself to a standing position holding onto a chair or the side of his crib or playpen. Between four and six months, he will reward your tickles with giggles and laughter. His ability to see and to grip has also matured. The 7- to 8-month-old is starting to finger feed himself and will take great pleasure in doing so. During this period, he will have better and better understanding of the day to night rhythm, and gradually you should be getting more rest again at night.

What Your Baby Can Do Now

Hearing and Seeing

At the end of the eighth month, your baby's perfect hearing is quite apparent. He can turn his head in any direction where an interesting sound originates.

He can't stand up yet—but the first attempts to crawl are not far in the future.

His vision is becoming increasingly sharp, and he can estimate distances. He even looks at television—but it is better to spare your baby that, since the rapid succession of images and the content are entirely too much for him.

His color vision, too, is well-developed by now. But his improved capacity for recognition and larger range of vision have something to do with his "shyness with strangers," also known as "stranger anxiety." This is manifested by clinging to Mom or Dad in the face of strangers, and starts around six months of age. At this point, the baby knows his surroundings and the familiar faces very well; as a result he also recognizes unfamiliar things as strange and takes alarm.

185

Slowly He Becomes More Mobile

In the fourth or fifth month, your baby learns to roll from his back onto his abdomen, and vice versa. He uses both hands to reach for toys and brings his hands together over his upper body. While lying on his stomach, he supports himself on his forearms. In the sixth month he makes paddling motions while lying on his tummy, holds his head in different directions, and discovers that he can play with his feet and the rest of his body. He has learned not only to grip but also to let go—an enormous advance. At six months, he will have good control of his head, and he is beginning to sit up without support—a good time to start thinking about the high chair. The "tongue protrusion" reflex—where babies will attempt to extrude objects from their mouth with their tongue—has disappeared mostly, and after the age of 4 months he is ready to be spoon-fed. He still has a great need to suck, and will use either his pacifier or a finger.

Ready to Crawl

In the seventh month, the baby will begin to make attempts at moving from one place to another. He turns from his back onto his tummy, then does a little push-up, and then tries—usually unsuccessfully at first—to move from his current position to another. Crawling, though, should not be used as a gauge of proper motor development. In reality, it is not even used by developmental specialists in assessing normal development. Some babies never crawl at all—they go directly from sitting to standing to walking.

What Stimulates Your Baby

Even if your child can already sit, his best playing position is still on his tummy or his back, because there he can move independently and freely. Don't put your child in his infant seat or baby chair; instead, lay him on his playmat or in the playpen.

With your support, your baby discovers new ways to have fun with a toy.

Exciting Toys: Rustling Paper and Yogurt Containers

Your baby's need for new toys is relatively small. Since he can transfer objects from one hand to the other, you should make sure he has *toys that are lightweight* and easy for a baby's tiny hands to grasp. Give him *different materials* to investigate. A fur glove, crinkly paper, an empty yogurt container, or a nail brush are more exciting than a rattle! Your baby can have fun with an *inflatable ball* that will float—even if he can't get his hands around it. Although plastic *play centers* that combine a number of different toys are very confusing, babies at this stage can do a lot with them. They are also useful when you are away from home, because you aren't going to lose a thousand individual pieces.

Important!

Remember, never leave your child playing alone, without supervision. Infants and toddlers are masters at getting into trouble!

Parents as Toys

Now that your child's vision is sharper, faces become increasingly important

for him. An unbreakable *baby-safe mirror* may become his favorite toy at this stage. His parents' faces, however, are the nicest playthings of all. Your child will never tire of seeing you make faces or of playing peek-a-boo (you put a cloth over his face, say peek-a-boo, and pull it off again), and he will do his best to imitate you. Your baby will display growing enthusiasm for verses and rhymes, in connection with finger games and touching games such as "10 Little Indians" and "Where is Thumbkin?" If you have forgotten these nursery rhymes, you can get an appropriate book at a bookstore or library that will not only contain the text but explain the finger positions as well.

Your baby is now stable enough for more *boisterous play* as well. Whether you choose to play airplane, ride him up and down on your ankle, dangle him on your knees, or let him sit on your shoulders, all these movements improve his sense of balance.

Important!
You also need to heed his protests. If he turns his head away, sticks out his tongue, or expresses some anxiety in his little cries of joy and ends up howling, you should give him a break.

Your Baby: Eight to Twelve Months

A toy telephone within easy reach will help keep your phone from becoming a toy!

Toward the end of the first year of life your child will become increasingly mobile. Now is the time to child-proof your home (see page 259). Some babies make the enormous leap from crawling to walking during the last third of the year, but most children don't take their first steps until they have passed their first birthday.

What Your Baby Can Do Now

Seeing and Hearing
Your child's vision becomes even more acute: At one year of age, he sees almost as sharply as an adult. He can spot the tiniest crumb on the rug and develops an increasingly good sense of spatial relationships, for what is up and down, inside and outside. His hearing matured during the preceding months, but now he begins to understand the meaning of words.

Creeping and Crawling
Over the course of the ninth month, your baby will get under way. He will worm along on his belly, often in reverse gear at first. Later on, he will move forward with increasing success. His movements become less jerky and better coordinated. Increasingly, he

grasps things with his thumb and finger—mainly his index finger—instead of his thumb and the palm of his hand.

In the tenth month, he moves from the prone position to the sitting position. He can already manage to "stand" on all fours, and sways back and forth in this position—a precrawling exercise. He uses furniture to pull himself up into a standing position. He takes hold of things in a growing number of ways. Now he grasps small objects between his thumb and index finger, in a pincer grip. With his two hands, he can strike objects together, and he enthusiastically flings everything he gets his hands on as far as he can.

Sitting Without Tipping Over: The First Steps

At the age of 11 months, the baby refines and perfects his abilities. He can sit up perfectly well, without falling over. In the twelfth month, he makes increasing efforts to stand upright. Holding your hand, most children now can take a few wobbly steps.

The baby now grasps things with precision, and loves to throw objects into openings. He puts objects into the hand of the person playing with him. He can drink unaided from a cup with a handle and feed himself with a spoon. Mobile and dexterous, he is ready to start his second year of life.

Important!

If you have a feeling that your child has poor vision, discuss it with your pediatrician. Prompt treatment improves the chances of repairing poor vision. This applies also to hearing problems. There are glasses or hearing aids made especially for babies. Such disorders are not outgrown; rather, they impair other developmental processes. A child who can't hear does not learn to talk, and a baby who can't see well has trouble getting around and taking hold of things.

What Stimulates Your Baby

His Radius of Action Is Growing

Now you need to put everything that could harm your baby and everything you place great value on out of his reach.

WHEN IS YOUR CHILD READY FOR THE SANDBOX?

Actually, your baby can move around fairly well in the sandbox by the end of the first year. The first prerequisite is that he be able to sit without falling over, because on his tummy or back, he is not in the right position for safe sandbox play! Many babies at this stage still explore objects by putting them into their mouths—so inspect the sandbox for small objects that may get him into trouble if swallowed.

But your baby wants, and ought, to discover, investigate, and try everything that is at his "level." Spread out toys, as well as suitable everyday objects, on the floor and on any shelves within reach: Old pots with lids, cooking spoons, egg spoons, empty containers, plastic boxes, and potholders are more exciting than the old, familiar toys.

Noises, Movements, and Music

Lightweight building blocks, stacking cups, baby-safe toy cars, and *toys that teach eye–hand coordination* are what the baby needs now. A *pull-toy* that possibly make great noises or special movements when dragged over the floor will delight your child at this stage. Sturdy *wind-up-toys* or *stuffed animals* that make noises arouse great enthusiasm. Your child now will examine a *doll* very thoroughly, but it needs to be quite uncomplicated and simple.

Best of All: Playing with Parents

Playing with human beings acquires increasing importance, since your baby now enjoys imitating. Simple *pantomime games* such as "How big am I?" or "Pattycake, Pattycake, Baker's Man" are no longer experienced passively; now your child copies what you do. Though at first it is great fun to throw things down in order to be handed them all over again, by the end of the first year, your child will enjoy putting objects into your hand. His motor skills are now so well developed that you can give him *primitive instruments* especially for babies: Chimes, a harmonica, a triangle, bells, a rattle, and drums will be a big hit with your child, once he has learned how to make noise with them.

Simple *picture books* may hold your child spellbound. The pictures should be as simple as possible, and the book should have only a few pages. Best of all are picture books with pages made of paperboard, which your child can look at on his own. This rule applies here as well: Repetition is helpful—too much variety is overwhelming.

As far as more boisterous play is concerned, playing tag now holds top ranking—but to play this game, you have to get down on your hands and knees. Maybe you can even play "wheelbarrow" with the baby at this stage (you hold his legs, the baby walks on his hands). Once he can sit without falling over, a car that will scoot is good—an ideal present for the baby's first birthday. Make sure that the car won't tip over, that your child won't fall down inside it, or that he accidentally drives it down a flight of stairs.

At this stage let your child play by himself at times—without constant supervision, but keeping safety in mind.

YOUR BABY HAS HIS OWN PERSONALITY

Your baby does not come into the world as a tabula rasa, a blank sheet of paper.
He develops within the framework of his heredity and in conversational interplay
with you and others. In the process, he accumulates experience and learns to
adapt to life with the people around him. This chapter presents the findings of experts
on childhood development who have studied this early phase.

What our babies can do physically at an early stage is quite obvious. What goes on inside their heads, however, is often a mystery to us. Although systematic research in this field began only about 20 years ago, we now are certain of this much—the intellectual and emotional capacities of an infant are greater than had ever been supposed. The "dumb baby" is an erroneous notion of the past, one that experienced mothers and nannies never believed anyway. However, a baby's means of expressing himself often are not able to keep pace with his knowledge. Consequently, the forms of communication between child and parents during the first year are largely nonlinguistic in nature.

Communication Without Words

Adults customarily use speech to express themselves to their equals. For this reason, it seems difficult to most parents at first to understand their baby and deal with him without words. Many mothers feel helpless or overwhelmed, especially when they sometimes cannot define their child's needs. But keep in mind that every baby, every mother, every father has an aptitude for nonverbal communication. Over time, you will learn to interpret your child's signs, body language, and behavior—and your baby, in turn, will react to your understanding.

If you succeed in developing these aptitudes and putting them to service, you can help your child find his inner balance. He first has to establish a sympathetic understanding of the new world, find his own rhythm, and develop suitable ways of self-regulation. If he fails to do all that, crying phases, sleep disturbances, and lack of understanding between parents and child are the results. You need to learn to understand your baby and to listen to your instincts. And don't get into a panic if that doesn't always work. He's your child, and he surely has a little bit of you in him—have confidence in this relationship. It is the best thing you have to offer your child.

The Infant's Consciousness

Psychoanalysts always have formulated theories about the early consciousness of infants. They were based on retrospective statements of patients, since babies themselves can unfortunately tell us nothing about their mind. But advanced technology made experimental research possible in the past few decades.

What We Know Now

Through the recording of glances and movements—the primary means being the monitoring of the intensity of the sucking motion to stimulus—researchers were able to measure babies' reactions to certain images and tones. The results are astonishing! From birth on, babies appear to understand that they can accomplish something with their actions. Between the second and sixth months they perceive themselves as a physical whole, a complete entity separate from others. At the age of about seven to nine months, they learn to share experiences and feelings with other people.

This finding may not be so amazing to you. For the experts, however, it is revolutionary: Freud saw the infant as a creature of instinct, intent only upon obtaining pleasure and avoiding the absence of pleasure. This is a view that is no longer tenable. Analyst Margaret Mahler's widely accepted theory about babies' symbiotic phase, in which a baby feels closely associated with his mother and is only able to distinguish between himself and others at about five months of age, was not confirmed by the research.

Instead, early childhood expert Daniel Stern has developed a new (psychoanalytic) model that gives an excellent explanation of the development of a baby's inner life on the basis of the latest research (see box on page 194). At first glance, his theory may seem a bit abstract, but its central message is this: Take your child seriously in his awareness of life, his expressions of emotion, and his wishes. Follow your instinct, and try from time to time to feel your way into your child's experiences and emotions. Simply try to imagine how he feels when he sees the bars of his crib or the glitter of a sunbeam, or when he feels gnawing pangs of hunger. Your effort can never be entirely successful, of course, but it will make you receptive to your child's signals. Perhaps you may simply understand him better afterward. If you would like to read more along these lines, I recommend *Diary of a Baby* by Daniel N. Stern.

No words are necessary: a conversation between mother and child.

How Your Child Establishes Relationships

Without the help of others, the newborn cannot survive. Thus the relationship to his mother, who feeds him in the first few months, is the focus of his bonding behavior for this time.

Over the course of the first weeks, however, he establishes more and more ties. Only by growing up in a community—in this country, the family—can he fully develop his potential and his personality. The patterns of behavior he employs, as a person connected with others, are innate. If these modes elicit no response from others, however, they wither away, as the sad examples of isolated or neglected children show. This is seen most clearly in the development of speech. But equally serious are deficiencies in relating to others, in dealing with other people, and in behavior in general. These developmental defects usually become noticeable only later on—too late.

THE BABY'S EMOTIONAL AND INTELLECTUAL DEVELOPMENT

Daniel N. Stern speaks of self-perceptions and differentiates four phases, which do not replace each other, but are founded on each other. His research is based on the idea that once the baby has learned something, it is never lost—a realization familiar to us from our adult life.

In the first two to three months, a baby is in the process of beginning to have the perception of an "emerging self." In this phase, the baby experiences each moment with all his senses. Thus he translates and processes everything that happens around him into physical sensations and reactions. He is not yet able to distinguish between outside and inside, between causative event and feeling.

Between the second and the sixth months, the "core self" develops; the infant becomes aware that he has his own feelings and his own will, apart from those of his mother. Thus he is able to enter into a relationship with her. The development of the "social smile," logically enough, occurs during this phase.

In the seventh to ninth months, the perception of a "subjective self" evolves, bringing another perspective with it. This self is not limited to observing actions, but also discovers feelings or even motives behind them. Only now do conscious "interactions" between the baby and others, especially his mother, become possible.

Only between the fifteenth and eighteenth months does the child develop the perception of a "verbal self," acquiring the capacity for objectivity and introspection.

The Key to a Good Relationship: Communication

If we take a critical look at the way we act with a baby, it's actually embarrassing: We change our behavior completely and become downright childish. Our behavior toward the baby is characterized by exaggerated facial expressions, a raised, high-pitched voice, nonsensical words, constant repetitions, and strange sounds. But what was considered totally impossible in the liberated seventies is back in fashion today. The truth is that this kind of behavior is exactly what the baby needs.

What Babies Already Understand

A baby does not yet understand the sense and meaning of words. He is more apt to comprehend feelings and moods and make his own sense of them. He simply needs stronger signals than older children or adults communicating with each other. Since babies hear especially well in the higher registers, we raise the pitch of our voice—surely also a tribute to the fact that babies prefer women's high voices to men's deeper ones. The exaggerated facial expressions are necessary so that the baby, with his still-blurry vision, can understand and mimic us. For the same reason, we quite instinctively bring our face toward the baby, to the best range of sight: a distance of 8 inches (20 cm).

The inflection, articulation, and melody of our words convey a message that the baby understands: Long drawn-out sounds have a calming effect, a falling intontation is comforting, and frequently repeated words or questions that rise toward the end cheer up or encourage the baby.

How a Dialogue Arises

We employ all these instinctive modes of behavior in interactions with the behavior of our child. The baby reacts in his own fashion, appears delighted or excited, produces sounds of his own in response—and reacts disapprovingly if it gets to be too much for him. Through this dialogue, understanding and trust between parent and child increase. This natural process of learning together can be inhibited by the fear of doing something wrong, by too much thinking and lack of faith in one's own abilities as a mother or father, or by unconscious worry about losing one's self to the child, forfeiting too much freedom.

The best preventive: Don't adopt a formula; instead, follow your intuition, learn to enjoy your "talk with the baby," and be receptive to all his ways of expressing himself.

How Your Baby Learns to Talk

From the first day on, your child learns in conversational interplay with you. In the first six months, however, his development is independent of his mother tongue. The sounds he produces have no meaning—the baby is, so to speak, practicing the formation

Our exaggerated facial expressions are just right for the baby.

of speech sounds by imitating us. The first thing we hear from our child is his crying. But by the age of roughly two months he begins to produce "eh" sounds. Then he practices "ah" and "ooh"; next come simple syllables with the letters *a, e, m,* and *n.* And in the fourth month, he often babbles to himself—even with no one else present. He shouts for joy and sometimes forces his breath through his constricted lips—resulting in sounds that our ears hear as *v* or *f.*

Talk to your baby—and give him time to answer.

The First Syllables

In the fifth month, the baby makes virtually no noticeable progress. Next comes a phase of syllable formation, in which the child strings individual syllables together apparently endlessly: dadadadadadada or dedededededede. In the process, he often changes volume and pitch as grownups do, though his babbling still has no meaning. In this phase, however, linguists have found differences in speech melody that correspond to the parents' native language.

At eight months, the baby discovers whispering. The next month, the emphasis is on forming words of two syllables—now he is slowly learning to see words in connection with meaning and to use them accordingly. Only about 3 percent utter their first conscious word by nine months of age, but 50 percent have done so by the end of the first year. Don't be disappointed, then, if your child fails to favor you with an enthusiastic cry of "Mama" or "Papa" on his first birthday.

Where's Mama, Papa, Teddy ...?

But you've surely noticed it by now: Your child understands the meaning of words long before he can speak them himself. At 10 months, he already knows simple concepts such as Mama, Papa, light, bed, Teddy, or milk, which have great significance in his daily life. If you ask him about them, he will look for them. Toward the end of the first year, he understands "no"—and promptly forgets it again. He's not able to remember what's forbidden yet! But he enjoys making a game of repeatedly provoking you to horrified "No's" by devoting his attention to the stereo system or to your flower pots.

He already understands simple directions such as "Come here" or "Let's take a walk" and frequently reacts correctly to them. But don't expect too much of your one-year-old: There are simply too many interesting things that distract him!

How to Encourage Speech Development

You do not train your child to speak as you would train a dog to perform tricks. Language acquisition is on an intellectually higher level. Even without any concerted effort on your part, your child would learn to speak by mere exposure alone. You can, however, exert a positive influence on your child's natural speech development.

■ Speak to your child from the moment that he is born. He will gain familiarity with the speech sounds and intonation. He will imitate these patterns long before he speaks actual words.

■ When he makes vocalizations, you should answer (with normal speech) so that he begins to understand the "give and take" nature of language.

■ Use simple words and phrases, and repeat them frequently.

■ Keep a running commentary of what you are doing when you interact with him (e.g., "Now we'll put your socks on.") As he grows, he will start to make the associations.

■ While you talk with him, pause frequently so that he may have a chance to respond.

The Power of the Smile

Baby humans, like baby animals, have characteristic features. Their rounded heads are large relative to their bodies, and they have big, wide-set eyes, a domed forehead, and a snub nose. Their bodies have a certain plumpness with well-rounded contours. These features arouse a protective instinct in us. When the baby looks at us, we are enchanted. Beyond the constant features, the baby soon develops a very significant behavior—he smiles. It is a profoundly human ability. In the first weeks we use the term "angelic smile" for this reflex, which can be triggered by touching the areas on either side of the mouth.

Over the course of the second month, the "social smile" develops. Your baby reacts to every human face—even pictures of faces—with a friendly smile. This behavior continues throughout the first six months. Never again will your child smile, laugh, and chuckle as much as during this period in his development. The smile and laughter are delightfully contagious. You and your baby will enjoy this time together.

Smiles Are Now Reserved for Friends

In the second six months, things get more complicated. During this period your baby develops the "specific smile." This means that he will no longer smile automatically at every face he sees. He has started to recognize certain faces and will smile at those that are most familiar. If a stranger approaches, he may wrinkle his forehead, stiffen, look away, or even cry out in horror. It is nice to reassure acquaintances that they've not done anything wrong, but that it is simply a stage that he is going through.

Smiles and certain physical characteristics that make us feel protective are nature's way of safeguarding babies.

Help, My Child Is Shy with Strangers!

This is not a backward step in behavior; rather it shows progressing development. Your child has learned familiarity with his parents and lack of familiarity with strangers. He no longer assumes that familiar people and places have all of the same qualities as unfamiliar people and places. He now assumes all that is unfamiliar is dangerous—a subconscious safeguard. In unfamiliar locations, he will cling to his parents, then slowly make brief excursions in the strange environment, returning frequently to "touch base" with Mom or Dad. Parents need to understand and respect this phase, which will end at $1^1/_2$ to 2 years old. Talk to your worried child and reassure him, but don't force the issue.

Important!

If strangers pick up, caress, cuddle, or kiss your child, this is probably going too far. The older child will likely not be comforted, no matter how well-intentioned the person may be.

If your baby is reserved with people who are close to you, it's not easy. Even getting used to baby-sitters or day-care providers may entail some problems at first. Here's how to help your baby warm up to "new people":

■ Don't intervene actively. Your baby needs you only as a security base—just make yourself available to him.

■ It is best for the "new person" to approach slowly from one side and then sit down, in order to seem smaller.

■ Let the baby take the initiative in making the initial contact. The "new person" should neither address nor touch the baby at first, but start a conversation with the mother instead: This will create trust.

■ When the baby begins to feel secure and starts to make the first overtures, the visitor can respond by smiling or handing the baby a toy.

■ Only frequent contact over several weeks will create real trust and make someone part of the baby's reference group. Give grandparents and others who take care of the baby such an opportunity; otherwise, his fear of strangers will increase.

■ If possible, try to meet with the baby-sitter or day-care provider for one hour initially and stay with your child for the first several encounters. This will help ease the transition and help your baby to gain trust in the people you've chosen to take care of him.

Do You Understand Your Baby?

The general public believes that every mother understands her child's needs instantly and magically—that she interprets his cries correctly, and thus is always able to satisfy his needs immediately—and that fathers, on the other hand, do not have this magical quality. These beliefs really have no truth. With each one of my children, I was much too excited, exhausted, and uncertain to be able to understand the nuances of their cries correctly every time. And I think many other parents share my experience.

What Does My Child Want?

As a rule, there are three standard answers to the question of why the baby cries: "He's hungry," "He has a tummyache, gas pains, or colic," and "He's tired." The crying of our babies is an expression of their adjustment to life. It often has concrete causes, like those mentioned above. Frequently,

however, it is a mixture of a great many feelings, a way of releasing tension—or a cry for help. And even if we don't understand the crying, we should never let it go unanswered (for more on this topic, see the section beginning on page 75).

Our inability to understand the baby is brought home to us painfully in such conflict situations. However, we fail to register how often, every single day, we do comprehend our child's signs of life and respond to them—which is only natural. After all, every minute we spend with the baby we are reacting to his smile, his movement of warding off, his amazement, and his anger without being aware that we are doing so. This is good, since constant monitoring of ourselves would create an intolerable distance between us and our child. But the fact that you repeatedly and quite unconsciously react "correctly" should also give you courage in building your relationship with your child.

Parents Have to Learn, Too

Basically, we can let our child guide us and observe him. From his first day on, he is concerned with finding an internal balance. Many of his manifestations have something to do with this search for self-regulation. To succeed, he needs our help and careful guidance: A lively, restless baby requires settling and calming down, and a placid child needs stimulation and diversion. It is not always easy to find the right measure. Not only the baby, but we as well are in a learning phase, after all. So don't be overly harsh and demanding on yourself; be patient—and open.

When Conflicts Arise

Mothers are under pressure: When their baby cries, when he won't sleep at all, when he throws the spoon across the room—then, in the eyes of many of your contemporaries, he is spoiled. You have failed to perform your "obligation" to bring up the child properly—as people's critical looks tell you. And what about you? Aren't there also times when you have the feeling that your baby is fairly intent

A crying baby needs comfort and closeness.

on a power struggle? When he blithely ignores your "No" with a provocative look in his eye? Doesn't that sometimes make you furious and ready to assume the role of disciplinarian?

When Is It Time for Discipline?
In both situations—when faced with other people's criticism and with your own fury—caution is a good idea. Don't let yourself get carried away; refrain from disciplinary measures, since they are of no avail. Your child doesn't become enraged deliberately, but because for some reason or another he has lost his inner equilibrium. He is actually desperate! And he doesn't throw the spoon in the air to make you angry. When he does something "forbidden" with a questioning look in his eye, he expects an appropriate reaction—he is looking for confirmation of the "naughty" act. But he is not yet capable of understanding or accepting such limitations. He is in a phase of constant testing and discovery; after all, this is the only way he can continue to develop.

Developing Within Safe Limits
At this age, bringing up your child can only mean making it possible for him to develop. This includes attaching safety devices to the drawers, if need be, or moving the stereo equipment one shelf higher to protect the baby. On the other hand, your behavior

should be unambiguous and should give your child emotional security and guidance. When he's tired, he should sleep—even if he fusses. And if he has just refused his applesauce, there is no need for him to sample a whole series of foods with other flavors.

In the second six months, you also can impart a certain rhythm of life to your baby.

In all situations, act deliberately and lovingly, even when it is difficult. Your child can make nothing of your rage and your punishments; they will only increase his desperation. He is at your mercy—for better and for worse.

Let's try to be understanding of this little creature who often drives us 'round the bend, and respect his personality just as we would that of an adult.

Give your child as much freedom as possible— and set as many limits as necessary.

HEALTHY FROM THE OUTSET

*Every parent's greatest wish is a healthy child.
It is not always fulfilled completely.
However, you can do quite a lot to strengthen your
child and support him through critical times.
Don't be overly fearful,
but keep a close eye on your baby.
This will help in recognizing developmental problems,
and you can then alert your pediatrician.
In this chapter you will learn how to keep
your child healthy and how to
help your sick child.*

PREVENTIVE PEDIATRIC HEALTH CARE IS VITAL

Prevention is the best way to protect your child against disease.

Checkups and vaccinations are an essential part of health maintenance.

Through preventive care, you can save your baby the trouble of illness and developmental problems. During regular visits to your pediatrician, you can ask questions and clear up areas of uncertainty. After all, it's fun to talk about your own child.

How can you tell if you have a healthy baby? The answer might be: by his contented mother. That tells us something important: You, as a mother, will notice that something is wrong with your child much sooner than an experienced pediatrician. A healthy baby is usually friendly, has a rosy look, follows a somewhat predictable pattern of sleeping and waking, consumes his feedings rapidly, and gains enough weight (see page 94).

Nevertheless, with your first child, you may be a little anxious, and some of your baby's behaviors may frighten or disconcert you. There are 6 scheduled checkups devoted to well-child care in the first year of life. This provides you with an ideal opportunity to talk about your observations and concerns with your pediatrician. During the examination, you will learn what "milestones" you can watch for as your child develops (see the section beginning on page 180).

Always go the checkup well prepared—ideally, with a note pad on which you have written down your questions. If you know ahead of time what the pediatrician is checking on, you can share additional observations with him. You and the pediatrician are a team in these checkups. The more effectively you work together, the better for your child. This applies to vaccinations as well. Your child's resistance to illness is increased, not reduced by these inoculations. It is better not to subject your baby to unnecessary and, in some cases, serious health risks. Have him vaccinated.

Preventive Medical Checkups

Prevention is better than a cure—this is especially true for infants and children. Chronic disease in children, if detected too late, can be fatal. Regular participation in preventive medical checkups will give your baby a good chance for a healthy childhood.

What the Standard Care Includes

The preventive care examinations for children (see the box that follows) are scheduled at regular intervals, so that the critical phases when chronic disorders tend to appear are well monitored. There are five scheduled office visits in the first 6 months. These are intended to detect hereditary problems—principally those involving individual organ systems such as the heart, kidneys, or nervous system. Later, the sensory organs, hearing and sight, and of course, overall development are targeted specifically. Many children deviate from the norm in their rate of development: They learn to crawl or walk late, or they have not started to talk by the time they are 18 months. All this may be quite normal. But very rarely, delayed stages of development many conceal disorders, some of which may be treatable. Not least of all, these scheduled checkups provide an opportunity to discuss proper nutrition, and of course, all the questions you've written down to ask your pediatric provider.

Important!

Each early detection system is only as good as the degree of participation in it. Take advantage of the opportunity offered you. Which of us would not find it reassuring to invest 15 to 30 minutes in order to know that "everything's all right," or that, for example, wearing a splint for a short time or doing physical exercises for awhile can ensure that your child's development will then proceed undisturbed.

PEDIATRIC PREVENTIVE CHECKUPS	
1	At birth
2	Within 24 hours of birth
3	At discharge from hospital
4	7–10 days
5	1 month
6	2 months
7	4 months
8	6 months
9	9 months
10	12 months
11	15 months
12	18 months
13	24 months
After 24 months, one checkup annually	

Extra Checkups for High-Risk Children

The phrase *high-risk child* refers to a child who before birth carried an increased risk of a disorder, or a child who was born during a difficult delivery. It is the purpose of prenatal care by your obstetrician to detect these potential problems, and to make allowances for any special care that may be needed after your child is born.

■ If you have had a high-risk pregnancy or if your baby is a high-risk child, you should present records to each doctor you visit. This way any further testing, if necessary, will not be overlooked.

■ If your baby was at risk and—like almost all high-risk children—was born without problems, you still may find that you are urged to have your baby checked at monthly intervals by the pediatrician, to rule out problems that may appear later (perhaps you had an accident while pregnant, and the doctor needs to see whether there are any consequences for your baby's development). Take advantage of this offer! The reassurance that everything is all right will soon replace your fear that some damage may have been done.

■ For these follow-up exams for increased-risk children, many pediatricians have a notification system that serves to remind tardy parents, so that damage does not go undetected on account of negligence. Gather information when you are asked for your consent to the implementation of a high-risk program for your baby.

The First Checkup

Even before you leave the delivery room, your baby has had his first (albeit brief) examination. This is to determine if your child is having difficulty making the transition to life outside of your body. A delivery room nurse will take notice of your child's breathing, color, and movements. With his first cry, he inhales oxygen into his lungs for the first time. As a result, his skin becomes rosy, his muscles tighten, and his breathing becomes regular.

The Apgar scores are considered the standard for estimating the general condition of newborns in the delivery room and are named after Dr. Virginia Apgar, who in 1953, proposed a method for evaluating newborns in the delivery room. In this scoring system, certain characteristics (skin color, reflex irritability, heart rate, respiration, and muscle tone) are tested at set intervals following birth (after one minute, after five minutes, and sometimes after ten minutes). If they are all completely satisfactory, two points are awarded for each category, then the scores are totaled.

An Apgar score of 10 is the highest, but 9 is also considered normal—and is the score most healthy babies receive. Scores below 7 after one minute and after five minutes require cautious intervention by the physician to accelerate the baby's adaptation to his new world. As the score gets lower, it reflects increasing difficulty of the baby's adaptation to his new world. If the difficulty is severe enough, a physician's intervention may be necessary. However, you will likely be aware of how the baby is doing before you know the Apgar score.

The Second Checkup

At the hospital, your child's pediatrician will visit you and your baby within the first 24 hours after birth. This is your baby's first real medical examination, which is more complete than the delivery room checkup.

■ The physician assesses the weight and measurements of your baby. He then gives your baby a thorough "head-to-toe" examination, looking at all "parts" and features. If your baby was delivered before term, his gestational age is assessed during the examination. In addition, his heart, lungs, abdominal organs, nervous system, bones, and joints—particularly the hips—are examined.

■ Occasionally, the pediatrician may have questions for you regarding the pregnancy. However, this is also *your* first opportunity to ask any questions and voice any concerns you may have.

And, you may ask to be present during the examination if you would like. In reality, today many mothers are rooming-in with their babies and the exam is done in the mother's room.

■ No one baby is exactly like any other baby. There is great variation in proportion, hair color, and so on. Furthermore, there are many "normal variants"—findings that are often not common, yet completely normal. For example, the so-called *stork bite*. In medical terms this is called a *nevus flammeus* and represents "swollen" or distended capillaries (small blood vessels), and appears as salmon or

PREVENTING VITAMIN K DEFICIENCY

Vitamin K is produced by bacteria inside the intestines. It is of vital importance, because it is an essential factor in the blood's ability to clot. In breastfed infants, production of vitamin K develops more slowly than in bottle-fed babies, who quickly receive an ample supply of vitamin K. To enhance the clotting ability of the blood—that is, to prevent excessive bleeding, all children need supplementary vitamin K in the form of an injection at birth. This is necessary since vitamin K deficiency can result in bleeding later on, with serious impairment of the baby's health.

reddish colored patches. About 40 percent of newborns will have this at birth, and it is usually located on the upper eyelids, between the eyebrows, below the nose, and on the nape of the neck. These markings will usually disappear before the end of the second year of life—and in many cases, before the end of the first year.

■ If your baby has something on his body that seems out of place or abnormal, you should ask your pediatrician to look at it and explain in detail until you are satisfied. You shouldn't be kept wondering or worrying.

Checkups in the Office

Before leaving the hospital you should ask your child's pediatrician to tell you when his next appointment should be made. You may be delivering at a hospital far enough from home that your pediatrician may not have privileges there and, therefore, your child will be seen by a staff pediatrician. In this case you should call your pediatrician's office and ask when your pediatrician would like to see the baby.

Generally, the first office visit will be when the baby is between 1 and 2 weeks old. Occasionally it will be sooner if there are feeding issues or jaundice, which needs more frequent assessment. All checkups in the first year of life include vaccinations, except the first, which is usually a weight check, physical exam, and opportunity to ask questions. Each checkup will include measurement of weight, height, and head circumference and assessment of your child's development, as well as a complete physical exam. In addition, and more important to many parents, this is an opportunity to ask questions and discuss anticipatory guidance and safety issues for now and the months ahead. Each new age brings with it new ways for your baby to get into "trouble."

The hospital or pediatrician will give you a booklet to keep track of your baby's immunizations and growth. Don't forget to ask at the end of the visit when the next checkup will be.

Vitamin D and Fluoride Supplementation as Preventives

Never again does a human being grow so rapidly as during infancy. To sustain that rate of growth, large amounts of calcium need to be absorbed and then deposited in the bones. Vitamin D is essential in guiding these processes. In its preliminary stages, it is produced in the baby's body and converted to active vitamin D when the skin is exposed to sunlight. Evidence shows that 10 minutes a day or 15 minutes twice a week in the sun is sufficient to provide adequate vitamin D.

All infant formulas contain sufficient vitamin D to prevent a deficiency in your baby. Breast milk, however, contains variable amounts of vitamin D. Usually with the supply from breast milk and that gained from ambient sunlight, the baby will have adequate amounts of vitamin D. Some pediatricians choose to supplement with vitamin D at about 6 months of age. You should discuss this with your pediatrician.

Fluoride is a trace element that the body uses to strengthen teeth and bones. It is present naturally in small amounts in food and water. In some areas of the country, however, it is not found in high enough amounts to prevent tooth decay. If you have private well water, it is unlikely to have much fluoride in it. If you have city water, your state health department can tell you if your town has fluoride in its water. Most spring water does not have fluoride unless otherwise labeled. Some "infant drinking water" will contain up to 1 ppm (part per million) fluoride, which is more than adequate. Ready-to-use and concentrated formula does not have added fluoride. Powdered formula will have only as much fluoride as you add with the water you use. Ask your pediatrician about fluoride supplementation—it is by prescription only. If it is needed, fluoride is usually started at the age of 6 months.

Selecting the Right Physician

Pediatricians, family practitioners, and pediatric nurse practitioners all provide preventive as well as urgent care for your child. It is optimal to choose a pediatric provider before the baby is born. Sometimes this choice will depend on your insurance plan. During a prenatal visit, get to know the office staff, the providers, and the philosophy of the practice. As with

CONGENITAL HIP DISLOCATION

One out of every 1,000 to 2,000 newborns suffer from this serious disorder of the hip joint. It occurs when the hip sockets don't form normally, and results in dislocation of the long bone of the leg out of the hip socket. The incidence is sixfold greater in girls than in boys, and more than 20 percent of affected children have a positive family history of congenital dislocation of the hip. Mechanical factors make it more frequent in breech deliveries.

Treatment for dislocated hips begins at the time of diagnosis; the earlier it is diagnosed, the shorter the course of treatment. Treatment usually consists of placing a harness around your baby's legs and abdomen that keeps the top of the long bone in place in the hip socket. The harness is removable and babies normally adjust to it quite well.

Diagnosis is by physical examination. Your pediatrician will check your child's hip until he is walking. If the physician suspects a problem, the diagnosis is confirmed by an ultrasound of the hip joint, and you will be referred to a pediatric orthopedist. There should be no reason why your child will not walk, run, and play sports after treatment for hip dislocation.

your well-child checkups, go with a list of questions that are important for you and your family. In many instances, the provider that you choose will come to the hospital for the baby's first examination and visit—this will depend on how far their practice is from the hospital and whether or not the physicians in the practice have privileges at that hospital. Most physicians admit their patients to hospitals local to their practice.

There are many aspects of a pediatric practice that might influence your choice. You want to look at location, office hours, practice philosophy, admitting hospitals, and the ease of getting an appointment. The doctor's type of practice needs to be in harmony with your personal preferences.

Tips for Stress-Free Visits to the Doctor

The first well-baby checkup, in particular, is stressful for both parents and child. The parents' nervousness not infrequently causes the babies to protest mightily against procedures such as measurement of length or testing of reflexes. Who enjoys laying naked on a cold scale—especially when it's actually time for a nap or a feeding?

Make careful preparations for the checkup:

■ Schedule your appointment so that you neither jolt your baby from sleep nor present him to the doctor when hungry. If you can't avoid scheduling a visit at the baby's feeding time, keep a bottle ready in a thermal container if your child is bottlefed. If you are breastfeeding, naturally you can nurse the baby in the doctor's office at any time!

■ Choose clothing that can be removed and put back on quickly and easily. Remember to pack an extra diaper, wipes, a bottle or snack, and a change of clothes.

■ Although hungry babies can make a doctor's appointment a horrible experience, please don't try to stuff your baby so full ahead of time that he won't make a sound, or that he is so stuffed that he will vomit when his abdomen is examined. It is optimal if it has been 2 to 3 hours since his last feeding, but in reality, many times this is not possible. So bring the bottle along or don't feel uncomfortable about breastfeeding if the baby is hungry—pediatricians are used to breastfeeding mothers in their office.

■ Your child may be ill on the day you have a scheduled checkup. It's a good idea to bring the baby anyway because he will then be looked at in terms of his illness and you can take the opportunity to ask questions you may have. Immunizations are not contraindicated for a cold or viral infection. Many pediatricians will choose not to give immunizations with a fever though, because it is one side effect of many vaccinations. Fever on top of fever is not such a good idea. This should not be a problem though, and you can schedule an appointment for the immunizations in 2 weeks.

Well Protected Through Immunizations

Immunizations are a potent form of preventive health care. It was through vaccination that smallpox was eradicated. Many other threats to your child's health still exist, however. Immunization works by exposing one's body to a vaccine, which is made from viruses or bacteria that have been killed or weakened. Through this exposure (generally by injection, or by mouth for polio), the body's immune system ostensibly learns the "enemy's secrets" so that it will be prepared for any future attack. In actual terms, the vaccination results in the production of antibodies and antibody-producing cells, which will act as an early defense mechanism against future infection.

Are Immunizations Really Necessary?

Parents may question the need for immunizations because they've never heard of anyone ever contracting the illnesses that the immunizations are supposed to prevent. Rather than deciding that the immunizations are unimportant, the correct interpretation is that the illnesses are rare *because* of the immunizations. You should note that some of the organisms are in the soil and everywhere in the environment, and therefore will *never* be eradicated. Others commonly affect adults in a mild form, but if contracted by your baby could cause severe illness or even death. Your pediatric provider can give you specific details.

And the Side Effects?

Mild side effects are frequent with immunizations. Tiredness, fever, rashes, poor feeding, and local swelling are the most common. Your pediatric provider can tell you what to expect. But remember, even though fever may be an expected outcome of immunizations, if your child is under 3 months of age and has a fever, then still call your pediatrician. With any vaccine, there are rare reported cases of serious side effects. The risk for serious side effects approaches one in a million. In all cases, you are safer getting the vaccine than not getting it because the same serious effects can be caused, and are much more frequent if one were to contract the illness that the vaccine is preventing.

Important!

Special consideration of added side effects must be given to children who either have an immune deficiency, or who have contact with an immune deficient person.

Required Immunizations

The table on page 213 lists the currently required immunizations, along with the schedule for the administration. Questions about the immunization schedule as well as the length of protection should be addressed to your pediatrician.

What if My Baby Has a Reaction?

In some cases, children will become restless or develop fever after an immunization. Acetaminophen may be given. If the fever is very high, however, or your baby is less than 3 months old, you should call your baby's doctor for advice. Sometimes the timing of the immunization is coincidental to the onset of an actual illness.

Additional Immunizations

The immunizations listed on page 213 are recommended for all children. Under certain circumstances your pediatric provider may recommend other immunizations.

■ Chicken Pox Vaccine—Some doctors recommend it to all children when they turn one year old. Others will recommend it to children who have not had the chicken pox by age twelve. Others only use it under special circumstances. It is not a required vaccine, but you will want to discuss the pros and cons with your doctor.

■ Flu Vaccine—Vaccination against influenza is recommended for children over 6 months of age who have certain underlying serious illnesses. Some people prefer to receive the flu shot even if they do not fall into this category; this is okay to do. The shot should be given during the autumn months before the onset of the flu season.

■ Travel Vaccinations—If you are planning to travel outside the country with your child, you should speak with your doctor about illness prevention and vaccinations. This should be done at a minimum of one month, and preferably several months, before you are planning to travel. Alternatively, in some areas, specialized "travel clinics" are available to help you plan your health needs while you are abroad.

REQUIRED VACCINES

Age	DPT/DTaP (diphtheria-pertussis-tetanus)	HIB (Haemophilus influenza type B)	Polio	MMR (measles, mumps, rubella)	Hep B (Hepatitis B)
Birth					Hep B #1
1 Month					Hep B #2
2 Months	DPT/DTaP #1	HIB #1	OPV/IPV #1		
4 Months	DPT/DTaP #2	HIB #2	OPV/IPV #2		
6 Months	DPT/DTaP #3	HIB #3	OPV #3 (optional)		
9 Months					Hep B #3
12–18 Months	DPT/DTaP #4	HIB #4	OPV/IPV #3	MMR #1 (12–15 months)	
4–6 years	DPT/DTaP #5		OPV/IPV #4	MMR #2	

So-Called Passive Immunizations

Your child is unlikely to ever need this other form of immunization. The term refers to the injection of antibodies against certain diseases that have been collected from the blood of people who have survived that particular illness. Passive immunizations are effective, but the protection lasts only a short time, because the "borrowed" antibodies usually are broken down within four to six months. Passive immunizations are possible against a number of disease-causing bacteria and viruses: measles, hepatitis A, hepatitis B, tetanus, rabies, chicken pox, and cytomegalovirus. Whether your child should receive any of these vaccines is a decision you and your doctor will make based upon your child's age and the likelihood of significant exposure.

Important!

The above table lists the most commonly followed timing and sequence of vaccine administration. Updates and changing recommendations occur frequently. For various reasons, your pediatric provider may choose to deviate slightly from this table. The chicken pox vaccine is recommended but not required; it is likely to be given at 12 to 18 months or 11 to 12 years old. Also, tetanus boosters should be given every ten years through adolescence and adulthood.

213

ILLNESSES IN THE FIRST YEAR

Barely in the world and already sick!

Few things worry new parents as much as their child's first illness.

Mild bacterial and viral illnesses are an inevitable part of normal childhood.

Your pediatric provider can teach you when and how to ease the symptoms of illness,

and will be available to intercede when more serious illness is present.

In the first weeks, the newborn has only to deal with the minor difficulties of adaptation to life "outside." These are usually quickly surmounted. However, infections represent an ever present threat.

Sooner or later it will happen: The previously eagerly taken feeding will be rejected, or even suddenly vomited up, or the baby will cry for no apparent reason, feel hot to your touch, and have a fever. These symptoms often take new parents by surprise, quickly producing a degree of panic. Feeding in particular is one of the most "maternal" activities of all—and if a baby refuses to be fed, one feels less able to nurse one's baby back to health.

Sooner or later, however, every child has to begin grappling with the large numbers of viruses and bacteria in his environment. This is an entirely normal course of events. Nature has equipped humans with a host of mechanisms for warding off and overcoming infectious diseases. Depending on your baby's age he will have varying ability to fight off an infection. As he ages, he will build immunity against various bacteria and viruses, he will be immunized against others, and you will gain experience in coping with his illnesses.

Getting Sick Is All Part of the Game

In the first weeks of life, many infants suffer from problems that are typical of this phase; jaundice, umbilical and dermatological problems, spitting up, and restlessness are among the most common complaints of newborns. In addition, sometimes there are also problems related to maturation or hormone mediated problems such as undescended testicles, or enlarged breast glands. As a rule, however, there is no need to worry; many of these complaints disappear without treatment. For additional information and suggested treatments, see the alphabetical listing beginning on page 218.

Most Common Cause: Viral Infection

By far the most common cause of relatively serious health problems in newborns and infants are viral infections. Inside his mother's body, the child is largely protected against them. Once he is born, the infant retains some of the immunity in the form of antibodies that were transferred across the placenta. These antibodies will stay in your baby's system for about his first six months while his immune system is taking time to mature. Eventually as your child grows older, each virus or bacteria that he has fought off previously will be met with a well-trained immune system the next time it tries to infect your child. The result is that as time goes on he will have fewer and fewer infections, and the ones that he does have will be milder and milder.

How Often Is It Healthy to Be Sick?

It can be quite upsetting to parents when they notice the early stages of a new viral illness before the last echoes of coughing of last week's illness are gone. Scarcely has one infection ended when the next one begins. It isn't always that bad, of course. Your first child, in fact, if kept safe from sniffling cousins and playfriends, is rarely sick at first. But you should be prepared for a small child who has older siblings or playfriends to catch as many as 10 to 15 illnesses in a year.

You can do little to prevent it. Antibodies in breast milk may help decrease the incidence of some infections. A day-care facility with strict guidelines about staying home when ill may be inconvenient when your child is ill, but may result in fewer illnesses overall for all of the children in attendance. In your own home, good hand washing will help keep illnesses from spreading from one sibling to another, from the baby to the parent, and vice versa. Finally, screening all visitors for illnesses is of paramount importance in your baby's first three months of life, and later on it can still be helpful.

No Need to Fear Childhood Diseases

Childhood diseases are caused by pathogens that can attack humans in any stage of life. Once you have contracted some of these illnesses, you will be immune to them for the rest of your life. With some of these diseases, unborn babies receive immunity on loan from their mother so that they are protected (against measles, for example) during early infancy. There are vaccines available that prevent the outbreak of a number of these diseases, and if the immunization program is followed properly, they can provide lifelong immunity against measles, mumps, rubella, tetanus, diphtheria, polio, chicken pox, and hepatitis B. For more information on immunization, see page 211.

But what if your baby does catch something? The childhood diseases listed here are by no means a stroke of fate. We are thoroughly familiar with their course. In any event, however, have your physician make a diagnosis, and find out what the treatment is, if

any. If you think that your child really does not feel well, then contact your pediatrician.

Evaluating the Symptoms Correctly

Many symptoms of disease are actually designed by your body to help clear the infection out of the body—actually a part of the healing process. Hiding the symptoms with medications will not cure your baby of the illness. Other symptoms are simply annoying accompaniments to the infection and should be soothed as much as possible for your baby's comfort. Although a disturbance of your child's well-being may give you a bad fright at first, you should try to observe him closely. When you talk to your pediatric provider, he will help you sort through which symptoms you should pay close attention to, which symptoms you should medicate, and which symptoms you should not worry about.

Fever
An increase in body temperature means that defense reactions are getting under way inside the body. Once a true fever of 100.5 degrees Fahrenheit (38.0°C) is reached, it is safe to bring the fever down with children's doses of acetaminophen or ibuprofen, if recommended by your doctor.

Letting the fever increase does not help fight off infection, while treating a lower temperature will raise concern as to whether a true fever exists, and may cloud the diagnosis. Remember that although a fever indicates infection, making a fever go away with acetaminophen does not mean that the infection is gone.

Important!

With any fever you should call your child's doctor immediately if your child is less than 3 months old or appears very ill.

Loss of Appetite

This is often an early indicator of illness. If this should happen, try to concentrate on administering liquids, which are more important than solid food to your child at this time. However, you will probably have more success at offering liquids on a more frequent basis, rather than trying to force the liquids down at any one sitting. If you are breastfeeding, you should continue to breastfeed rather than substitute any other liquids.

Vomiting and Diarrhea

Vomiting is the body's response to a variety of illnesses. It is a highly coordinated, efficient, and important mechanism for removing undesirable substances from the stomach, as in the case of food poisoning. However, it is also an annoying and unnecessary symptom in many other illnesses. Diarrhea, on the other hand, is usually the result of bowel inflammation caused by infectious agents, or noninfectious bowel irritants. If these symptoms occur, you need to make sure to avoid dehydration by replacing the lost fluid. Always consult your pediatrician for help in the case of these symptoms.

Coughing

Coughing is a natural reflex that serves to expel harmful substances from the respiratory passages. By keeping your child from coughing, you can cause these substances to accumulate inside his body. Loosening the cough is a more appropriate treatment (see page 236). Once your child is older, cough suppressants can be used to treat coughs that persist after the illness is over.

Pain

Pain is an alert signal. The baby usually announces pain immediately to his parents by crying. Continuous crying at night, especially when your baby has cold symptoms, may be an indication of a middle ear infection (see page 227). Very severe pain leads to intense crying. No one can bear to listen to this type of crying without calling the doctor immediately—which is the appropriate thing to do.

Problems and Illnesses from A to Z

Allergies

An allergy is a hypersensitive reaction to one or more substances:

■ Food allergens (for example, milk proteins)

■ Airborne particles (for example, dust or flower pollen)

■ Contact substances (for example, synthetic fabrics worn next to the skin)

Typical Symptoms

The degree of a hypersensitive reaction depends on your child's immune system. The reaction varies from harmless itching and rash, to severe—even life threatening—forms that cause breathing difficulty and circulatory shock (anaphylaxis). Allergies are also at the root of the so-called "atopic" diseases such as asthma, eczema, and hay fever. They have a strong hereditary component and tend to run in families.

The Cause

The immune system ferociously attacks what are otherwise harmless substances in contact with the body. The excess inflammation that results is the cause of the discomforting and occasionally dangerous symptoms listed above.

What You Can Do

■ Cow's milk, fish, eggs, and nuts are the worst offenders. Breastfeeding mothers should avoid them if allergies run in the family, because they can be transmitted through breast milk.

■ When you start your baby on solid foods, avoid cow's milk products, eggs, fish, citrus fruits, peanuts, other nuts and seeds, berries, and chocolate until okayed by your baby's doctor (usually at 1 to 3 years old).

COMMON ALLERGIES

Allergies are on the increase today as technology creates new food additives, propellants, and perfumes. The following forms are the ones most likely to appear in infancy, especially if allergies run in the child's family:

■ *Allergy to cow's milk or soy protein. Diarrhea and occasionally vomiting and abdominal discomfort are seen with these allergies.*

■ *Eczema: blotchy, scaly, itchy red rash, frequently on the cheeks, chest, elbow, and the backs of the knees. Moisturizers are helpful.*

■ *Asthma: inflammation of the breathing passages leading to difficulty breathing and the characteristic wheeze. This condition always demands a visit to the pediatrician.*

Your child's doctor can help confirm the presence of allergies and begin both a course of treatment and further prevention.

■ Avoid perfumed soaps and detergents.

■ **Never allow cigarette smoking in the presence of your child.**

■ Keep your house as free of dust as possible.

Bronchiolitis

Inflammation of the small passageways within the lungs. It is usually caused by a virus.

Typical Symptoms

The symptoms typically include a spasmodic cough, and sometimes fever and runny nose. If more severe, you may notice wheezing or poor appetite. It may be every bit as severe as asthma.

What You Can Do

■ Keep young infants away from other sick children.

■ Avoid excessively hot and dry air in your house.

■ Treat the fever with acetaminophen.

■ Always go to the pediatrician for treatment.

Chicken Pox

This childhood disease is an infectious illness. Newborns and young infants are not completely protected from it from their mother's antibodies received through the placenta. Generally however the antibodies make for a milder illness. Milder symptoms are not the case, however, if the infant's mother never had chicken pox. If an infant's mother should develop chicken pox around the time that the infant is born (5 days before or up to 2 days after), your pediatrician must be told immediately so that passive immunization can be arranged (see Passive Immunization on page 213).

Always call ahead if you are bringing your child with chicken pox or a case of suspected chicken pox to your doctor's office. Otherwise, you may start an epidemic in the waiting room.

Typical Symptoms

A fever often precedes the rash. When the rash appears, it will usually start on the face, then move to the trunk and finally to the arms and legs. Each spot of the rash will begin flat and red, but soon a liquid-filled bubble will form on top. Eventually, the bubble will dry out and crust over. The spots are characteristically very itchy on most of the skin, but painful if on the mucus membranes (mouth, eyes, or genitals).

What You Can Do

■ Fever control with acetaminophen is helpful. **Never use aspirin.**

■ Anti-itch lotions and bath additives, such as colloidal oatmeal, are extremely helpful.

■ Oral antihistamines are also useful. Ask your pediatrician for your child's age-appropriate dosage.

■ Keep your child's hands well

washed, his fingernails clipped, and give him a soapy bath daily.

These measures will help decrease the likelihood that any of the open sores will become infected.

Constipation

If the stool is too hard, it can cause your child a great deal of discomfort. If the anus is irritated, or the hard bowel movements cause pain when they come out, your child may try to avoid the bowel movement as long as he can. If he holds the stool inside long enough, it will only become drier, harder, and more painful to evacuate. So, a vicious cycle can develop.

Breastfed babies tend not to have true constipation. Often their bowel movements are relatively more frequent as compared to their formula-fed counterparts. They are typically soft, sometimes runny, mustard-colored with little seeds, and do not cause discomfort.

Typical Symptoms

The consistency of the stool, as well as the discomfort that it causes, are the best ways to tell if your baby is constipated. An infant who is becoming constipated will have bowel movements less frequently than is typical of his previous pattern. Some babies will have a stool pattern of 1 stool every 3 days, and this is perfectly normal as long as the stool remains soft. Therefore, the definition of constipation is more directed at what the stool itself looks like and not the frequency. With severe constipation, hours of crying are typical, and less commonly, blood streaking in the stool from injury to the anus wall can occur.

The Cause

Usually the problem is dietary (inadequate fluid intake once solids have been introduced); rarely is there a physical problem with a child's bowels.

What You Can Do

■ If your baby is less than four months old you may add 2 to 3 ounces of water per day (spread across the day) to his feedings. If this is not adequate, ask your pediatrician for a more aggressive approach (juices or formula additives are sometimes used).

■ Often constipation occurs when cereals are introduced. If you notice your baby's stool getting harder, infant juices may be added to provide extra dietary liquid.

■ If your baby has progressed beyond cereals, you can add softened, pureed prunes, pureed pears, or strained apples to get his digestion back on track.

■ Persistent constipation problems that are present right from birth need to be evaluated by your child's doctor to consider the rare case of intestinal constriction, which would require surgery to be fixed.

Cradle Cap

This common, benign skin condition first appears on the scalp between 6 to 8 weeks of life. It looks like light yellowish scales, which cover the baby's scalp. It may be caused by overactive sebaceous glands, although some feel that there is some fungal component.

■ If you do nothing, it will eventually resolve itself.

■ You can, however, speed its disappearance by rubbing the scalp with baby oil or mineral oil several hours before bath time. Just before the bath, gently comb the softened scales away. Twice a week, shampoo with a selenium sulfide or zinc containing shampoo, carefully avoiding the eyes, and rinse away.

Diaper Rash

The term "diaper rash" is used to describe various conditions that tend to occur in the diaper region. Diaper rashes, if severe, can be quite painful, especially when urine or stool seeps onto sensitive raw skin.

The Cause

There are a number of different causes of rashes in the diaper area. Irritation from watery diarrhea is common, and will be centered around the baby's bottom. Yeast will often be widespread and be accompanied by small red dots. However, telling the difference between yeast, contact dermatitis, and seborrhea can sometimes be difficult, even for an experienced pediatrician. On rare occasions, bacteria can invade the raw skin and cause further problems.

What You Can Do

■ Simple reddening of the skin can be cured quickly with an ointment (zinc oxide ointment, for example, which is available in most drugstores).

■ Frequent diaper changes and leaving the diaper off for 20 to 30 minutes at a time, to expose the diaper area to air, can also be helpful.

■ You can help your child by paying attention to your diet as well, if you are breastfeeding. First, eliminate acidic fruits such as citrus fruits and berries, acidic vegetables such as tomatoes and peppers, and all acidic juices, nuts, chocolate, and processed foods. If that doesn't help, try replacing milk with hard cheese and yogurt.

■ If your baby is already eating supplementary foods, make sure you give him low-acid juices such as white grape juice and mild fruit purees, such as strained pears.

■ If you suspect that the diaper rash is caused by yeast (see Thrush, page 231), you should consult your pediatrician. If your suspicion is confirmed, you will be given an antifungal cream or ointment to apply to the diaper area until the rash is clear.

What the Doctor Can Do

The doctor will help by prescribing the proper medication. There are several ways to treat a diaper rash caused by the thrush fungus, *Candida albicans*. Ask your doctor for advice.

Diarrhea

By diarrhea, we mean a noticeable, roughly twofold increase in stool volume. Diarrhea may be watery, contain blood or mucus, and/or have a foamy appearance. Take a close look, so that you can inform your pediatrician, and if need be, take along a soiled diaper for inspection.

Typical Symptoms

Increased frequency of bowel movements is the key symptom. Diarrhea may be accompanied by fever, abdominal pain, restlessness, and a refusal to eat. Frequent movements, in combination with fever and a refusal to drink or a decrease in urination, should always be a reason to see the doctor.

The Cause

Diarrhea usually is caused by viruses, more rarely by bacteria or other illnesses. Not the infection itself, but the loss of fluid has to be kept under observation.

Because infants need large amounts of fluids, sudden, acute diarrhea can become dangerous quickly, due to the often substantial loss of fluid. Loss of fluid is also exacerbated by fever, vomiting, and refusal to eat.

Important!

If an infant under seven weeks old has diarrhea, he always should be taken to a pediatrician. If your baby has vomiting in addition to the diarrhea, notify your pediatrician immediately.

What You Can Do

As long as your baby is willing to take liquids, the following guidelines apply:

■ If you are still breastfeeding, keep on nursing the baby. If your baby is formula-fed, you should also continue to give the baby formula. Your pediatrician may ask you to give your baby clear liquids or a balanced electrolyte solution. In some circumstances, with a prolonged diarrheal illness, your pediatrician may recommend changing to a soy-based formula for a couple of weeks. This is due to the fact that some babies will become transiently lactose-intolerant after prolonged diarrhea.

■ Balanced electrolyte solutions are available in pharmacies and supermarkets for the replacement of salts and nutrients in babies with vomiting and diarrhea. It is now the practice to "feed through" a diarrheal illness, meaning that you should, in most instances, continue breast or bottle feeding. You may want to supplement your feeding with an electrolyte solution to replace the important salts lost in the diarrhea.

■ Avoid the temptation to give any over-the-counter antidiarrheal medications to your child.

■ Notify your pediatrician for any

diarrhea that has blood or mucus in it, or is accompanied by fever.

What the Doctor Can Do

Usually the parent is really providing the bulk of the medical care in diarrheal illnesses. If the diarrhea lasts for more than a week, your pediatrician may consider ordering tests to determine if there is any other likely cause besides a virus. Rechecking the child's weight in the event of a prolonged diarrheal illness is also important.

Dry Skin

Some babies have dry skin that is rough to the touch. If it is moisturized regularly, two or three times a day, its appearance quickly improves and it feels smooth and supple once again. Dry skin may be an initial indicator of an atopic skin condition—eczema. Predisposition to this condition is hereditary (see Allergies, page 218). If your baby has dry skin, smoothing moisturizers on it or using bath oils has to become part of your daily routine. Ask your doctor to recommend suitable products.

Febrile Seizures

You've just put your soon-to-be one-year-old or even older child to bed. Though he was cheerful up to this point, he feels a little warm now. Scarcely have you shut the door behind you when you hear him flailing in his crib. When you look in, you are terribly alarmed, because your child is twitching all over.

Typical Symptoms

The child makes rhythmic convulsive movements of his arms or legs. He may stiffen. He will be unresponsive to voice or touch until it is over. The duration of the seizure is usually a few moments, but, although rare, can be longer—up to a half hour or more.

The Cause

Febrile seizures usually occur between the age of 6 months and 4 years, most commonly in the second year. They occur with rapidly rising fever in children who usually have a hereditary susceptibility to this condition. Sometimes the upper respiratory infection, ear infection, or other infection is just getting underway, and may be unnoticed by you.

What You Can Do

■ Place your child on a soft surface from which he can't fall, such as a carpeted floor.

■ Don't try to stop the convulsive twitching.

■ Loosen his clothing if it is tight around his neck.

■ If the seizure stops quickly, try to bring the fever down quickly with acetaminophen suppositories, sponge baths, or cold compresses to the body.

Important!

If the seizure ends after one to two minutes, call your pediatrician. If the convulsion lasts longer than a minute, or if the seizure begins again, call your local emergency number.

■ After his first febrile seizure, every child needs to be evaluated to determine the cause.

Fever

Fever is an indication that the body is mounting a response to an infection. It is not certain if the fever itself has any value in fighting off the infection—if it does, it is very small. Evaporated water loss contributing to dehydration, risk of febrile seizures, and the discomfort that it produces makes it worthwhile to treat a fever in a child.

The Cause

The fever is both a by-product of an increased metabolic rate during illness, and a resetting of the body's thermostat to fight the infection. Remember, it is the body's response to an infection, not the bacteria or virus itself, that is causing the fever. Thus, how high a fever is does not correlate directly with whether or not it is a severe infection.

What You Can Do

Stay calm! Even if the thermometer's reading is 105 degrees Fahrenheit (40.1°C) your baby will not boil! Reducing the fever with acetaminophen or ibuprofen (if recommended by your pediatrician) is a good idea. If your child seems to feel fine, then the infection is less likely to be serious, but if he is lethargic or irritable, then your doctor should know right away. In any case, if your child is less than 3 months old, an immediate phone call is mandatory.

What the Doctor Can Do

The physician will make a diagnosis and decide if the illness requires any treatment other than fever-reducing medication. Fever due to bacterial infection can be eliminated after 1 to 2 days of antibiotics. Viral infections, the most common cause of a spiking fever, do not respond to antibiotics. They last 5 to 7 days and then disappear on their own. Have the doctor tell you what the course of the illness is likely to be, to spare yourself unnecessary worry.

Fretfulness

Not all babies are peaceful little angels all of the time. There are some "fidgeters" among them who often rattle their parents with their constant restlessness. This kind of temperament may already have announced itself when the child was in his mother's womb.

Many poorly understood factors play a role here. Level of alertness, ease of arousability from sleep, discomfort thresholds, and "nervous energy" probably contribute to this temperament. There is probably a hereditary component.

What You Can Do

■ Ask the baby's grandparents if either the mother or the father had similar temperaments as a child.

■ If the baby's fretfulness takes the form of sleep problems and irritable crying, it can be quite trying on the parents. See pages 75–78 of this book, where you will find additional tips for fidgety babies.

Gas Pains

Almost every baby has to deal with a little gassiness from time to time. Particularly in the first weeks and months, however, the pains can be uncomfortable for your baby and disquieting to you. The gas pains themselves are not harmful.

Typical Symptoms

The gas pains usually begin when the baby is two to three weeks old, and often occur in the afternoon and evening. The child becomes restless, cries, and has a distinctly bloated abdomen. He tries to force out the gas, drawing up his legs, contracting down his abdomen, and closing his vocal cords—turning red in the face and causing a high-pitched cry in the process. Eventually the gas will be expelled, sometimes with a bowel movement, and the child will quiet until the gas reaccumulates.

The Cause

Gas pains are caused by the distention of the bowel, by gas that is swallowed and by gas that is produced in the intestine. Occasionally, a baby does not break down milk sugar—lactose—completely. If this occurs, bacteria in the bowel will ferment the excess sugar, causing gas. Some components of the diet of a breastfeeding mother can contribute to gassiness. Some babies swallow more air when they feed than others, and still others do not burp as well as they might. Unfortunately, once the abdominal discomfort begins, your baby will cry—which only leads to even more swallowed air and a downward spiral.

What You Can Do

Before you try anything, come to terms with the fact that although you can sometimes help ease the discomfort, nothing that you do will make the pains vanish for good—only time will take care of that.

■ Carrying the baby around—often belly down is helpful (see flying position, page 66).

■ Burping your baby as you carry him around can help to dislodge the air that he has just swallowed while crying—thus helping to prevent as much pain tomorrow.

■ Simethicone antigas drops do not

COLIC

For the severe, rare form of gas pains, with crying bouts of up to three hours per day and more, we use the term "colic"—that is, intestinal spasms. It begins gradually—about the fourth week—and stops sometimes abruptly at around four months old. Parents are then amazed to see how cheerful their baby can be.

work in the short run—they are preventive and will help your baby separate the gas from other bowel contents so that it can be expelled more easily.

■ If you are breastfeeding, avoid broccoli, cabbage, eggs, cauliflower, and brussels sprouts, as well as hyperallergenic foods, such as cow's milk, fish, and nuts.

■ Occasionally a switch in the type of formula can be helpful, but this should be done with the help of your pediatrician so that you're not just switching brand names, but actually the content of the formula.

Hip Dislocation

Hip dislocation (dysplasia) can be present at birth or develop over time. If untreated, it can lead to limping and the need for corrective surgery later on. The causes are both genetic and physical, such as with breech delivery (see page 209).

What You Can Do

If you know that you or the father's side of the family has members with congenital dislocation of the hip, you should let your baby's doctor know so that he can pay extra close attention to the hips at your regular visits.

What the Doctor Can Do

Your pediatric provider will examine your child's hips at every visit until he is walking normally. If there are any indications of a dislocation, then an ultrasound or x-ray tests may be performed to help diagnose the disorder, although sometimes the diagnosis is clear without these studies. Treatment is in the form of an abduction splint (also known as a Pavlik harness).

Important!

Consistently wearing the harness early on is necessary to make sure that your child develops normally. Generally after a few months it will no longer be necessary, but wait for the specialist to give the "okay" to stop using it.

Hydrocele (Swollen Testicle at Birth)

Usually it is the right testicle, but it may be both. It will be present at birth. The swelling will generally disappear on its own within the first year, but if you notice an enlargement or if it persists after 1 year, you should visit your pediatrician, because some children will need corrective surgery.

Jaundice

"Physiologic jaundice" in newborns is not a true disease. Rather, it is a symptom that occurs in two-thirds of healthy newborns in the first days of life. You will notice a yellow-tinging of his skin and the whites of his eyes. As a rule, if there is no underlying disorder causing the jaundice, it will subside without treatment in the first week of life.

The Cause

The yellowing is caused by a pigment called *bilirubin*. The bilirubin is produced as a by-product of the breakdown of excess blood within your baby's bloodstream. The baby's immature liver, whose job it is to remove the bilirubin from the blood and expel it with the stool, becomes overloaded. The bilirubin then can build up in the baby's system and show itself in the skin and eyes. All babies do this to a greater or lesser extent, but sometimes the jaundice is so slight that it goes unnoticed by parents. Sometimes the jaundice is more pronounced in breastfeeding babies.

What the Doctor Can Do

While physiologic jaundice is not a disease, if your baby is yellow enough, your doctor may want to determine that there isn't another cause and blood tests will be necessary. If you notice any jaundice, your baby's doctor should know, so that these tests, if needed, can be performed right away.

Other Causes of Jaundice

If the jaundice is severe, it may be that the excess blood is being broken down too fast, which can occur with an incompatibility between the mother's and the baby's blood type, bloodstream infections, or inherited weakwalled blood cells. Alternatively, if there is a problem with the liver, even a normal amount of bilirubin production will result in overly high levels of bilirubin.

■ If treatment is needed, it is best performed early—special lights shined on the baby can have great results.

■ Don't worry if the bilirubin lights (also called *phototherapy*) are being used—this is a preventive measure.

■ Your baby can come out of the lights for frequent feedings (which is also helpful for removing bilirubin), but should go right back in soon afterward. The treatment of jaundice with lights is easy, but if it fails, further treatment is more drastic, so the time under phototherapy should be maximized.

Middle Ear Infection

Usually middle ear infection is rare in the first three months. Later on, it can be associated with colds and upper respiratory infections.

Typical Symptoms

Ear pain is often present, although your child cannot tell you about it. Sometimes the child will pull at the affected ear, although children will pull at their ears when there is nothing wrong as well.

The Cause

The middle ear is an air-filled cavity that lies beyond the extremely sensitive eardrum. Air is supplied to it through a narrow cartilaginous tube (eustachian tube) from the nasal part of the pharynx. If the nasal mucous membrane is inflamed and swollen, air cannot travel through this tube into the middle ear. Pain can result from infections of the cavity that involve a build-up of fluid or pus.

What You Can Do

Your child's doctor will need to see your child. However, if the pain develops overnight, using acetaminophen or ibuprofen is helpful. If you have leftover anesthetic eardrops from a previous ear infection, it is okay to use them overnight, but they will not cure the infection, so a visit to the pediatrician is still needed.

What the Doctor Can Do

Only an evaluation of the eardrum and canal can establish the diagnosis conclusively. Your doctor will choose an appropriate antibiotic and dose it according to your child's most up-to-date weight.

Roseola

This is a harmless viral infection that affects children usually between 6 and 18 months old. It makes a lasting impression on parents because it may be the first time their child gets a high fever.

Typical Symptoms

Roseola is sometimes known as "three-day fever," and true to its name, it will usually produce fever for three to four days, which may get as high as 104 to 105 degrees Fahrenheit (40–40.1°C). Typically, the fever has little influence on the child's well-being (although sometimes a febrile seizure will result). Most children will continue to eat, drink, and play, just as usual. When the fever disappears on the third or fourth day, a rash appears. Generally the pale pink rash appears on the neck and trunk, does not affect the face and extremities, and lasts for 1 to 2 days.

The Cause

Roseola is caused by a virus. It is not highly contagious, but like any other virus, it can be passed to other susceptible children. Roseola occurs mainly in the spring and fall.

What You Can Do

Since children with roseola usually do not feel sick, treatment is necessary only if the high fever is making the child uncomfortable, with symptoms such as irritability, sweating, lethargy.

Then an antipyretic (fever-reducing) agent such as acetaminophen or ibuprofen can be given. Ibuprofen is usually indicated for fevers higher than 102.5 degrees Fahrenheit (38.7°C), and should not be given to a child who is dehydrated. A warm or lukewarm bath may also be helpful in bringing the fever down temporarily.

Skin Problems in Newborns

After a baby has spent nine months floating around in the amniotic fluid, the dry indoor air to which his skin is now exposed may cause considerable irritation. As a result, the complexion of many newborns is a colorful expanse of blotchy, reddened areas that come and go quickly and have no pathologic significance.

There is, for example, a rash called *erythema toxicum neonatorum*, which typically consists of red blotches with tiny central yellowish bumps that can occur anywhere on the body. It usually appears in the first few days of life and disappears in the first 1 to 2 weeks. It is a benign rash that needs no specific treatment.

Another very common newborn rash is *milia*, which consists of tiny, yellowish, raised dots on the nose and chin and results from clogged oil glands.

All of these conditions disappear without treatment and are no cause for worry. For information and tips on treating cradle cap and dry skin, see pages 221 and 223.

Spitting Up

Spitting up is one of the most common symptoms in infancy. Some babies spit up so frequently that parents gradually become frustrated, because the baby's clothes and bed linens, as well as his mother's blouses, constantly have to be laundered to remove the sour smell of gastric juice.

Spitting up—the easy, painless bringing up of small amounts of food— is almost a natural event, something quite different from real vomiting (see page 237).

Spitting up when the baby burps sometimes occurs hours after a feeding. Even when the baby is lying on his stomach and wiggles back and forth a little, or when he simply tenses his stomach muscles slightly when crying or laughing, something may "come back up."

The Cause

In infancy, the sphincter or muscular bundle between the stomach and the esophagus does not yet function properly. In addition, the tube leads directly into the stomach at this stage, while later on it bends in such a way that the contents of the stomach can flow backward only with great difficulty.

The process is reminiscent of a full bottle that lacks a cork: Shake it a little and the contents will spill over the top.

What You Can Do

■ Ask your doctor whether there is any cause for concern. If your baby continues to gain weight despite spitting up, which is usually the case, only patience and time will help in the final analysis. As a rule, the symptom disappears on its own once the baby begins solid foods and begins sitting up on his own.

■ If your baby seems to be spitting up more than average, you should discuss this with your doctor. He may recommend thickening the formula with $1/2$ to 1 tsp. of rice cereal per ounce of formula, and/or elevating the head of your baby's crib to a 45 degree angle for 1 hour after feeding.

■ If you are bottlefeeding, ask your pediatrician if your baby is taking excessive volumes in one sitting.

Swollen Breasts in Your Newborn

Some newborns, especially those born after their due date, have enlarged breasts from the second or third day on. Both boys and girls are affected equally. In rare cases, the breasts even secrete a few drops of milk, the so-called "witch's milk."

This occurrence, though rare, is completely normal. It is triggered by residual maternal hormones, which were cleared from the baby through the placenta during pregnancy, but now have a temporary effect inside the baby's body.

What You Can Do

■ Here, your motto should be wait and see. Don't press on the swollen breasts. By applying pressure, you could allow bacteria to gain entry, and that would produce inflammation.

■ If the breasts become reddened and sensitive to pressure, inform your pediatrician immediately. Antibiotics may be required to prevent the formation of an abscess (a pocket or collection of infection).

Tear Duct Blockage

It is not rare at all for one of the baby's eyes to be stuck shut in the morning from blockage in a tear duct.

Typical Symptoms

Yellowish mucus mixed with tears collects in the corner of the eye. Sometimes, both eyes may be affected. Constant tearing when the baby is not crying is another sign of tear duct blockage.

The Cause

If present from birth, the cause of the blockage is delayed development of the lacrimal duct (tear duct), which drains fluid from the eyes down into the nose. In older infants, upper respiratory illnesses can often cause temporary blockages.

What You Can Do

■ Even though this is a benign condition, you should always consult your pediatrician if your baby has a collection of mucus in the eye or excessive tearing.

■ After washing your hands thoroughly, you can massage the inner corner of the eye with the tip of your little finger, making downward movements.

■ If the eye develops redness or the discharge from the eye becomes thick, you should check in again with your pediatrician—antibiotic eye ointment may be necessary at this time. You should always check in with your doctor's office before using the ointment, since it should not be used on a chronic or ongoing basis.

Teething Pain

Teething pain is a mild discomfort of the gums, beginning sometime before the teeth actually begin to break through the skin at 5 to 7 months of age.

Typical Symptoms

The earliest symptom of teething is heavy drooling. There may also be a certain irritability and wakefulness, which may concern parents. Many babies enjoy biting on hard objects at this time—"gumming." You can occasionally see the reddening and swelling of the gums that heralds the eruption of a new tooth; the child will be very sensitive to touch in this spot. Remember that teething is not a cause of fever or diarrhea, and these symptoms should be evaluated at the doctor's office.

What You Can Do

■ Sometimes a teething ring is enough.

■ Your baby may feel better if you rub a pain-relieving ointment on his gums (available over-the-counter in pharmacies and drugstores). These ointments work well, but the effect doesn't last very long.

■ If none of that helps, and your child is restless and wakeful, help him through the night with a dose of acetaminophen. It is best though, before giving the acetaminophen to check his temperature—you don't want to mask a fever by giving acetaminophen frequently.

■ Do not give teething pills; your baby could choke. Remember that teething pain is normal and will pass!

Thrush

This yeast infection can affect the mucous membranes (mouth) and diaper area in infants (for treatment, see also Diaper Rash, page 221).

Typical Symptoms

Your baby suddenly has white patches in his mouth, not only on his tongue but on the insides of his cheeks and gums as well. Most babies are not at all bothered by thrush, but others may cry while eating or not eat well. If you try to scrape off the white patches with the handle of a small spoon, you will note reddening of the underlying lining of the mouth.

The Cause

Thrush is a relatively harmless yeast, which very quickly builds up in the oral cavity. Yeast is ubiquitous in our environment and loves the mouths and diaper areas of infants. It is a rare baby that does not have at least one bout of thrush in the mouth or diaper area during infancy.

The use of antibiotics can predispose your baby to this condition. It is also seen in children who share toys or pacifiers and who use nipples dropped multiple times without cleaning.

Many times you will see both thrush and a yeast diaper rash at the same time. The yeast in the mouth are swallowed and travel into the intestines. When they pass into the stool, they can cause diaper rash.

What the Doctor Can Do

■ You should pay a visit to your pediatrician: He or she will confirm the diagnosis and select an appropriate antifungal medication.

■ There are various oral solutions with which you dab the baby's mouth, using a cotton swab or your clean finger, several times a day, and which you should allow your baby to swallow.

You should administer these drops after a feeding, not before; otherwise, they will get washed away quickly.

■ It takes several days for the patches of thrust to disappear. Should no improvement be apparent within 7 days, however, take your baby back to the doctor's office. You may need to change to a different medication.

Umbilical Hernias

If you can feel a weakness in the umbilical area (belly button) or the navel, protrudes when the baby cries, he may have an umbilical hernia. This is not uncommon. Your pediatrician should follow up on this at your checkups. Rarely does this type of hernia result in the kinds of complications that hernias cause elsewhere in the body. The situation usually

THE TEETH AREN'T ALWAYS TO BLAME

Many parents tend to blame all their baby's problems on teething. But the teeth are only rarely the real culprits. Fever, diarrhea, and irritability simply happen to be common symptoms in infancy. Keep this in mind: While teething, babies are also susceptible to all kinds of infections.

resolves itself completely by the time a child is 2 to 3 years old or by 5 years old for larger hernias.

Other Umbilical Problems

Every few years, our ideas of what constitutes proper care of the healing navel, or umbilical stump, change. Today we are advised that keeping the area dry and clean with rubbing alcohol and exposed to air is the best method (for more on cord care, see page 52). The area at the top of the cord stump usually dries up and offers no breeding ground for bacteria. Concentrate your efforts on the base of the cord. Keep it clean with rubbing alcohol. Your baby may cry when you clean it, but this is only because the rubbing alcohol is cold; your baby is not feeling pain. Don't worry if the stump is still a little wet and sticky or even bleeds slightly from time to time before it is completely dry. Other problems are rare, but may appear: The site may continue to ooze, or infections or other changes may appear in the umbilical area.

The Cause

The cord itself is no longer alive, and it does not receive blood flow or any protection from your baby's immune system. Bacteria may like the warm, moist, unprotected area at the base of the cord. If the skin around the cord becomes red and swollen and if yellowish material is draining from the cord stump, you should consult your pediatrician immediately! This is an infection in the skin around the cord and requires antibiotics.

What You Can Do

■ If the navel continues to ooze and the cord does not dry up, expose it to air for at least five minutes every time you change the diaper, and clean the area with isopropyl or rubbing alcohol.

■ If the navel continually discharges small quantities of clear fluid, the baby has to be seen by the pediatrician.

■ If bleeding occurs days after birth, you should consult the doctor.

■ If there is redness surrounding the umbilicus, a foul smell, or pus, call your pediatrician immediately. Infections of the cord are a true emergency.

Undescended Testicles

In newborn boys born prematurely, it is not uncommon for one or both testicles to fail to descend into the scrotal sac by the time of birth. In full-term baby boys, this is less common. If both testicles are undescended at birth, this should be evaluated while still in the hospital. Your pediatrician will decide if any tests are needed to determine the location of the testicles. If only one is undescended, then watchful waiting is usually adequate.

In the next few weeks to months, the other testicle will appear. If one testicle remains undescended after the sixth month, your pediatrician will consult a pediatric urologist or pediatric surgeon for further treatment options.

Upper Respiratory Tract Infections (URI or Colds)

Upper respiratory tract infections are probably the most common cause of illness during the first year of life. Luckily, these infections rarely are serious. You just have to learn how to handle them.

Typical Symptoms

The early signs may be difficult to interpret: Often the rhythm of sleeping and waking is out of kilter, and the baby is fussy. Vomiting is not uncommon at the beginning of the illness. Soon, the hallmark nasal congestion and runny nose followed by coughing will appear. Decreased appetite because of the stuffed nasal passages or throat irritation is not uncommon. Fever, if present, should last only a few days, and if your baby is under the age of three months and has a fever greater than 100.4 degrees Fahrenheit (38°C), he should be evaluated by the pediatrician.

Important!

Even with harmless viral infections, complications are possible.

■ *Continual crying may indicate that your baby has the beginnings of a middle ear infection.*

■ *In infants under 3 months old, fever over 100.4 degrees Fahrenheit (38°C) is always a reason to have the baby seen by a doctor.*

■ *Restlessness and shortness of breath could indicate bronchiolitis or pneumonia. These symptoms also warrant a trip to the doctor's office.*

The Cause

Viruses are almost always the cause of such infections (see page 215). Typically, in infancy the symptoms do not confine themselves to the upper respiratory passages. The younger the child, the less able he is to localize an infection. Sometimes, lower airway inflammation develops, in addition to the symptoms in the nose and throat area. Difficulty breathing may sometimes show up as poor feeding. Usually, however, it is a throat inflammation or stuffy nose that causes discomfort and interferes with the baby's ability to feed well. The baby may have a stuffy nose through which he cannot breathe properly. Infants less than 2 months old don't know how to breathe through their mouths, so a stuffed nose may be worse than a runny nose. Upper airway mucus will give your baby a raspy breathing sound, which reverberates in his lungs although there is no real chest congestion. This is different than wheezing or the sounds of pneumonia.

What You Can Do

With minor infections, especially as your child grows older, you rarely need to intervene.

■ If your baby is less than 3 months old, you should have him checked at the pediatrician's office.

■ Check for difficulty in breathing—if you are not absolutely sure, then have him seen at the doctor's office.

■ Saltwater drops or spray can help wash the mucus out of the nose of younger infants—sometimes initiating coughing and sneezing, which also helps to clear the baby's nasal passageways.

■ If there is a fever and your baby is less than 3 months old, he should be seen immediately—that day—by his doctor. If he is older, the fever goes away quickly, and there are no other problems—poor appetite, vomiting, diarrhea, lethargy, or irritability—you can probably nurse him through the illness on your own.

■ Avoid excessively dry hot air in your house. A vaporizer or humidifier may help—especially in the dry, winter months. Increasing fluids orally will also be of benefit.

■ Ask your doctor before using any over-the-counter remedies. In small babies, they may have undesirable side effects, including an increase in irritability.

Vaginal Discharge of Mucus and Blood

Whitish mucus discharge is common during the first few days of life in newborn girls. Sometimes, after several days, blood may appear. The same body physiology that occurs with the menstrual cycle is occurring. During pregnancy, the mother's hormones crossed the placenta and built up the lining of her daughter's uterus. With the cord cut, the hormones dissipate and the uterine lining breaks down, causing newborn vaginal bleeding. This usually appears in the first several days after birth and disappears by 7 to 10 days of age.

Vomiting

Vomiting is one of the most common symptoms of illness in infants. It is different from "reflux" or spitting up, in that it is forceful evacuation of the stomach contents, usually preceded by a wave of nausea.

Typical Symptoms

Your child cannot tell you about the nausea, but it may be noticeable in the form of refusal to eat. The vomit itself will smell sour, appear to be the food or formula that was recently consumed, but becomes more clear and contains gastric juices and mucus with repetitive vomiting as the stomach empties.

235

Important!

If your child spits up or vomits several times a day, you should consult the pediatrician. If the child loses substantial amounts of fluid, there is a danger of dehydration. Keep an eye on the frequency of urination. The pediatrician will want to know this information because it is a good gauge of your baby's hydration status.

The Cause

There are many different causes. The most common cause is a gastrointestinal upset from a "stomach virus." However, in the appropriate setting other causes should be considered,

---

CHECKLISTS FOR COLDS (URIs)

What the pediatrician will want to know when you phone for advice:

■ *How long has the baby been sick?*

■ *What was the first sign of illness?*

■ *Is he refusing to eat or drink?*

■ *Has he vomited or does he have diarrhea?*

■ *Does he have a cough or a runny nose?*

■ *Does he have a fever? If so, have you given him any medicine and how much?*

■ *Is anyone else at home or in contact with the baby sick?*

---

especially if it is green, if it is projectile (traveling a couple of feet), lasts for more than 2 days, is associated with unrelenting abdominal pain and fever, or if your child is refusing all

fluids. With any of these symptoms, your child should be evaluated in the doctor's office.

What You Can Do

It is advisable to wait about 1 hour after a bout of vomiting. At this point you can give your child a clear feeding—diluted apple juice, diluted white grape juice, or an electrolyte solution. The best approach is small, frequent feedings of clear fluids at first. You can give 1 teaspoon every 5 minutes for the first 2 hours and then slowly advance to a larger volume and include bland foods such as crackers, toast, applesauce, or clear soup.

Whooping Cough (Pertussis)

Whooping cough is a respiratory illness caused by a bacteria. All newborns are routinely immunized against this bacteria included in the 5-dose DPT/DTaP vaccine series given at 2, 4, 6, and 12 to 18 months and a booster at age 4 to 6 years. We still see whooping cough in children who have not yet been fully immunized, or never immunized, and more recently in adolescents and adults with waning immunity from the vaccine.

Pertussis occurs worldwide. The word *pertussis* means intensive cough. In China it is called "cough of 100 days." Pertussis infection can be very serious in young infants, whereas in adolescents and adults it is considered a minor infection, but one that includes a bothersome, long-lasting cough, with the potential of spread to unimmunized young babies or the elderly.

Typical Symptoms

Whooping cough has three phases. The first stage consists mainly of runny nose and low-grade fever; the second includes the coughing spells (5 to 10 forceful coughs in a row) with or without a whoop attached at the end of the spell (younger infants tend not to have the classic associated whoop); and then the last stage is the convalescent or recovery phase of the illness. The illness lasts approximately 6 to 8 weeks. Also noteworthy is that vomiting may occur after the coughing spell. Many older patients look and feel quite well in between the coughing spells.

In young infants (less than 6 months old), whooping cough can be more serious and, therefore, should always be evaluated and followed closely by a doctor.

What You Can Do

■ It is essential to have the pediatrician confirm the diagnosis. Is it really whooping cough? If the diagnosis is confirmed, then treatment with antibiotics is necessary since after 5 days of treatment the child can no longer spread the disease. If antibiotic treatment is started in the first phase of

SPITTING UP OR VOMITING?

Spitting up is different from true vomiting. It is the result of inadequate closure of the muscle at the junction of the esophagus and stomach. Spitting up is very common in infants. Some infants may spit up a little after each feeding. As long as it is only a small amount (1 to 2 teaspoons), and doesn't have a greenish color or travel in the air across the room, it is the normal spitting up of infancy.

whooping cough, then the duration of illness will be shortened. If the child is already in the coughing stage, the duration of illness will not be affected, but the communicability will be decreased.

■ Family members should also receive prophylactic antibiotics to prevent further spread of the disease, even if they have been recently vaccinated.

■ Unfortunately, there are no truly effective medications to make the coughing less explosive. The presence of the child's father and/or mother, who can make the attacks less agonizing by providing comfort or diversion, is still the best and most helpful measure for getting through this disease in early infancy.

SIDS: FACTS AND PREVENTION

Until a few years ago, about three out of every 1,000 newborns died suddenly in their sleep—at night or during an afternoon nap—in the course of the first year, usually before the sixth month of life. Subsequent investigation yielded no indication of the cause of death. These mysterious circumstances caused all new parents to dread the possibility of crib death, or sudden infant death syndrome (SIDS).

Since then, medical scientists have been working aggressively to combat this horrible occurrence and with some success. Extensive research worldwide is showing that there are probably many contributing factors to SIDS including:

■ Certain children are at increased risk for SIDS. They are premature infants or those who had a low birth weight and tend to have spells of apnea—temporary suspension of respiration—while sleeping. Infants with these risk factors will be watched closely in the neonatal nursery with specialized monitoring devices. They are not released until these spells resolve. Sometimes infants who have outgrown the apnea spells will be sent home with

monitors that sound an alarm if the baby's rate of respiration or heartbeat drops too low.

■ Respiratory viruses have been isolated from up to 20 percent of SIDS cases. These same viruses, so harmful to young infants, cause nothing more than cold symptoms in adults and older children. Hence, keeping people with cold symptoms away from your young baby is of paramount importance. All infants less than 3 months old with cold symptoms should see their pediatrician.

■ Always lay your baby to sleep on his back on a standard firm infant mattress. If he has frequent or severe spitting up, discuss this sleep position with your baby's doctor.

■ Infants of mothers who smoked during and after pregnancy carry increased risk. If you are nicotine addicted, quit or smoke outside the house—smoking in the presence of your baby will further increase the risk.

■ Crowded living conditions increases risk.

■ Feeding the baby formula rather than breast milk increases risk.

THE ESSENTIALS OF CARING FOR A SICK BABY

Loving care makes everyone healthy faster, including your sick baby.

At this time especially, he is in need of your attention, your presence, and your warmth.

However, it takes a little know-how as well to look after a sick child.

On the pages that follow, we will tell you all you really need to know about

helping an infant through an illness.

Actually, you don't have such a lot to learn about taking care of your sick baby: After all, he is completely reliant on your care even when he is in good health. You are already used to keeping him clean, feeding him, and keeping him safe and comfortable. You just have to do those things to an intensified degree when he is sick:

■ Your baby doesn't know what is wrong with him.

■ Often he is incapable of making his needs known.

■ Illness makes him even more passive than usual.

For these reasons, it is especially important that you stay close to your child and pay attention to him at this time. If you can concentrate on your baby during his illness, without being distracted, then the essential things— like adequate fluid intake and regular elimination (that means soiled, or at least wet, diapers)—will not escape you. Further, if you've paid close attention, your observations can help the physician make the diagnosis.

Often, the baby's illness will be mild because of the maternal antibodies, which crossed the placenta during pregnancy, that help protect him. However, if infants do become seriously ill, they do not have the same reserves as older children and adults.

239

The trick lies in being able to evaluate the situation correctly and, even in an emergency, to avoid panic. With your doctor's help, you can do this successfully. Everything else you need to know about handling a sick child is presented on the following pages.

■ One last tip before we get started. Protect other children, too, against contagion. Don't take your sick baby to places where other children are likely to be!

At-Home Care

It is nicest for both you and your sick child if he can be treated at home. In his familiar environment, he can recuperate best, and you, too, will find things easier to manage in your own home. One requirement, of course, is that someone keep an eye on the baby 24 hours a day. Under no circumstances should you or anyone else, leave him alone at this time. Naturally, you can take turns with your husband, your mother, or a friend, but it is your company that your child wants most. He doesn't feel well—and he wants comfort and support from you. That doesn't mean that you have to spend every minute beside his crib, but do stay nearby or take him with you to other rooms in his bassinet or carriage. Turn on the baby monitor (see page 260) if your child is in a different room. And while he is sick, let him sleep in your room next to your bed at night.

The Sickroom

■ Your baby will sleep best at a room temperature of 68 to 70 degrees Fahrenheit (20–22°C). Hot, dry rooms can dry the nasal passages and make an already congested baby more uncomfortable.

■ Fresh, not overly dry air is especially pleasant. If it is warm outside, you can leave the window open. In cold weather, air out the room when the baby is not in it.

■ Cool mist humidifiers or vaporizers that are cleansed at frequent intervals can help keep the air in your baby's room from becoming too dry. If your baby has croup, you can turn on the hot water in the shower to create *steam* and then sit in the bathroom with your baby for 10 minutes. This can have a calming effect for your child.

Handling a Sick Baby

■ Don't immediately put your child in quarantine: With minor illnesses, being out in the fresh air will do the baby a great deal of good; you can continue to take him out as usual.

Even cold air will not harm your baby at this time!

■ If your child is seriously ill and has a high fever, you should avoid all extreme stimuli: The baby should be shielded from heat, sunlight, wind, cold, wet, noise, and commotion.

■ If he has fever, don't wrap him up too warmly. He could become over-heated, since he can't regulate his body temperature the way an adult does. Dress him in the usual way, and cover him loosely.

■ If the fever is making your baby uncomfortable, choose antipyretic medications rather than sponge baths or compresses. Your baby's body has sent a signal to his thermoregulatory center in his brain saying that it wants a certain temperature. The medications erase that signal. Cold compresses and baths help only temporarily. The child may shiver and shake to try to regain that temperature again.

The Office Visit

Call first if you are uncertain that your child needs to be seen by a doctor. If your child has a contagious disease, you should let the doctor know, since some practices have a special waiting room for sick children. If the office is not open on weekends and holidays, you should call your doctor's office to speak to the covering physician to decide whether to meet in the office

—— ESPECIALLY FOR FATHERS ——

Caring for a sick child is your job also. Particularly if both you and your spouse work, you will need to help out as well. This is especially true if your wife is ill or has professional commitments. Start participating in your child's care now, during your free time—whether he is sick or well; then you won't be at a loss in an emergency. This assurance alone will take a huge burden off your wife.

or go to the nearest walk-in clinic or emergency room.

Tricks for Managing the Baby

Reassured by your talk with the doctor, you are ready to begin treating the baby "as the doctor ordered." And you find out that it's not that easy. How can you give the baby his liquid medicine, suppository, or nose drops without causing crying and fussing, and prevent the little bundle of energy from bringing it all right back up?

Giving Liquid Medicine

■ Your baby is not yet able to swallow tablets or pills, nor will they be prescribed for him. However, occasionally a medication is available only in pill

241

form. It should be crushed between 2 spoons or in a garlic press. It can then be placed in the baby's formula or pureed fruit.

■ The majority of medications for infants—antipyretics, antibiotics, and so on—come in liquid form and are easy to administer. Some babies fight taking medicine and will readily spit it out. This is usually an older baby, and you can try to disguise the medicine in juice or his favorite foods. Antipyretics—such as acetaminophen—come in a suppository form as well, which is an effective and easier way to administer this medicine to some babies.

■ You may want to purchase a needleless syringe (usually a plastic, tubelike apparatus) for administering liquid medicine. Many pharmacists will dispense one with your medication. You can draw the medicine into the syringe, without the needle of course, and give it slowly, by squirting small amounts of medicine into one side of your baby's mouth, taking breaks to let him swallow.

Giving Saline Nose Drops

■ *Hold the baby on your lap or on the changing table on his back with his head slightly bent back. Place one or two drops in each nostril, one nostril at a time. Wait for a few seconds as gravity works to settle the drops into the nasal passages, then use the bulb syringe you received when the baby was born, and suction at the tip of the nose. Take care not to insert the bulb syringe into the baby's nose—it will worsen the blockage and cause irritation.*

Giving Suppositories

Suppositories have a soft surface that is designed to melt easily inside a body cavity. You can lubricate the tip of a suppository with petroleum jelly if so desired. There is a rich network of blood vessels in the rectum, making absorption of medicine very efficient.

■ *Lay your baby on his back on the changing table. Hold both ankles between the thumb and index finger or between the index finger and middle finger of one hand, and bend the baby's legs slightly. With your free hand, slowly but firmly push the suppository into the rectum, then press the baby's buttocks*

together and lower his legs to the table surface. Wait two minutes, distracting your child by cuddling and playing all the while; otherwise, the suppository may pop out again in a flash! Don't be afraid that inserting a suppository will hurt your baby—it won't!

Taking the Temperature Without a Fuss

A baby's temperature can be taken rectally, under the arm, or digitally in the ear. Under the age of 3 months, it is best to take the temperature with a rectal thermometer. In children, normal body temperature measured rectally ranges between 98 and 99.6 degrees Fahrenheit (36.8–37.5°C). If the baby's illness is accompanied by

fever, you should check his temperature several times a day.

A digital thermometer is the fastest and safest method, though more expensive, with a beeper sound to indicate that the reading is complete. The standard mercury thermometer is more difficult to read, but is okay to use if great care is taken so that it does not break while in your baby's bottom. The mercury is in a nontoxic form, but the broken glass may cause a small cut or scrape. Clean the thermometer afterward with lukewarm water and soap.

To Take the Temperature Rectally:

■ *Lay your baby on his back on the changing table. Hold his feet together with one hand, with his knees flexed up toward his abdomen—this is a comfortable position for babies and thus he will be less likely to fight you. The insertion of the thermometer does not hurt, but an uncomfortable position will annoy him.*

■ *Lubricate the tip of the thermometer generously with petroleum jelly. Insert the thermometer about $^1/_2$ inch and leave it in place for 2 minutes. If it is a mercury thermometer, remember to shake the mercury down into the silver-colored base before beginning. Also remember never to use an oral thermometer rectally.*

Compresses and Baths for Fever

Generally antifever medication is preferred. But if it is not adequate, sometimes compresses or baths can be helpful.

■ *For the compresses, moisten a clean washcloth and lay it folded across your child's forehead. You can also pat other parts of his body to cool him. Don't force him to keep it on if he isn't comfortable with it there, because the purpose is then defeated. If your child is older, immersion in a warm tub for a few minutes will be helpful. The warm water will dilate the blood vessels close to the surface of his skin and allow for better heat dissipation—a cold bath will make him feel uncomfortable and make him shiver. As the water evaporates from his skin, his temperature will be reduced. Sponge baths will help increase evaporative heat loss, but the blood vessels in his skin won't dilate like they do during a bath, so the effect is less.*

Taking a Urine Sample

Rarely will you be asked by your doctor to collect a urine sample from your child at home. On occasion when your child is older, he may need to give a first morning sample to be brought into the office. But on most occasions, if your doctor needs to examine your child's urine, the sample will be collected in the doctor's office.

What to Keep an Eye On: Fluid Intake and Elimination

Babies are especially susceptible to fluid loss. If vomiting or diarrhea is present, the loss can be dramatic. If he has fever as well, the baby's body loses even more water. And in addition, if your baby is too lethargic to drink, dehydration can quickly become a threat.

■ As long as you are breastfeeding, you should keep on nursing consistently and feed the baby at least every four hours—even if he doesn't indicate that he's hungry.

■ Continue feeding through diarrhea, making no changes unless instructed to do so by your doctor. Cutting down on apple, pear, and peach juices can lessen the severity of a diarrheal illness.

■ If there is vomiting, oral rehydration solutions are easier on the stomach and will replace the salts that are lost when your baby vomits (see the section on vomiting, page 237).

■ Infrequency of bowel movements is no cause for alarm (see the section on constipation, page 220). If the diaper stays conspicuously dry, however, you should notify your physician at once.

Stocking Your Medicine Chest

Your home medicine chest should contain medications with which you can relieve your sick baby's discomfort without masking the nature of the illness. The following list is only a suggestion. All doctors have favorite medications that they prefer their patients to use. Before you plan your medicine chest, ask your pediatrician for advice once more. He or she may also give you a prescription for some additional appropriate medications.

BASIC SUPPLIES FOR YOUR MEDICINE CHEST

Fever

Have one package of acetaminophen drops and one package of acetaminophen suppositories. At each visit with your pediatrician, ask for the updated dosage appropriate to your child's weight. **Do not give aspirin** to infants and children for fever. Rarely is aspirin used in this age group, and if needed, it will be ordered by your doctor.

Diarrhea

One bottle of oral electrolyte solution. This is a rehydration fluid designed to restore the ideal balance of salts and minerals. There are several products available commercially. For dosage and use, follow manufacturer's instructions and your doctor's directions.

Colds

One small bottle of simple saline solution (0.9 percent, available in pharmacies and supermarkets), to soften crusted or hardened nasal mucus. Oral decongestant medications formulated for infants are available at drugstores, but should not be used in infants without consulting your pediatric provider.

Diaper Rash

One tube of simple zinc oxide ointment and one jar of petroleum jelly.

Dry Skin

Add one of the many mild, nonfragrance moisturizing creams or bath oils to your medicine chest (ask the pharmacist or your pediatrician for suggestions).

Injuries

Because collisions will be occurring once the baby learns to walk, if not sooner, you need to keep an assortment of Band-Aids on hand as well. Brightly colored Band-Aids are especially consoling, by the way! Babies love the distraction that the bright colors attached to their bodies provide.

Accidental Poisoning

Have a bottle of syrup of ipecac to induce vomiting in the event of an accidental ingestion. Remember, always call your pediatrician or poison control center before using ipecac.

245

Your Child in the Hospital

There are serious emergencies for which the baby has to be taken to the hospital. And there are scheduled hospital stays, on account of a necessary operation or even extensive tests. Both types of situations will be upsetting and frightening to you. At first you may even feel completely helpless, but the same basic rules about caring for your child still apply, except that you have the additional expertise of a trained nursing and physician staff assisting you.

Ground Rules for Being in the Hospital

■ Don't be separated from your child. He needs your support and reassurance now more than ever. Don't let the hospital personnel send you away and keep you out. If you are still breast-feeding, your presence is even more necessary: A change in diet would only place additional stress on your baby at this time.

■ Behave calmly and collectedly, so that all the necessary treatment procedures go more smoothly. An agitated mother or father can keep medical personnel so busy that the sick baby gets less than his fair share of attention.

■ It is important to remain calm because your anxiety is transmitted to the baby, and can cause him additional

EXTRA-TIP

Most hospitals today allow one or both parents to room-in with their child in his hospital room. Even if he is in the intensive care unit, there is usually a parents' room where many parents spend the night. If the hospital cannot provide accommodations, you need to ask your insurance carrier whether your coverage might include a stay in a nearby hotel.

trouble. You and your spouse should both be available as much as possible for your child's support. You can take shifts, so that one of you can go home to shower and take a walk. In addition, you may have other children at home who will need your attention as well at this time.

Important!

If your baby has to be rushed to a specialized pediatric hospital shortly after birth, it may entail a physical separation. If you are nursing, you should nevertheless try to keep milk production going. Express milk with a breast pump every four hours, and store it in sterilized bottles in your refrigerator and freezer (see page 110). Once a day, the milk has to be taken to the hospital. If this is not possible, you have to pour it out or freeze it for later use. This will enable you to retain the ability to breastfeed, which will make your baby's convalescence easier later on. And you will feel that you can do something, that you're not a helpless bystander.

If the Hospital Stay Is Planned

Choose a hospital with mother-and-child rooms. If you have several children, you will have to organize their lives for the duration of your absence.

With operations, your presence is especially important before anesthesia is administered, since this situation could frighten your child. But waking up again will be much less scary for your baby if he senses your proximity. Moreover, a mother who is observant may notice things that will help the physician make a diagnosis.

Try to "play on the same team" as the doctors and the medical personnel. You should lend each other mutual support: Your common goal is your baby's well-being. The nurses in particular can give you many valuable tips on caring for your child at home.

What to Pack for the Hospital
■ Find out whether the hospital supplies diapers. If your baby is used to cloth diapers, you will probably need someone to pick up the diapers every day and launder them. Or, more practically, switch to disposables for the duration of the hospitalization.

■ Have sleepers or pajamas for the expected length of stay. The hospital will supply child-size "Johnnies," but in some instances your child will be allowed to wear his own more familiar sleepwear.

■ Bring one clean, full set of clothes for the day that your child is discharged from the hospital.

■ Be certain to have pacifier, toy, doll, musical clock, or other objects that are important parts of your bedtime ritual.

■ Food will be provided for your child in the hospital. If your baby is on a special diet, however, take some of his food along, and don't forget to tell the hospital staff about special needs in his diet and allergies, if any.

Be Prepared for an Emergency

Everyone hopes that there never will be one. But should an emergency occur, you need to know which hospital is closest to your home or vacation destination, and if it is equipped to treat babies. Your pediatrician surely can give you a few pointers. The address should be within easy reach at all times, since you will have little time to search for it in the excitement of the moment.

Important!

If the emergency is that your child is pulseless or not breathing, you need to call an ambulance (see the section on CPR, page 250).

Making an Emergency Call

Every time your baby's health is suddenly affected, you feel anxious and fearful, and you instinctively seek expert assistance at once. That's how it should be!

But before you reach for the telephone, first safeguard your child against additional danger by taking some *immediate steps*:

A safe position in an emergency: the secure side position.

■ Place the baby on his side in a stable position.

■ Loosen his clothing to let him get more air.

■ If he seems to be unresponsive and to have stopped breathing, start mouth-to-mouth resuscitation. If you are alone, perform CPR for 1 minute, then call 911 (see section on CPR, page 250).

What to Say on the Phone

The dispatcher needs to know what the emergency medical assistance personnel should expect. Provide the following information:

■ Your name and your address
■ Your child's age
■ What happened
■ When it happened

First Aid for a Baby

Breathing Difficulties

The following illnesses may be accompanied by difficulty in breathing, and speedy action is required:

Viral Croup

Your child wakes up suddenly during the night, is hoarse, and squeaks every time he breathes in. He seems restless, stands up, shakes the side of his crib, and is obviously afraid. In addition, you hear a barking, seal-like cough.

Viral croup, which results from a viral infection in the trachea, is usually accompanied by low fever. If affects older infants and young children and is especially common in winter, as well as in the fall and spring.

■ First, try to calm your child down. Take him out of his bed and carry him around with you; this will reduce his anxiety and thus reduce his need for oxygen and relieve the respiratory distress.

■ Usually croup occurs in the winter months—going outside in the cold night air will often soothe the inflamed airways.

■ Humidify the air in the bathroom by turning on the shower to the hot setting and let the bathroom get steamed up. Your child can then sit on your lap in the bathroom—this will help to calm him and improve his breathing.

■ Call your pediatrician or go to the nearest emergency room if your child can't be calmed down and continues to suffer from breathing difficulty and anxiety.

■ If your child has moderate croup symptoms one night, but is better by the next morning and seems fine all day—don't be fooled into not visiting the pediatrician. Your child should be examined, and sometimes there is a need for some helpful medications that your pediatrician may prescribe to help with the inflammation in the upper airway.

Epiglottitis

Epiglottitis is a bacterial infection of the top-most portion of the breathing tube. It is an infection that interferes with normal breathing in much the same way as viral croup. Affected children, however, are more seriously ill, have high fever, and usually lie exhausted in their bed or sitting up with their arms supporting them in front and their chin pointed outward. They are drooling, have a muffled voice, and are unable to swallow. They also have difficulty breathing, especially when inhaling, but the noise differs somewhat from the typical squeaking of viral croup.

Epiglottitis is an emergency. Even the slightest suspicion is cause enough

249

to take your child to the nearest emergency room, by ambulance if necessary.

Epiglottitis is not nearly as common as it once was; in fact, today it exists but is quite rare. This is a result of widespread immunization with the vaccine Haemophilus influenza type b (Hib). This is the bacteria that causes epiglottitis, and it is because of this serious, potentially fatal infection that widespread immunization was implemented.

Swallowed Objects

Babies and toddlers love to put everything in their mouths. Whatever is in reach is fair game from their standpoint. Signs that warrant concern are sudden violent coughing, difficulty getting air, choking, or turning blue (cyanosis). What should you do if you suspect your child has swallowed and aspirated an object into his lungs?

■ Call for help immediately.

■ If he can breathe effectively and easily, encourage him to cough.

■ If he has trouble breathing, turn his face down and hold him with his head lower than his trunk, and give 4 strong blows to his central back with your hand. Then turn him over and thrust against the center of his chest with your fingers 4 times. Continue until he either improves or stops breathing. If he stops breathing, try to provide mouth-to-mouth resuscitation (see section on CPR).

CPR (Cardiopulmonary Resuscitation)—For Infants Up to 1 Year Old

A course in infant CPR is strongly recommended to all new parents. The basics provided below are not meant to replace such a valuable course.

If your child appears not to be breathing:

1 Quickly stimulate him and call out for help if he does not rouse and start breathing.

2 Visually inspect the inside of his mouth and sweep away any objects that you see.

3 Tilt his head back by pulling up on the corners of his jaw.

4 Place your mouth over his mouth and nose and give 2 breaths. If air is not getting in, you need to try repositioning his head and reinspecting his mouth. If air still does not get in, use back blows and chest thrusts as you would do for choking. Repeat these steps periodically.

5 If air enters, then check his pulse by feeling the inner part of his upper arm about one-third of the way down. If there is a pulse, continue providing breaths at about 20 per minute.

6 If there is no pulse, alternate one breath for every 5 chest compressions. A chest compression is performed by placing 2 to 3 fingers in the center of the chest just below an imaginary line made between the nipples, and pressing down approximately one inch.

7 Continue until help arrives or your baby breathes on his own and recovers his heartbeat.

Falls

Almost every baby has fallen off the changing table or out of the front carrier at least once. Usually these little ones have a guardian angel, and everything is fine.

■ First, comfort your child. Then try to determine whether he is hurt or behaving abnormally. Even if everything is all right, inform your pediatrician and ask whether you should bring the baby in to be examined.

■ If you suspect a serious head injury (he remains irritable, lethargic, or vomits more than 3 times in a row after the fall), you should take him directly to the pediatrician's office or an emergency room.

Scalds

If your baby has been scalded by hot water, then you've had a bad fright. You should:

1 Quickly remove the clothing covering the scalded areas of skin, and hold the affected part of the body under cold running water for several minutes. Then try to calm your baby by talking to him and rocking him back and forth.

2 Then go immediately to the hospital for further treatment.

Poisoning

Things that are part of everyday life for us adults can become a threat for your baby. This includes pills, tobacco, alcohol, and cleaning fluids in particular.

■ You may be able to tell at a glance what your child has swallowed. If there is any doubt, first examine the inside of his mouth. Often some of the swallowed substance will still be in evidence there.

■ Next, call the poison control center and follow their instructions.

■ Depending on what your child has swallowed, they may instruct you to give syrup of ipecac (a vomit-inducing liquid). Alternatively, if the substance can burn the eating or breathing tubes, they may instruct you to go to the emergency room without inducing vomiting.

■ Keep your pediatrician informed about what is happening. Some pediatricians will feel comfortable enough with poisoning to instruct you on their own.

Important!
If you know what was swallowed, always take along the container of liquid or pills to the emergency department with you. It is helpful if you know how many pills are remaining and how many there were to start off with. This will help the emergency staff gauge the seriousness of the poisoning.

GETTING THE HANG OF IT ALL

Life with baby completely upsets your daily routine. If you can bring some order into the chaos, things will be easier for you. In this chapter, you will find suggestions for organizing your household more efficiently and keeping your baby safe; tips to make getting out of the house with the baby easier; lists of foods to keep on hand; essential clothing items and baby equipment; and information about your legal rights.

GOOD ORGANIZATION IS A STRESS-RELIEVER

*As in all fields of management, good organization can save you
a great deal of work and time. The management of a household
with a young child sometimes requires outside help.
In this chapter, you can find out about the various options.*

Your household has to be adapted not only to the baby's daily schedule but to his safety requirements as well. Every outing and every trip has to be organized in a different way now that the baby is here. For these reasons, you need to plan carefully; you cannot rely on feelings and instincts alone to get the job done.

Take the time to get organized and make lists, even in the first exhausting months of parenthood. It can be really liberating to write down all the problems that have to be solved—this raises them to a more businesslike level. Together with your husband, you can formulate possible solutions in the same way. It sounds complicated and fussy, but it is very helpful. And it may well get your partner into action faster than his feelings of guilt over your fatigue and your complaints.

The sooner you have your life under control, the faster you will get back on your feet. Nevertheless, you'll need to develop a good knack for improvisation, and sometimes you won't have the energy for what needs to be done. But if you get your life in order more quickly, it will benefit your child as well.

Household Help

What we once took for granted has become a luxury today: household help. Certainly, machines and low-maintenance equipment have made housework easier, but our demands for a comfortable standard of living have risen at an equal pace. And in many homes today, both parents are working. Thus we expect that life after childbirth will proceed in the same well-ordered fashion. We think that we can manage the "little bit of house-work" on the side. But first, calculate how much time you will spend nursing and diapering in the first months: easily four to six hours a day, not counting all the cuddling, rocking to sleep, singing, and carrying around. Add to that the increased expenditure of time whenever you get ready to leave the house and the inability to stick to a set work schedule, in combination with great weariness and a huge change in your body. Don't get ambitious and think you can do it all alone. Instead, start as early as possible to think about what you need to get done in the next few months and what help you will need with these tasks.

You may want to start by getting someone to come into the house and help you with the cleaning and the laundry once a week or once every other week.

——ESPECIALLY FOR FATHERS——

This chapter probably will be of special interest to you, because it contains a wealth of practical and factual information. Starting on page 267, you will find a list of all the things you really need to buy. If you are enthusiastic about fixing up the baby's "nest" yourself, you need to check page 260 for information on materials that are safe for children.

And if you need someone to look after the baby, it will help if you participate in the search yourself. Husbands often have excellent professional contacts, which they use too little for personal concerns. Do not be embarrassed about putting a notice on your company bulletin board to advertise for a sitter. All contact with the outside world is much easier for you than for your wife at this time anyway. If you do the grocery shopping dependably and promptly, that will be a blessing for your wife! If you cannot manage it during the week, you should at least do large-scale shopping during the weekends. Encourage your wife to delegate duties in general; you will both profit from sharing the load.

If you are going to be returning to work you will need to arrange for someone to help take care of your baby. Many options exist, including neighborhood family day-care, your parents, a day-care center, someone who comes to your house daily, or a live-in nanny (see below for further details). Remember, if outside help is not available, then you have to fall back on your own resources: your family. The baby's father or other close relatives (and possibly other children) will have to lend a hand. The important thing is that this help be reliable and regular. Only delegating things completely and being able to forget about them will give you real relief. Make a list of tasks that can be assigned, from taking out the garbage to shopping. And then hand them over to someone else.

What Your Options Are

■ You may be able to be reimbursed with tax-free dollars for some child care expenses if your company participates in a flexible spending or cafeteria account. This plan allows the employee to have a certain amount of salary withheld without payment of taxes on that amount. This non-taxed money can be used to reimburse the employee for certain medical, dental, or child care expenses. Having child care in your home has certain advantages for you and your child. However, this option is very expensive.

■ *Au pairs* or *nannies* are an option for many families, especially if you have more than one child. You can seek au pairs internationally or through the Mormon community in Salt Lake City, Utah. There are a number of domestic agencies that provide trained nannies. In addition to watching the children, they can help with household tasks. They are entitled to their own room and (for the au pair) an opportunity to take courses. The advantages: individual attention to the child; relatively lower costs if you have two or more children; possible international contacts; and possibly a foreign language for older children. The disadvantages: no trial period; room has to be available; high cost for experienced nannies; you may need to provide transportation and vacation expense/time; you may need to pay Social Security tax, unemployment, disability, and so on; limited availability; high turnover rate; no state regulation.

■ *Self-help groups* often benefit the insecure or harried mother. A group of mothers may already exist in your area, offering each other help, providing a baby-sitting service, and keeping a list of good household helpers. You can locate such a group through your church, synagogue, or various community organizations. Or a "mother's center" may provide a meeting place for contacts. If necessary, found one yourself—every mother in the neighborhood certainly has a need for such a group. The advantages: no or low costs; benefits your private life. The disadvantages: takes involvement and requires dealing with other people; not always a helpful resource.

■ *Part-time help* is still the usual solution: Such helpers can be employed when needed, and you have no additional responsibility. You can ask a teenager from the neighborhood to come in after school as a mother's helper. High school and college students are always looking for ways to earn extra money. The advantages: They can be used when and as needed,

and the monthly rate is moderate. The disadvantages: The hourly rate can be high, and dependability may be an issue.

For information on any of these services, contact an employment agency, the job placement office on college campuses, and your local high school guidance office. Check community bulletin boards and the daily newspaper. Be sure to find out what your tax obligations are.

Organizing Your Household

With my first child, I thought organizing my private life was unnecessary—and I sank without a trace. As my family continued to grow and my level of professional involvement increased, I learned to organize, to delegate, and to structure my obligations. This gave me more space to spend time with the children, as well as space for myself (and sometimes for my husband, too . . .).

Shopping: Not Every Day!

Every outing with the baby becomes a small expedition: He needs to have a fully tummy and be freshly diapered, as well as be properly dressed for the weather and in good spirits. In other words, you no longer can plan your

errands in advance; you have to seize the opportunity quickly when it presents itself. Consequently, you should always maintain a buffer of extra household supplies. That way no one particular shopping trip is crucial. On a bad day, when your child is crying a lot and you are overtired, you should be able to stay at home or take only a short walk for pleasure and not worry about running out of any necessities.

Planning Successfully

■ Keep certain *basic items* on hand in your pantry. Include plenty of staples, and an array of quick dinners that require little in the way of preparation. Keep a list on the refrigerator door, so that you know what needs to

257

be replaced. You or your husband should automatically purchase them at the next opportunity and cross them off your list.

■ *Home delivery:* Look for a grocery store that will deliver to your home. Although these days such services are a rarity, they are appearing on the World Wide Web. The service may cost a bit more, but you may save by getting only what is needed and avoiding making spur-of-the-moment purchases. Furthermore, the time it saves is more precious than you can imagine. However, you first have to get used to making a shopping list systematically and promptly.

■ *Help from family members:* If your husband, the grandparents, or your children are going to take over the shopping for you, don't make them flounder unnecessarily. Make a complete grocery list and include the brand names that you prefer. Don't expect your loved ones always to choose the exact same things you would—the main thing is that they do the shopping. In the first months with a new baby, you need to set different priorities, even if it takes some doing.

Delegating Chores and Improving Efficiency

Don't try to do the same amount of housework you were used to doing before the baby was born. Do away with the delusion that you have to do everything yourself.

■ Pay for labor and services of certain kinds: having the windows washed, taking the bed and table linens to the laundry or dry cleaners, having mending done by a tailor, buying a cake at the bakery.

■ Buy a clothes dryer if you don't already have one. A microwave oven is also an enormous help when mealtimes are irregular. A dishwasher, too, would be a useful acquisition.

■ Simplify things in regard to ironing: Use place mats instead of a tablecloth. Send shirts out—cleaning and pressing is usually inexpensive. Woolens that require hand washing can be sent to the dry cleaners.

WHAT TO KEEP ON HAND

Foods of high nutritional value predominate in this list. Grains are especially nutritious and quick to prepare.

Vegetables: 8 potatoes; I lb (0.5 kg) carrots; I head cabbage; I head broccoli; I head romaine lettuce; 4 onions

Fruits: I dozen oranges; 3 lemons; I dozen apples; 3 bananas

Dairy Products: I box nonfat dry milk (equal to 3 quarts [3 L] liquid); ¹/2 gal. (2 L) fat-free milk; I (32-oz.) container [900 g] fat-free or low-fat yogurt; 4 oz. (110 g) Parmesan cheese

Cereals: I (18-oz. [450 g]) package oatmeal; I lb (0.5 kg) rice, preferably brown; I lb (0.5 kg) spaghetti; I box bran cereal; I lb (0.5 kg) whole wheat couscous

Fats: I (32-oz. [900 g]) bottle canola oil; I (8-oz. [225 g]) bottle olive oil; ¹/2 lb (0.25 kg) unsalted butter; ¹/2 lb (0.25 kg) of unsalted margarine

Meat and Fish: I (6-oz. [170 g]) can water-packed tuna; I (8-oz. [225 g]) can salmon; I (5-oz. [140 g]) can chicken; I lb (0.5 kg) sliced low-fat ham; I (10-oz. [280 g]) package sliced turkey breast meat

Miscellaneous: I dozen eggs; ¹/2 gal. (2 L) orange juice; 2 (11-oz. [310 g]) cans condensed tomato soup; I (26-oz. [725 g]) jar spaghetti sauce; I (24-oz. [675 g]) loaf sliced whole wheat bread; I (1-lb [0.5 kg]) bag frozen vegetables; 8 oz. (225 g) raisins, figs, and other dried fruit

■ During the baby's first year, reduce all your large-scale plans to a minimum: Housecleaning, canning and preserving, family celebrations, and holiday baking all be postponed until further notice.

A Safety Check Indoors and Out

Safety is spelled in capital letters where babies are concerned. Manufacturers of products and equipment for babies—from toys to car seats—have already taken this into consideration. But what about your home environment? Is the pretty baby furniture really safe? And have you ever explored your home from the baby's perspective—on all fours? By the crawling stage (see page 186), your child will be exploring corners and nooks behind and under furniture— places adults would never think to go.

DELEGATING PAPERWORK

Running a household entails far more than just doing housework. Paperwork, too, has to be attended to: the daily mail, including bills or other official notices. Beyond that, you might wish to inform neighbors, friends, and family members of the birth, accept and respond to congratulatory messages, and select godparents for your child. This sounds straightforward, but it involves a lot of work. As far as possible, delegate these jobs to your husband.

If you get a lot of mail, it will be difficult to answer each congratulatory card or letter personally. When you have some quiet time, sit down and write a family newsletter with a little account of your first days with the baby. Enclose a small photo and a handwritten personal message at the end.

Taking precautions ahead of time will save your nerves, as well as many of your favorite possessions, and above all will prevent accidents and eliminate health hazards.

The Nursery—Redone with Good Health in Mind

A freshly decorated room with new furnishings looks wonderful, but it has certain drawbacks: Newly painted walls and furniture, in some cases, create irritating fumes. Make sure that the room has good ventilation and that if the room is repainted, it is thoroughly dry well before delivery. Many parents choose to keep the newborn in their room for the first 3 months. In this case, make sure that there is adequate room for the infant and the infant supplies. A crowded room, if not kept orderly, may lead to unsafe footing and a dangerous accident.

Security Control

■ Nursery or baby monitors are commonly used today. They allow you to check on your baby even when you are on a different floor of the house. If you want flexibility, choose a cordless model. If you plan to use the monitor only inside your home, models that use the electric power supply system for transmission are appropriate. If all you want is a connection between the kitchen and the nursery, you can install an intercom yourself.

■ A smoke alarm and carbon monoxide detector in the nursery provides additional security, especially in a large apartment or a house. The alarms can be easily plugged into a wall plug, as high off the ground as possible, and they will emit an ear-piercing howl upon detecting smoke or carbon monoxide gas.

Important!
Never place a nursery monitor directly in your child's crib! Make sure there is at least 3 feet between your child and the transmitter or the power unit.

Never depend solely on the equipment; look in on your child at least every hour (except at night, of course).

Caution, Baby Traps!

Toward the middle of the first year, when your baby becomes mobile, you should go through your home again with a fine-tooth comb, looking for possible "baby traps." All kinds of security systems are commercially available. Here's what you need:

■ *Caps or shields for electrical outlets:* Tests showed that stick-in disks that can be turned to the open position are the hardest for little hands to figure out. Covers designed to block sockets should not be easy to remove. Disadvantages: They are expensive and you have to keep a key for each cap. If you are completely overhauling the room, you can have concealed sockets with shields built in.

When furnishing the nursery, choose natural materials wherever possible. The colors and textures of the walls, curtains, and floor also have an influence on your child's well-being.

■ *"Kiddy locks"* for doors, drawers, and the refrigerator not only keep the baby safe, but protect you against utter chaos as well. Door stoppers and door and window locks are vital necessities in many cases.

■ *Safety gates* keep doorways and stairs safe. For the kitchen and the nursery, a rigid gate that is easy to remove is sufficient; for doorways and staircases, flexible gates are more practical.

Important!
Many things that are part of our adult life are dangerous for your baby: cigarette butts, tobacco, alcohol, perfume, scented oils, nail polish, medications. Don't leave anything lying around, and check for such hazards when visiting in someone else's home. For first aid, see page 249.

Caregivers and Extra Help with the Baby

Physical closeness between mother and child is a vital and beautiful thing, but sometimes a separation of several hours is unavoidable. It may be that you are going back to your job, have important appointments scheduled, or simply want to go to the hairdresser. Maybe you also need to create some distance for a few hours, to "recharge your batteries." Don't feel guilty about wanting to do that; it is completely normal. In generations past, the large extended family made finding a helping hand easy.

It is important for you to be able to arrange a good temporary alternate caregiver for periods of time when you and the baby's father cannot be there. (Refer to the final chapter in addition to the section below.)

Child Care Alternatives

■ *Grandparents* are always an ideal source of help. In the first weeks, the father usually takes some leave from work. But after that, when the daily routine begins, temporary "postpartum care" provided by a grandparent can be a great help. If the grandparents can arrange to provide the family with help of this kind over the long

SAFETY RULES AROUND PETS

If you already have a cat or a dog before your child is born, you need to eliminate hazards and observe certain rules of good hygiene.

■ *Dogs in particular may react with jealousy to the arrival of a baby. Be very careful here. Don't make your pet feel excluded by keeping it away from the child or ceasing to pay attention to it. Extra petting and a chance to participate in family life are the best ways to prevent situations with bad consequences. Usually it takes a few months for the dog to accept the new family member. Nevertheless, never leave the dog and the child together unsupervised, even later on.*

■ *With cats, you need to make sure that they don't jump into the cradle or crib unobserved and lie down on the sleeping child. He could suffocate!*

■ *It is also important to check and treat your dogs and cats regularly for worms, parasites, ticks, and fleas. Ask your veterinarian to recommend appropriate products.*

■ *Especially for children in the crawling stage: Don't leave food and water bowls on the floor; always feed dogs in a separate room.*

term as well, this solution probably is the most agreeable for all those involved.

■ *Baby-sitters* will be needed in the first two to three years whenever you want to go out in the evening (and you should do so!). Think in terms of the long run, and line up your sitters now. The more mature the baby-sitter, the better. Alternatively, trading off double duty with another new mother may ensure even more reliable care. Always leave them the telephone number of the place where you can be reached. If you very seldom need a baby-sitter, you should contact your friends for recommendations.

■ *Family child-care providers* are very popular. Studies give good marks to this type of caretaking arrangement. Although these providers are highly regulated, as a rule, you have to check them out for yourself. When visiting a family child-care provider consider the following:

• Is it safe? Are the toys age appropriate? Is there an adequate number of mature adults present?

• Is the outside play area safe from cars and car exhaust?

• Will my child be comfortable here? Is it brightly lit? Are there plenty of colorful toys?

• Is the food palatable and healthy? Do I need to send my own food?

• What type of teaching or early stimulation takes place?

Despite all their curiosity, babies really are not able to play with each other.

• One must also consider the cost. The rate may range from 150 to 200 dollars per week or more for full-time care.

■ *Day-care centers* are becoming more common. One indicator of a good day-care center is the ratio of children to caregivers. The younger the children, the larger the number of personnel should be present. A caregiver should be responsible for no more than 4 children under the age of two; if some of the children are older, she can manage 5 to 6. The look of the facility itself will also tell you a lot. Warm colors, cozy corners, free-play zones, outdoor play areas, and quiet rooms where the babies can nap are positive signs. Other favorable indicators are a relatively flexible daily schedule and a

If you're well-equipped, diapering is not a problem even when you're away from home.

year old. Nevertheless, these groups are an ideal basis for play groups later on, and they keep the mothers from becoming isolated. Consider having half the mothers leave their babies with the group and take some time off; then the group will have an actual caregiving function as well.

■ Tip: Make a written contract with the daycare provider, spelling out all rights, duties, and terms of notice.

Going Out with Your Baby

Today, babies are no longer raised in relative isolation from the rest of the world. This is due partly to the lack of domestic help, partly to the change in mothers' self-image, and our current conception of babies themselves. We want to remain independent and self-reliant, even as mothers, and we also want our child to participate in our life as fully as possible. The ideal probably lies somewhere between these two extremes. If you're always on the move with the baby, you're asking too much of him; if you pamper and protect him, you're asking too little. Here are a few tips to help you avoid most of the stress.

week-long adjustment period, during which special attention is paid to the new child. Also consider the six points previously listed.

■ *Peer groups (baby play groups)* are not a solution to the caregiver problem for working mothers. However, they do make life easier for at-home mothers, especially with the first child. You can start a group yourself or get in touch with existing groups through a community center, kindergarten, breastfeeding group, or community newspaper. Usually, both children and mothers are present at these sessions. The mothers can exchange information and give encouragement and advice; the children, however, don't get much out of being together before they are one

In an airplane, keep the baby's bottle of water or his pacifier within easy reach upon takeoff and landing. The change in pressure could cause ear pain. Swallowing will aid in equalizing the pressure once more.

Little Outings

■ Write down a checklist of the equipment that you need to pack to be able to travel out of the house with your baby for a few hours. Fasten it to the front door—then you're guaranteed not to forget the pacifier!

■ Keeping a small bag packed with things you'll need when out with him will help you get out of the house faster. Everything you need for diapering, a pacifier, a burping pad, toys, and some emergency provisions for you (trail mix, bottled water), should be inside.

■ Don't set out at rush hour.

■ For quick trips, the infant carrier is all you need; for longer ones, your baby will be better off in his carriage once you have arrived at your destination. (For more on this topic, see page 80.)

■ Ideal for short excursions: a thermos bottle for the baby's formula. Experiment to see how hot the formula should be when poured into the bottle, so that it will be at the right temperature one or two hours later.

Longer Journeys

■ On longer trips away from home, you have to pack your child's hand

A family vacation at the beach can be fun with a baby who is at least a few months old.

luggage with great deliberation. In addition to sufficient diapering supplies, fresh clothing, and formula, you should have a bassinet or the detachable top of a carriage (designed to be usable as a fabric bassinet) with you, so that you can put your baby down to sleep from time to time.

■ If you are traveling by car, it is best to drive at night. You will avoid possible traffic jams; it won't get too hot in the car; and your baby will probably sleep. If you travel during the day, be sure to protect your baby against the sun (see page 87) and take a short break at least every two hours. Don't drive extremely long distances without a break, and reserve a room in advance in a hotel that welcomes babies (even better: stay with friends or relatives). Remember never to continue driving when you begin to feel tired.

Airplane Travel

■ Arrange for tickets well in advance. Let the travel agent or airline booking agent know that you are traveling with an infant—you will get preference for a bulkhead seat, which has the benefit of no seats in front of you so there is increased foot room and, in some planes, a pull-down bassinet.

■ You will need to hold your infant on your lap or, if there's an empty seat next to you, you can strap your child in with his car seat.

■ Alternatively, you can book an additional seat for your child, but you will usually have to pay full price.

■ Check into the gate early so that any special arrangements can be made promptly.

■ Check with your pediatrician about 1 to 2 months before traveling out of the country so that travel immunizations, if needed, can be arranged.

Eating on Trips

If you are not breastfeeding exclusively, you will need to have enough formula for several feedings with you in any event.

■ You can take one bottle, already warmed, in a thermos. The others should be prepared, refrigerated, and warmed in the bottlewarmer as needed on car trips. Alternatively, you can have bottles warmed in a pan of hot water in the railroad dining car or in the galley kitchen aboard the plane.

■ Another possibility is to take along a large thermos container full of boiled water, and use it to mix fresh formula for the baby's bottle each time.

WHAT YOU REALLY NEED TO BUY

Industry has made life with babies easier, albeit more complicated!

You should be well equipped when your child arrives.

But don't overdo it: Judge and evaluate carefully,

to avoid spending money needlessly in your initial enthusiasm.

Anyone who looks at a baby catalogue will be impressed by the wealth of products offered. For every situation, there's a solution to your problem, and sets of matching items ensure that both the nursery and the baby will be in perfect style. But not everything that looks pretty is also practical, and often less is more.

At some point in the second half of her pregnancy, every woman allegedly goes through a "nest-building phase" and wants to get everything ready for her child. Don't go too far in your efforts. Keep asking yourself what you really need, and get only the most essential things at first. Some things you can borrow from friends or buy secondhand—a notice posted on the bulletin board at the nearest kindergarten is sure to get results. Then, over the course of the first months, you can buy the remaining items or let people know you would like them as gifts. It is better to invest the money you save for your child, because soon enough he will be more of an expense, and in a few years you can use your savings to treat him to music lessons or hockey equipment that otherwise would not be in your budget.

■ One more tip: Before your delivery, go ahead and pick out in your mind the things that the baby will need later, after the first few weeks. Visit the appropriate stores and make a list of the articles that you will want. If you don't change your mind, your husband can go back and purchase the things you still need.

Essential Baby Equipment and Clothing

You should have a basic layette together at least two months before your due date. You need to decide how you want to diaper your child, and you will need the crib or bassinet, baby carriage, changing table, and infant bathtub from the outset as well. It's not too early to start planning for the first car trip, too—the ride home from the hospital. If you plan to breastfeed, you can postpone buying feeding supplies until later.

■ In the following section are tips on essential early acquisitions; more information and guidelines for decision-making will be found in the chapters on baby care and feeding (pages 36 and 88).

The Diapering System

It is best to decide on a certain diapering system (see page 39) before your baby is born and to buy the necessary supplies. This will give you less to worry about in the first weeks after the delivery. If you are still undecided, you can either buy a package of disposable diapers to keep in reserve or make arrangements with a diaper service that are subject to cancellation. This might mean, however, that you would not buy the diaper supplies you

What you need at first:
- *Two dozen washable diapers with one dozen diaper inserts (liners) and two pairs of water-repellent pants made of breathable material*
  or
- *One package of disposable diapers (smallest size, from 6 to 11 pounds)*
  or
- *Two dozen gauze diapers and two pairs of pants*

In addition:
- *One roll of adhesive tape or diaper pins (for washable diapers only)*

Even if you decide to use washable diapers, it is still wise to keep a small package of disposable diapers on hand.

268

finally choose until the baby is several days old—which could be exhausting. Keep in mind that it is becoming more and more difficult to find functioning diaper services. You may be able to locate a company that will sell you cloth diapers, but it is becoming very difficult to find a company that will also launder them for you.

Layette for a First Child

Here is a list of the essential items for the first weeks. It is based only on the bare minimum, because you are sure to get more things as presents. In addition, the washing machine will be running every day anyway, and your baby will quickly outgrow his first wardrobe.

In making your selection, keep the baby's tender skin in mind as well. Give preference to natural materials such as cotton or wool, and always wash baby clothes before the baby wears them. Use a mild soap and do not add fabric softener.

Baby's first wardrobe:
- *4 short-sleeved pullover tops*
- *4 cotton sweaters*
- *4 stretchies (one-piece outfits) with feet*
- *2 sleepers or 2 pajamas or 2 additional stretchies with feet*
- *2 cotton caps*
- *2 pairs of baby booties*

In winter, these are needed as well:
- *1 bunting or snowsuit*
- *1 pair of thermal mittens*

In summertime, these are needed as well:
- *1 sun hat*
- *2 pair of short pants*
- *2 short-sleeved pullovers*
- *2 pair of cotton socks*
- *1 cotton cardigan or jacket*

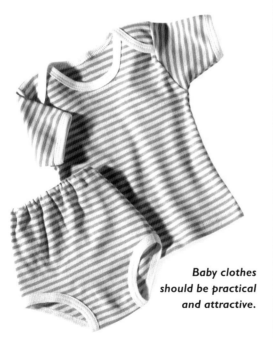

Baby clothes should be practical and attractive.

269

Tips for Shopping

■ Undershirts in particular should not be too big; otherwise, the baby will get cold. Stretchies and rompers can easily be a size larger.

■ Especially at night, infant sleepers are practical (see page 71). They will fit until the baby is about one year old, and they leave plenty of room for his legs to move around.

■ For daytime wear, rompers without feet are a good idea. They will fit your child far longer than styles with feet. Then you need to think of little socks and booties, however. Training shoes are for style only. Your child will be just as happy with soft shoes—even socks alone are adequate.

Bed linens for your newborn:
- *2 cotton-coated, waterproof mattress covers*
- *2 to 3 fitted sheets*
- *2 washable crib or bassinet blankets—light-weight for summer and heavier material for winter*
- *6 thick gauze diapers to put at the head end for protection*
- *1 set of bumper pads for a crib with bars*
- *1 quilted playmat*

The Baby's Bed

The selection is large: bassinets on wheels, cradles, basket-type bassinets, and cribs are available. On page 68, you can read about the advantages and disadvantages of the different types of furnishings for your baby.

From a financial standpoint, the acquisition of a crib that the baby can grow into is the most economical solution. If you are planning to have a second child soon, however, a bassinet on wheels or a cradle would make sense. Basket-type bassinets are relatively expensive and entirely too unstable a means of transportation.

If you or your husband suffer from allergies, make sure all your new acquisitions for the baby's bed are allergy-tested products. Wool, feathers, horsehair, and coconut-shell fiber are not good choices in your case.

If there is already some baby equipment in your family, it makes sense to give it a try and see how it works for you. But make sure that it is consistent with current safety standards.

From Tub to Changing Table

An enormous range of practical, attractive, "problem-solving" products having to do with bathing and diapering have been developed. But here, too, you can get by with a minimum of acquisitions:

■ You are sure to have a small plastic dishpan somewhere in your house. If need be, you also can bathe your baby in a washtub, though portable baby tubs are quite inexpensive and have a drain. Especially in the cold months of the year, you will want to bathe your baby in the warmth of the bathroom, yet often there isn't enough room there, and you therefore may want to bring the bathtub to the kitchen where there is more counter space.

■ For diaper changes, a changing table with drawers for supplies is optimal. Alternatives include a well-stocked diaper bag that you can use both while traveling and in the house. The baby can then be changed on the bed, carpet, or any other stable surface.

In addition, you will need a thick piece of fabric (e.g., terry cloth) as a changing pad and an extra plastic bag for soiled diapers. All of this can be put in a backpack, basket, or elegant shopping bag—whichever you prefer.

■ For more information about the changing area, see page 46; for more on bathing, see page 53.

For daily care, you need:
- *baby bathtub with stopper*
- *dishpan*
- *possibly a baby tub frame or stand for the big bathtub*
- *changing area at least 28 inches wide and 32 inches long*
- *soft, washable changing surface*
- *1 diaper pail with lid*
- *1 small trash container*
- *1 small laundry bag*
- *2 bath towels—with hoods if possible*
- *6 cloth washcloths*
- *1 soft baby brush*
- *1 pair of blunt nail clippers and emery board*
- *1 tube of ointment for the diaper area*
- *mild soap for the bath*
- *rectal thermometer*
- *1 bottle of isopropyl (rubbing) alcohol*
- *diaper wipes or disposable washcloths*

When the Baby Is More Mobile

Over the course of the first months, the baby expands his range of activities. Slowly he comes to need an infant seat, a playmat, and a playpen. If you are interested in finding out what toys are appropriate at what stages, see the section beginning on page 179.

■ For the transitional phase between lying and sitting, and for the times when you want to keep your baby where you can see him, an infant seat is helpful (see page 73). A simple, basic model is the most portable.

■ A large, thickly quilted playmat is ideal for the initial "floor exercises."

■ A playpen (see page 73) makes sense only if you really have enough room for it in your kitchen or living room, because it should measure at least 48 by 48 inches. If your kitchen is tiny, it is wiser to install a gate (see page 261) in the doorway when things get too dangerous for your crawling baby.

Feeding Supplies

■ If you want to breastfeed, there's no real need to bother with bottles and nipples at this point. But you may wish to give the baby water if he has constipation. On the one hand, you will feel better knowing you already have everything you need. On the other hand, having bottles and other supplies ready may tempt you in moments of weakness to go ahead and give the baby an unnecessary bottle feeding. Everything else you need to know about bottles and other feeding supplies is presented in the section beginning on page 120.

Important!
Be careful with the thermal baby bottles: Make sure they are unbreakable, and test the temperature of the formula on the inside of your wrist before feeding the baby.

If you want to breastfeed, consider having on hand:
- *2 water bottles with nipples (silicone, smallest size)*
- *1 bottle brush*
- *1 thermos container*
- *bottled water suitable for preparing baby formula*

If you are going to bottle feed, you also need:
- *4 bottles for formula*
- *4 nipples (smallest size)*
- *1 sterilizer or pressure cooker (optional; dishwasher cleaning is adequate)*
- *1 insulated container*
- *1 bottle warmer*

■ There is no need to acquire the following utensils in the first weeks; their turn won't come until your baby is getting supplementary solids (see page 129). Buying a high chair (see page 140), too, doesn't make sense until your child can sit securely and is eating his meals with you.

■ The training cup and plate should be plastic, lightweight, and designed not to tip over. A hot-water plate or electric heating disk are not essential for a baby just learning to eat. They will, however, keep your baby's food nice and warm while he takes an inordinate amount of time to consume a few morsels. We used the hot-water plate for our youngest son until he reached kindergarten age, whenever we ate as a family—simply because he was a slow eater.

■ If you use a bib for the baby, make sure it is large enough to cover his shoulders and arms, and is long enough to cover his lap when he is being fed. Especially practical: If you are handy with the sewing machine, cut bibs out of old hand towels, and hem and border them with matching cloth or lace.

A training cup is one of the many practical products available to make feeding easier.

Going Out: Carriages and Carriers

You won't be able to get by entirely without a baby carriage. See the section beginning on page 83 for "do's and don'ts" when shopping for one. Parents in urban areas will almost certainly need a baby carrier of some kind as well. Both front carriers and back carriers are available. Try the models your friends use to see what suits you best, and get the father involved in the decision-making, since he also must be able to carry the baby. For pros and cons, see page 86.

Utensils for the first solids:
- *1 spillproof training cup with drinking spout*
- *1 training dish with suction base*
- *1 hot-water plate with partition, or electric warming dish (optional)*
- *2 to 3 narrow, shallow plastic spoons*
- *1 baby spoon*
- *1 hand blender*
- *1 high chair*
- *7 bibs*

Baby carriage and accessories:
- *I baby carriage*
- *mattress, rain shield, and sun shield (all of which usually come with the carriage)*
- *blanket from his crib as a cover for the baby*
- *terry cloth hand towels to protect the mattress*
- *tote bag and shopping basket for the carriage*

And/or
- *I baby carrier*

For the car:
- *I car seat*
- *sun shades*
- *bottle warmer for the car (optional)*
- *portable crib*

portable crib until the end of the first year, at the earliest. Think twice about whether you really need one: Hotels usually have cribs available, and when visiting grandparents and friends, children often much prefer to sleep in "nests" on the floor. By the age of four, if not sooner, you child will be too heavy for a folding crib anyway.

On a Big Trip

If you're traveling by car, a car seat for the baby is always necessary! (For more information, see page 86.) Sun shades are also nice to have in the car for the side and rear windows. A bottle warmer that plugs into the cigarette lighter is handy on longer trips, but certainly not necessary.

For spending the night on the road in a hotel, the removable top of the baby carriage is adequate for the first few months. Simple fabric bassinet styles, however, are not safe enough for use in the car. You won't need a

Never leave your child unattended!

Checklist for Mothers

■ Your breasts will be bigger than they were once your milk comes in. Before the delivery, buy one or two simple, expandable nursing bras one or two sizes larger than your regular size, in a style that closes in front.

■ Your breasts are not absolutely "leakproof." Purchase several nursing pads—round, absorbent inserts for your bra—to keep moisture from leaking out and to prevent your clothing from developing the infamous wet stains. There are disposable pads, which are relatively expensive, but save time. Washable pads, however, are easier on your skin: Cotton and microfiber mixtures are especially leakproof, while wool and silk are easy on your skin.

Important!
Iron the nursing pads—especially the insides—after washing (follow manufacturer's instructions) to sterilize them.

What to Wear After Delivery

Don't be disappointed if your favorite dresses still don't fit in the first months. Your body needs time to return to its former condition. In summer, simple dresses that button in front will help—look for stylish designs in stores that carry clothing from India. There you will also find

What to pack for the hospital:
- *1 or 2 nursing bras*
- *10 nursing pads made of cotton, or 1 package of disposable nursing pads*
- *2 pairs of pajamas or nightgowns with buttons in front*
- *slippers*
- *robe*
- *1 lightweight wool cardigan*
- *underpants*
- *hairbrush*
- *toothbrush and toothpaste*
- *1 package of sanitary napkins (for lochia)—most hospitals will provide these*
- *book or magazines*
- *writing paper and pens*
- *clothing to wear home*

pants with elastic at the waist and blouses in inexpensive, fun designs. In winter, knit outfits are good—look for styles with front buttons, if possible.

If you want to nurse your child in public as well, you need tops that open in front. Pulling up a sweater to nurse doesn't allow your baby any eye contact, and it also exposes your abdomen. You can also bring along a large cotton shawl to cover yourself in public while breastfeeding.

YOUR LEGAL RIGHTS AND OTHER MATTERS

Mark A. Goldstein, M.D.

Until 1978, there was no national legislation on maternity leave; parental leave was only legislated in 1993. Early in the twentieth century, laws were enacted that were "protective" of women. These included state laws prohibiting married women from paid work and state policies allowing employers to terminate women who became pregnant. Teachers were very often forced to leave once the pregnancy was made known to school authorities.

Title VII of the 1964 Civil Rights Act prohibited discrimination on the basis of sex. However, it was not until 1978 that Title VII was amended to make it quite clear that sexual discrimination on the basis of pregnancy, childbirth, and related medical conditions was illegal. The Pregnancy Discrimination Act of 1978 required employers to consider disabilities from pregnancy and related conditions as they would other short-term disabilities.

It was not until 1993 that the Family and Medical Leave Act (FMLA) was enacted into law. Certain employers must provide up to 12 weeks of unpaid, job protected leave to eligible employees (men and women) for certain family and medical reasons, including:

■ for the care of the employee's child (birth, through adoption, or from foster care)

■ for the care of the employee's child who has a serious health condition (for example, if your child has to be seen weekly for a serious medical condition, you should be able to take FMLA leave to take the child to the appointment)

The employee may be required to provide advance leave notice and medical certification. Upon return from FMLA leave, most employees must be restored to their original or equivalent positions with equivalent pay, benefits, and terms of employment. For the duration of the FMLA leave, the employer must continue the employee's medical insurance coverage.

The FMLA gave legal rights to the mother and father to take parental leave without the fear that one's job security could be sacrificed.

■ It would be unusual for the mother to sustain a permanent disability from pregnancy and childbirth. However, the Americans with Disabilities Act (ADA), which became law in 1993, applies to permanent rather than short-term disabilities. This law states that your employer may not discriminate against you on the basis of your disability, such as in the area of promotion. Furthermore, your employer has a duty to make reasonable accommodations for your disability provided you can perform the essential functions of the job with or without accommodations.

■ For the *infant who has a disability*, a number of programs are available. As an example, a child born with a congenital infection may be eligible for early intervention programs. These programs offer a variety of services to children and parents, including medical and nursing assistance, physical and occupational therapy, home visits, and parenting skills. The Education for the Handicapped Act of 1975 was extended recently to provide special education for handicapped children from birth to 3 years of age.

■ If you decide not to return to work after your FMLA leave, then your health benefits may be continued under the Consolidated Omnibus Budget Reconciliation Act of 1985 (COBRA). Under COBRA, your portion of the health insurance premium will increase. The law allows an employer to require employees to pay for any health care benefits the employer paid during the leave if the employee does not return to work.

Medical Insurance for Your Baby

Because national health insurance has not been enacted in the United States, it is vitally important that every infant be covered by medical and hospitalization insurance. Employer provided plans include health maintenance organizations (HMOs), indemnity plans, managed indemnity plans, and preferred provider organizations (PPOs).

■ An *HMO* provides a defined package of services to a patient in return for prepayment of a premium. The patient generally receives services from a select group of providers.

■ *Indemnity plans*, because of their cost to families and employers, are disappearing. These plans allow the patient to select their providers, and the providers are paid a fee for services.

■ A *managed indemnity plan* includes an arrangement where the use of services and procedures is monitored closely, and there is significant cost-sharing by the patient.

■ In a *PPO*, physicians or hospitals contract with employers or insurers to provide services to patients at a negotiated lower fee. The patient has more choice in selection of his or her providers.

You should decide carefully which plan is best for your family. There are no convincing studies that prove that one type of plan over another provides better services to infants. You should contact your employer's benefits office for further information.

Maternity Benefits

If you are an expectant parent, you should speak to your employer about the maternity health benefits offered under your hospital insurance program. In Massachusetts and some other states, it is now mandated that the new mother have a 48-hour length of stay in the hospital for a vaginal delivery and a 96-hour stay for a cesarean section. Any discharge earlier than these times must be agreed to by the mother as well as the physicians. For an early discharge in Massachusetts, it is also mandated that a health care provider perform a home visit within 48 hours of discharge.

■ The COBRA law enacted in 1985 required all states to provide Medicaid coverage to pregnant women and children to the age of 5 years who met a definition of low income. The Supplemental Program for Women, Infants, and Children (WIC) enacted in 1972 provides supplemental food to pregnant and postpartum women, lactating mothers, and children from newborn to 5 years. Again, certain low income levels must be met. For certain low income children, the Headstart Program is designed to improve their development and other skills.

Never draw back from having a relationship with your child: Fathers are important!

Returning to Work

If you are returning to employment, there are a number of considerations for the new mother, especially in regard to day-care and work arrangements. If you do not have your spouse, a parent, or another relative available for child care, then you will be seeking outside care.

■ *In-home care* for your new baby is preferable. There is very close attention from the provider, convenience, lack of other children's germs, and a sense of comfort and security. This care can be provided by a sitter, an au pair who actually lives with you, or a professional nanny. Although this option is ideal for many families, the trade-offs include the expense and potential lack of privacy.

Important!
Thorough screening and background checks should be performed on individuals who will care for your baby. Generally, au pair agencies do carefully screen their candidates for positions in families. Remember, au pairs are European women between 18 and 26 years of age who may not have had any significant child care experience. They are not usually trained in the care of babies. The agencies may give them only minimal training before placing them in a home. Despite careful screening and background checks, tragedies have occurred when au pairs have been caring for babies. If you have any qualms after an au pair is placed in your home, contact her agency immediately and consider obtaining another source of child care.

■ Extended families are playing a more important role recently in the care of new babies. In many young families, both parents may either be in work or in school, and family finances will not allow for a day-care option. Often a grandmother or occasionally a grandfather is called in to help. In fact, it is not unusual for young international families residing in the United States to have a grandparent come over for several months to a whole year after the birth of a new baby. Many new mothers are relieved to have an experienced parent help them in the first few months. A grandparent can devote an incredible amount of time and love to a newborn. The baby, his or her parents, and the grandparent benefit greatly from this situation.

■ In rare instances, some international families residing here send their relatively young baby back to their homeland. This is especially common among Chinese who may send their baby back to China for up to a year.

■ The next best option for the infant is *family-centered day-care*. This care occurs in the caregiver's home; state law may require licensing, and the

279

number of children allowed in the house is restricted by law.

■ *Group day-care* has certain advantages. Some of the caregivers may be trained in early childhood education; the cost is less than in-home care, and there is backup in case the caregiver is ill. However, because of the larger number of children in group day-care, your child will be exposed to some infections.

■ Some employers have their own day-care centers. This allows the new parent to continue nursing, to see her baby during the day, and to have a certain peace of mind. Often the costs are subsidized by the employer.

Needless to say, whatever your source of day-care, you must select the provider with the utmost care. Interview the provider, obtain references, speak to others who have used the provider, and observe children in her care. You need to be absolutely comfortable in your choice for this very important part of your new baby's life.

■ Some employers allow new parents to reorganize their work arrangements to allow for more at-home care of their new babies. These arrangements include flex-time, compressed work weeks, extended work weeks, telecommuting, job sharing, and voluntary reduced time programs. Generally, each of these will allow more flexibility to the new parent's work week with the goal of having more at-home family time.

Other Legal Issues

Previously, couples who were unable to conceive went childless or tried to adopt a baby. In vitro fertilization (IVF) has brought joy to many previously infertile couples. Some mothers are able to carry their pregnancy and some have a surrogate carry the baby. A natural pregnancy is not available to all.

■ Couples considering *adoption* should work with a reputable agency. As much information as possible should be obtained about the birth father and mother. Medical records should be reviewed with your pediatrician before the birth. As soon as the baby is available, have your pediatrician review the records and examine the baby. If your baby is coming from another country, special testing will be required to rule out infections and metabolic diseases. Often the baby will come weeks or months after birth. He or she may not have optimal growth and development, but often the baby begins to thrive quickly under the attention and care of loving parents. You should work very closely with your pediatrician during the beginning months to anticipate problems and be certain all immunizations are brought up-to-date.

■ *Single parent* pregnancies and adoptions are also emerging. The concept of what constitutes a family has been changing over recent years. Through artificial insemination, some single women are obtaining their goal of starting a family. Furthermore, some states are allowing single parent adoptions. There are special sets of issues that pertain to the single parent of an infant. Besides being the only parent and wage earner, as well as head of the household, somehow you need to do everything else around the house. Close linkages with relatives or friends are needed for support. Contingency plans if you are injured, ill, or hospitalized must be made in advance. Efforts should be made for your new baby to have close contacts with other caregivers.

■ Some *lesbian and gay couples* are also adopting babies. Often they go through the same agencies as straight couples. Political climates in some foreign countries may discourage this practice. If these obstacles can be overcome, then there are issues to address in this country. The legal parent, i.e. the nonbiological parent who becomes the child's legal parent through adoption, must consent to adoption by the co-parent without giving up his or her parental rights. Co-parent adoption continues to forge legal paths at this time.

Some lesbian and gay couples decide to conceive a child through artificial insemination. The biological birth mother will have to work out the legal issues with her domestic partner. Unless there is a legal adoption, it is extremely difficult to obtain health insurance through the "unrelated" parent. If the biological parent became unemployed, then the child could lose his or her health insurance.

In the past 20 years, there have been a number of changes in U.S. laws, health insurance, and day-care options. Changes in the laws try to make life and parenting easier for the new mother and father. Health insurance should promote comprehensive medical care for mother and child from the pregnancy through the first years. With increasing regulation of day-care, it should become even healthier and safer. More must be done to promote parent and child welfare in the first year. However, we have made a good start.

Parenthood: Getting a Good Start

National Center for Fathering, 10200 West 75th Street, Suite 267, Shawnee Mission, KS 66204. (913) 384-4661; (913) 384-4665 ncf@aol.com

The Expectant Father: Facts, Tips, and Advice for Dads-to-Be, Armin Brett and Jennifer Ash, Abbeville Press, 1995

Choosing a Nurse-Midwife: Your Guide to Safe, Sensitive Care During Pregnancy and the Birth of Your Child, Catherine Poole and Elizabeth Parr, John Wiley and Sons, 1994

Around the Circle Gently: A Book of Birth, Families, and Life, Lynn Moen and Judy Laik, Celestial Arts Publishing, 1995

The National Association of Postpartum Care Services. (800) 453-6852

National Organization of Mothers of Twins Clubs, Box 23188, Albuquerque, NM 87192-1188. (800) 243-2276; (505) 275-0955

Making Your Baby Feel Good All Over

Babyworks (cloth diapers), 11725 NW West Road, Portland, OR 97229. (800) 422-2910; (503) 645-4349; (503) 645-4913

Guide to Baby Products, Consumer Reports Books, 1996

The Safe Nursery, U.S. Consumer Products Safety Commission, Office of Information and Public Affairs, Washington, D.C. 20207 The Catalogue For Safe Beginnings, Box 1265, Burlington, MA 01803. (800) 598-8911

Kid Natural (Clothing), 4302 224th Place S.W., Mountlake Terrace, WA 98043. (206) 778-0418

"The Parent/Child Sleep Guide," Sleep Products Safety Council, Box 19534, Alexandria, VA 22320-0534. (include business size SASE)

Helping Your Baby Grow Big and Strong

The Nursing Mother's Companion, Kathleen Huggins R.N., Harvard Common Press, 1995

The Womanly Art of Breastfeeding, Plume, 1991

La Leche League International, Box 4079, Schaumburg, IL 60168-4079. (800) LA-LECHE; (708) 519-7730; (708) 519-0035 (fax)

Vegetarian Baby: A Sensible Guide for Parents, Shoron Yutema, McBooks Press, 1991

Wellstart (lactation program), P.O. Box 87549, 4062 First Avenue, San Diego, CA 92138. helpline: (619) 295-5193

The New Parents Sourcebook, Hilory Wagner, Citadel Press, 1996

Help for the Entire Family

Motherwell, 1106 Stratford Drive, Carlisle, PA 17013. (800) MOM-WELL, momwell@epix.net

Father's Resource Center, 430 Oak Grove Street, Suite 105, Minneapolis, MN 55403. (612) 874-1509; FRC@winternet.com

FEMALE (Formerly Employed Mothers at the Leading Edge), Female National Headquarters, Box 31, Elmhurst, IL 60126. (708) 941-3553

American Baby. (303) 604-1464 (subscriptions)

How Your Baby Develops

Games Babies Play: From Birth to Twelve Months, Vicki Lansky, The Book Peddlers, 1993

How to Soothe and Amuse Your New Baby: 0–3 Months, Judith Bestt, Remedios Publishing, 1995

Best Guide to Your Growing Baby,
   Remedios Publishing, Box 324 - NPS,
   Folsom, CA 95763-0324.
   (408) 226-1859 (phone, fax);
   remepub@netcom.com

Healthy from the Outset
American Academy of Pediatrics,
   141 Northwest Point Blvd., Box 927,
   Elk Grove Village, IL 60009-0927.
   kidsdoc@aap.org; http://www.aap.org

National Health Information Center, Box 1133,
   Washington, D.C. 20013-1133.
   (800) 336-4797; (301) 565-4167 (in Maryland);
   (301) 984-4256 (fax), nhicinfo@health.org

National Women's Health Network, 514 10th St.
   N.W., Suite 400, Washington, D.C. 20004.
   (202) 347-1140

Getting the Hang of It All
Family Resource Coalition, 200 South Michigan
   Avenue, 16th Floor, Chicago, IL 60604.
   (312) 341-0900; (312) 341-9361

Consumer Product Safety Commission, "Baby
   Safety Checklist," Publication Request, U.S.
   Consumer Product Safety Commission,
   Washington, D.C. 20207.
   info@cpsc.gov; http://www.cpsc.gov

"Family and Medical Leave Act," Women's Legal
   Defense Fund, 1875 Connecticut Avenue N.W.,
   Suite 710, Washington, D.C. 20009.
   (202) 986-2600; (202) 986-2539 (fax)

Women's Bureau Clearinghouse, U.S. Department
   of Labor, Room South 3306, 200 Constitution
   Avenue, Washington, D.C. 20210.
   (800) 827-5335; (202) 219-4486;
   (202) 219-5529 (fax)

Adoptive Families of America, 3333 Highway 100
   North, Minneapolis, MN 55422.
   (800) 372-3300; (612) 535-4829;
   (612) 535-7808 (fax)

Gay and Lesbian Parents Coalition International,
   Box 50360, Washington, D.C. 20091.
   (202) 583-8029; (202) 783-6204 (fax);
   glpcinat@ix.netcom.com

Single Mothers by Choice, Box 1642, Gracie
   Square Station, New York, NY 10028.
   (212) 988-0993; mattes@pipeline.com

National Association for Family Childcare,
   725 15th Street N.W., Suite 505,
   Washington, D.C. 20005.
   (202) 347-3300

Au Pair Care, 1 Post Street, 7th Floor,
   San Francisco, CA 94104.
   (800) 4-AUPAIR; (415) 434-8788;
   (415) 986-4620 (fax)

Family Travel Times, TWYCH, 40 Fifth Avenue,
   New York, NY 10011.
   (212) 477-5524; (212) 447-5173 (fax)

General References
Beck, W. W. *Obstetrics and Gynecology: The
   National Medical Series for Independent Study.*
   2nd edition. John Wiley and Sons, Inc., 1989.

Behrman, R. E. and R. M. Kliegman. *Nelson
   Essentials of Pediatrics.* 2nd edition. W. B.
   Saunders Co., Philadelphia, 1994.

Guide to Baby Products. 5th edition. Consumer
   Reports, 1996.

Oski, F. A. et al. *Principles and Practice of
   Pediatrics.* 2nd edition. J. B. Lippincott,
   Philadelphia, 1994.

Palfrey, J., et al. *The Disney Encyclopedia of Baby
   and Child Care.* Hyperion, New York, 1995.

Shelov, S. P. Editor-in-Chief. *The American
   Academy of Pediatrics: Caring for Your Baby and
   Young Child—Birth to Age 5.* Bantam Books,
   New York, 1991.

Wagner, Hilory. *The New Parents Source Book.*
   Citadel Press, 1996.

Index

About the Authors

Baroness Dagmar von Cramm has a degree in home economics. As a journalist, her areas of expertise are nutrition, children's topics, and cooking. Gräfe and Unzer has published several of her books, including two volumes of culinary advice: *Fur Babys (For Babies)* and *Fur die Stillzeit (For Breast-Feeding Mothers)*. The mother of three kindergarten- and school-age sons, she knows the problems of the first year from experience.

Professor Eberhard Schmidt, M.D., is a member of the National Commission on Breast Feeding and the Nutritional Committee of the German Society of Pediatric Medicine. For many years he was director of the Dusseldorf University Children's Hospital, and he now is head of the Neonatal Department of a Dusseldorf maternity hospital.

He is the coauthor of *Die Kunst des Stillens (The Art of Breast Feeding)*. The father of four children and now a grandfather, he also has a great deal of hands-on experience in private life as well.

Mark A. Goldstein, M.D., is an Assistant Clinical Professor of Pediatrics at the Harvard Medical School and Chief of Pediatrics at the Massachusetts Institute of Technology in Cambridge, Massachusetts. He is a published author, and together with his wife is planning a book on the many issues of adolescence. Raising two children, in addition to his pediatrics practice, has also given him much hands-on experience.

Photos

Sigrid Reinichs

Other photos:
Alete: pages 6, 174–175; Eva Hehemann: page 19; Milupa: pages 138, 139, 141, back cover (bottom left); Penaten: pages 40, 264, 268, 274; Rainer Schmitz: pages 113, 258; Fotostudio Teubner: pages 112, 135, 136; Tony Stone Bilderwelten/David Hanover: pages 4, 36–37, back cover (top left); Ron Sutherland: page 83; Chris Harvey: pages 5, 88–89; Bruce Ayres: page 110, front foldout flap; Laurence Monneret: page 152; Frank Herholdt: pages 7, 252–253; Philip and Karin Smith: page 263; Andy Cox: back foldout; Walz: pages 39, 47, 57, 68, 84, 93, 123, 124, 179, 187, 269, 271, 284, 285, 286; SuperStock, Inc.: pages 6, 180, 186, 195, 202–203; Simmons Juvenile Products Co., Inc.: pages 70, 261; Augustus Butera: back cover (top right); Barron's Educational Series, Inc.: pages 131, 273.

Drawings
Helene Schwab

Acknowledgments

For their kind permission to use their photos, we thank these companies: Alete, Milupa, Penaten, and Walz.

Our special thanks to all the mothers, fathers, and babies who posed for our photos.

Published originally under the title: *Unser Baby—Das Erste Jahr* from the Series *Der Gross GU Ratgeber*

All inquiries should be addressed to:
Barron's Educational Series, Inc.
250 Wireless Boulevard
Hauppauge, New York 11788

Library of Congress Catalog Card No. 97-26565
International Standard Book No. 0-8120-9778-5

Library of Congress Cataloging-in-Publication Data

Von Cramm, Dagmar.
  [Unser baby. English]
  Our baby : the first year / Dagmar von Cramm, Eberhard Schmidt ; Mark A. Goldstein, consulting editor ; Ellen Bass, Dante Pappano, consulting authors.
      p.   cm.
  Includes bibliographical references and index.
  ISBN 0-8120-9778-5
  1. Infants (Newborn)—Care. 2. Infants (Newborn)—Health and hygiene. 3. Maternity nursing. 4. Child rearing. 5. Child development. I. Schmidt, Eberhard, Dr. med. II. Goldstein, Mark A. (Mark Allan), 1947– III. Title.
RJ253.V6513   1997
649'.122—dc21   97-26565
                                CIP

Printed in Hong Kong
98765432

THE FIRST YEAR AT A GLANCE

7 MONTHS | 8 MONTHS

DEVELOPMENT

Your baby transfers toys from one hand to the other.

The constant smiling is over: Your baby is shy with unfamiliar people. For ways to deal with his hesitancy, see page 198.

Now the baby can sit without your help: time for the high chair! For shopping tips, see page 140.

HEALTH

Now is a good time to childproof your home.

The immunity acquired in utero has worn off (see page 215). But an illness now won't bowl your baby over anymore.

The baby's hearing and vision are very well developed now. If you suspect developmental delays, arrange for an examination!

FEEDING

You might offer some pureed chicken or turkey.

YOU AND YOUR FAMILY

Travel plans? During the second six months, it's all right to take the baby along on vacation.

Gradually you are able to lose weight. For tips and aids, see page 172.